Edwin Herbert Lewis

An introduction to the study of literature

For the use of secondary and graded schools

Edwin Herbert Lewis

An introduction to the study of literature
For the use of secondary and graded schools

ISBN/EAN: 9783337206086

Printed in Europe, USA, Canada, Australia, Japan

Cover: Foto ©Paul-Georg Meister /pixelio.de

More available books at **www.hansebooks.com**

AN INTRODUCTION

TO THE

STUDY OF LITERATURE

FOR THE USE OF

SECONDARY AND GRADED SCHOOLS

EDITED BY

EDWIN HERBERT LEWIS, Ph.D.

ASSOCIATE PROFESSOR IN THE LEWIS INSTITUTE; AUTHOR OF
" A FIRST BOOK IN WRITING ENGLISH "

New York

THE MACMILLAN COMPANY

LONDON: MACMILLAN & CO., Ltd.

1899

To A. H. L.

I HAVE TRIED TO MAKE A BOOK THAT
YOU WOULD HAVE APPROVED, HAD IT
BEEN GIVEN ME AT FOURTEEN.

E. H. L.

PREFACE

IT would seem that literature ought to serve as a prime agency in the education of the emotions and, indirectly, of the will. This is particularly true of the early adolescent age, with which the upper grammar and the lower high school grades are concerned. If the study of English during this greatest crisis of the student's life is merely formal, he loses one of the best influences school can ever give him. To say so is not to underestimate the value, ethical or commercial, of formal training in composition. There is need for Spartan severity regarding chirography, orthography, punctuation, syntax, and logic. The task of securing correctness by Spartan methods, and, at the same time, of arousing an unconstrained love for noble literature, is the almost hopeless labor set for the English teacher. Gradgrind and enemy of Gradgrind he must be within the same hour. But there is no escaping the double duty, and no denying that the second part of it is the more important. No greater danger can beset secondary education than the notion that its true aim is merely the acquisition of instrument knowledges; but, of the twin evils resulting from the information cult, the neglect of ideals is worse than the neglect of scholarly method.

But literature is in the schools; the problem is, How should it be graded? There is no solution in following the procrustean principle of chronology. However valua-

ble an historical view of representative authors may be to
the pupil of eighteen, it has little value for the younger
pupil.   Were the authors of the seventeenth and eigh-
teenth centuries interesting to fourteen-year-old boys and
girls, the case would be different.   Shakspere interests
this age, and so do very many authors of our own day;
Milton and Pope and Addison usually do not.   In grades
eight to ten, systematic literary history is hardly a defensible
subject ; yet some such table as that appended to this volume
may prove useful, on any indication that the student is be-
coming interested in the historical significance of a writer.
If the instructor utilizes his chances to speak of the authors
as men, the knowledge he conveys of such things as
Lamb's heroism and Franklin's thrift will repay the stu-
dent better than learning of Lamb's place in the Eliza-
bethan revival, and of Franklin's relation to the English
deists.

The student's *highest normal interests* are the chief
things to regard in grading.   It must be ascertained by
what stages the imagination, the emotions, and the char-
acter develop.   Imagination is strong throughout youth,
but it is developed now by one interest, now by another.
Emotions which are embryonic to-day are blossoming to-
morrow.   To discover the stages is the first task.   The
second is to furnish the particular masterpieces "indi-
cated."   Theoretically there is a masterpiece (written, or,
alas ! unwritten) for every month of the student's life.
The surest way of learning where the masterpieces fit is
to allow the student to "browse" in a library.   Lamb
and Ruskin approved this method, with limitations ; for
though Lamb would have all girls educated as Bridget
Elia was educated, by being "turned loose in a roomful
of *old books*," the phrase just quoted meant with Lamb
the Elizabethan dramatists ; and though Ruskin is thankful

for having been allowed the run of a library, it was a library carefully chosen by a man whose tastes were inherited by Ruskin. Various classes in the Lewis Institute have been encouraged "to browse," to see if they might not hit upon a body of literature that would remain a constant interest to their equals in age. However imperfect and incomplete these investigations, the sifting process, upon which the students entered actively and honestly, has been of the greatest value to all concerned. It has shown that noticeable differences of interest exist between ninth and tenth, tenth and eleventh grades. In the nature-sense, for instance, as it appears in the youth not hopelessly hardened by "business" aims, there are usually marked changes between thirteen and sixteen. The change is first from the child's scientific curiosity about nature to a half-poetic, but objective, interest in her; the boy becomes capable of direct, unreflecting joy in nature, or even of direct displeasure with her, in something of the Homeric manner; then he slowly grows to sympathize with the modern view, so much more imaginative and sometimes so much less wholesome than Homer's.

The present volume is offered as a tentative body of lyrics, ballads, and short stories, for the eighth, ninth, and even tenth grades. It draws mostly upon nineteenth-century authors. In spite of hundreds of rejections on the score of form alone, it includes pieces of very different value as to form, a fact which should never be allowed to escape the student's attention, — as it certainly will not the critic's. The works are grouped by subjects according to what are believed to be the healthy interests of the early adolescent period. An introduction is prefixed to each chapter with the aim of pointing out, not too ingeniously, a thread of meaning common to all the pieces. Although most of the hundred and fifty compositions are complete, it is by no means supposed that short works should suffice for these years. Not later than the eighth grade the boy should doubtless become acquainted with Homer in rhythmical or metrical translation. Not later than the ninth he should doubtless be introduced to Cooper's Leatherstocking in at least one complete novel of the series. Not later than the tenth he should read a play of Shakspere. Homer, Shakspere, and Cooper are not only essential experiences of the youth, but by mere length compel him to consider the architectonics of art.

The present volume contains a great many poems, all of which should be read aloud, except the few (italicized in the table of contents) which are perhaps too delicate for oral interpretation by young students. Those starred are particularly good for learning by heart.[1] Difficult words should be pronounced by the instructor and doubtful passages orally interpreted before the pupil is asked to prepare (always overnight) the piece he is to read facing the class. It will be better still to rehearse the whole piece for the pupil before he studies it. The vigorous poems should be given to the vigorous; the swift poems to the sure of speech; the pathetic to the self-controlled; and the dröll to those who are risible.

The best results will be secured with the book if it is not taken too rapidly. It will yield ample material for three hours a week of recitation for forty weeks; these weeks may be successive or may be divided into twenty for one year and twenty for another. Every precaution must be taken not to let the poetry pall, particularly in Chapters III and VI, where the emotional element is large, and wherever the didactic and artistic elements

---

[1] The songs may properly be sung, wherever good music is obtain able — like Schubert's for *Hark, hark, the lark.*

are imperfectly fused. It is assumed that the student is writing themes frequently, and perhaps on such questions as may be suggested by the notes. But he should not be allowed to lay violent hands on the poetry for topics. That is, paraphrasing and set criticisms should be discouraged. It is better for the teacher to do whatever paraphrasing is necessary for the understanding of the work, and to change the diction of the poet as little as possible. Three hours a week to the literature for its own sake, and two hours (on consecutive days) for composition, is probably a better division of time in these grades than half an hour daily to each subject.

Now a word as to the analytical , parts of the book — the general introduction, the notes, and the " plans of summary." Their perhaps overambitious purpose is to suggest a very elementary, but sound, method and vocabulary of criticism. They are here to be used or not used as every teacher thinks best. At fifteen the boy or girl persists in a certain amount of self-analysis, and perhaps a little analysis of literature may be a legitimate discharge for this impulse. Just how much of this kind of study is healthful in the eighth, ninth, and tenth grades is a question not for theorists, but for teachers. It is a question on which the experience of other teachers is entreated by the present editor. In the eighth grade it may be best to omit all the editorial matter. In the ninth it may be best to omit only the general introduction, or a part of it, or to give it after the literature has come to be liked and felt. One thing is certain, *that the analytic notes should not be studied by the student till he has read and enjoyed the piece itself.*

The editor's thanks are due to the following gentlemen, the publishers whose courtesy has made this work possible : Messrs. Charles Scribner's Sons, Messrs. Harper and

Brothers, Messrs. D. Appleton and Co., Messrs. Longmans, Green, & Co., Messrs. Little, Brown, & Co., Messrs. G. P. Putnam's Sons, Mr. John Lane, Messrs. Henry Holt and Co., Messrs. Small, Maynard, and Co., Messrs. Robert Bonner's Sons, Messrs. Doubleday and McClure Co., Messrs. The Macmillan Co. Detailed credit will be given in the proper places for permission to use the pieces printed. If any selection has been taken without securing permission from the owners, the mistake has been due to inadvertence.

In conclusion the editor must thank many friends for counsel. Particularly must he acknowledge the welcome assistance, criticism, and sympathy of his colleagues, Miss Jane L. Noble and Miss Charlotte N. Underwood, and of Director George N. Carman.

E. H. L.

CHICAGO, November 17, 1898.

TABLE OF CONTENTS

xiii

CHAPTER III

THE HEROISM OF PEACE

CHAPTER IV

THE ATHLETE

CHAPTER V

THE ADVENTURER

CHAPTER VI

THE HEARTH

CHAPTER VII

THE MORNING LANDSCAPE

CHAPTER VIII

THE GENTLEMAN

CHAPTER IX

WIT AND HUMOR

CHAPTER X

THE FAR GOAL

AN INTRODUCTION TO THE STUDY OF LITERATURE

INTRODUCTION

1. Literature is, etymologically, something written ; *litera* is the Latin from which *letter* is derived. Yet it was late in the world's history that songs and stories were actually written down. Homer's poetry was the better for being tested a thousand times by audiences before any of the reciters of it (rhapsodes) thought of writing it out. In the dawn of the world there was only oral literature. To this day, old ballads, like *Adam of Gordon* (page 93), are handed down by Scotch women who can neither read nor write. The tales of Uncle Remus were literature even before Mr. Joel Chandler Harris conceived the admirable notion of giving literary form to what he had heard from the lips of illiterate negroes.

2. The songs and stories which we heard as children were literature, but we were probably unaware of the fact. In childhood we enjoy whatever appeals to us, but do not ask ourselves its scientific name, or why we like it. Nor are such questions vital. It is surely more important to enjoy a book than to know by what tricks the author makes us enjoy it. If no man ate his dinner till he understood why he liked it, the world would be a grave-yard in a month. Yet in studying literature there are certain principles of appreciation which may help us in

B   I

getting the full flavor of what we read.   First, then, let us ask ourselves what literature is.

3. Evidently such a question is not to be answered in a breath; yet we probably agree that literature is an art, — whatever that means.   It is allied to painting, sculpture, and music.   These are sometimes called the fine arts, to distinguish them from practical arts like cooking and architecture.   Perhaps a better distinction would be that between higher arts and lower.   Cooking is a lower art, — lower than it might be if cooks knew hygiene.   Sculpture is a higher art, yet not unpractical; statues were often compelled by the Greeks to support roofs.   Music is a useful art when it nerves soldiers for a righteous fight, or quiets a mob, or refines the vulgar, or puts a miser in a mood to think of eternity.   Music is far from useful when it throws people into hysterical raptures and unstrings the will.   Architecture is a useful art, but architecture would probably be more useful if it considered certain laws of beauty; if built of poor material and ornamented with tin cornices, a house is neither honest, useful, nor beautiful.

4. We must now define more closely what is meant by art, as applied to painting, sculpture, music, and literature.   What is the chief end that these arts try to accomplish?   The great artist aims at something better than tempting dishes and water-tight houses.   Consider a line or two of real poetry: —

> Golden lads and girls all must,
> As chimney-sweepers, come to dust.

What effect is Shakspere trying to produce upon us? Clearly he is endeavoring to convey to us one of his personal feelings, or rather several of them.   He has been thinking about one of his characters, a golden-haired woman, who, disguised as a boy, is lying unconscious in the forest. The shepherds call her dead, and sing a dirge over her. Shakspere is composing that song. As he looks with the shepherds upon poor Fidele,[1] he remembers that not all children are fair and white. The chimney sweepers, poor little imps, are both amusing and pitiful in their grime and soot. Suddenly it sadly flashes upon him, remembering his own dead child, that, golden-haired or grimy, all the children must one day turn to dust. Into his song he pours all this mixture of feeling — admiration, humor, pity, and grief. On reading, we suspect immediately that transmission of feeling is one chief function of the higher arts. We recall lines that pretended to be poetry, but that were prosy, because cold and unfeeling. To show that metre does not make poetry, Dr. Samuel Johnson improvised these verses : —

> I put my hat upon my head
> And walked into the strand;
> And there I saw another man
> Whose hat was in his hand.

Here no emotion is conveyed — unless it be unintentional humor.

5. Let us see if the transmission of feeling is characteristic of the other fine arts. Certainly it is of music. Music makes us laugh, or weep, or quicken step. Something similar is true of painting. Before the Sistine Madonna the peasants shed tears, or stand in breathless awe. Sculpture, too, moves the feelings, though fewer than are reached through pictures. The statue of a Greek god awakes our admiration for the human form, and our appreciation of majestic repose. It rouses, too, a sense of awe, for it stands looking out on life to-day with the same divine steadiness it has shown for a thousand years. Evidently all artists aim at the heart. They may stir the merest quiver

---

[1] Three syllables, accent on the second.

of pleasure, regret, hope; or they may arouse the fiercest throbbings of joy, remorse, ambition.

6. Of course, with all these emotions thought is mingled, especially with those aroused by literature. Whereas music is the natural language of the heart, words are the natural language of the head. If the orchestra plays fear, you feel it at once; if the poet writes "fear," the word does not immediately move you; it is merely the idea of fear. Not until you fall to thinking on the subject, calling up the pictures of things that you fear, does literature get you to feel it. Literature therefore gives a calmer, a more thoughtful pleasure, and often a healthier pleasure, than does music. Literature is a sort of finer thinking about life, — the thinking that comes more from the heart than from the head. The poets tell us their wisest and tenderest thoughts about life.

7. It may seem unfortunate that the arts put so much weight on emotion; but only bad art makes people hysterical, or sentimental, or visionary. Good art, at least good art in reasonable quantity, never does that, for it does not forget to express all the stronger emotions that are noble, and these are the sworn enemies of the hysterical. Fine natures are bundles of feeling, though they seem outwardly calm. The coarse man does not show grief, because he does not feel it; the fine man feels it, but masters it with another emotion, — pride, faith, courage. Our sensibilities are numberless, and very few of them can receive expression; yet they are the most important part of us. Children do not think of their father as a walking volume, or a walking industry, though he may have written a profound book or built up a great business. They think of him as a person made chiefly of humor, patience, sympathy, and love. His learning is a mere adjunct to himself.

8. Obviously, our possibilities of noble feeling need development. Not to have experienced all the legitimate sensations of youth, beginning with the love of fun, the love of adventure, and the love of success, is to be uneducated. Literature is a recognized means of widening our range of feelings. How is a boy to know the hopes and fears of shipwreck but from Crusoe and Jim Hawkins? How is he to imagine the sensations of journeying to the moon, save by the help of Verne? Ordinary life will not invite us to dinner with the queen, or to go on secret messages after her diamonds, or to fight in armor, or to see ghosts, or to descend into the inferno. If we wish to imagine these experiences, we must turn to literature. If we are not to be content with drudgery, we must go to books for means of multiplying our imaginative pleasures. I say "imaginative" pleasures distinctly, not meaning the pleasures of information. The novel or poem that has no object except the sugaring over of useful information is usually poor stuff.

9. It is not pretended that every emotion <u>transmitted</u> by art is desirable. It would be a great mistake to suppose that every beautiful style embodies noble feeling. The photographer can use a lense that heightens the brutish forehead. So the novelist can disguise the bestial qualities of hatred, cruelty, cowardice, and lust, if he mixes a little courtesy with the hatred, a little wit with the cruelty, a little policy with the cowardice, a little nonsense about "wild oats" with the lust.

10. Have, then, these evil qualities no place in literature? Yes; but only in the hands of a few masters. Shakspere and Hawthorne can show the horror of them; most writers merely succeed in presenting degrading pictures. The virus of hydrophobia will not more surely cause its victim to act like a dog, than will the memory of beauti-

ful images expressing bestial feelings degrade him who cherishes them.

11. Each time of life has its peculiar emotions. Old age has its pleasures of memory, its quiet sadness of sorrows dulled by time, and its serene hope of the future life. Middle age has its anxiety for the welfare of the young generation. Young manhood has its ambition, its sentiment, and its passion of love.

12. Perhaps we may say that the feelings normal to fourteen and fifteen are as follows: a wholesome sense of fun; a love of nature in her fresh and woodsy moods; courage, endurance, fidelity, loyalty; a reasonable sense of bodily vigor; love of adventure; a desire for practical success; aspiration, hope, perseverance, faith; a strong love of one's parents and home, if one is not treated like a child; admiration for courtesy, mercy, and heroism. All this does not mean that the youth is a saint with a formidable list of virtues. It does mean that he admires in others any manifestation of these emotions, many of which are among the noblest that human nature can feel; and that he is entirely capable of developing many of them in himself.

13. The poems and stories of this volume have been selected because they exhibit these feelings as they have appeared in actual men, or in personages of the imagination. Note that artistic exhibition is very different from preaching a moral. One can draw a moral from anything in this world, if one has the habit. Most of us are fortunately able to see the robin in the sunrise without reflecting that the early bird catches the worm. Perfect poetry, like nature, never preaches. If all the poetry in this book were perfect, there would not be a single moral, directly stated, in it. Nearly every piece included has been recommended by some hundreds of students of the age for which it is here intended. These did their best to keep out everything

unpleasantly didactic. They regret that they could not find more perfect expressions of some of the emotions, for example, those of football. The search convinced them that great poets must find it very hard to remember their boyhood. It is comparatively easy to remember one's thoughts, but it is hard, even for the poet, who recalls his emotions better than do other people, to remember feelings long since dead.

14. We have now seen that literature transmits thoughtful emotions. It does this not by stone, or pigment, or musical sounds, but by words. Yet how by words? Suppose that a dry philosopher one day feels the emotion of sadness at the thought that all things must perish. An emotion of any sort is so rare in him that he fancies his dreamy youth coming back, and sits down to express in poetry his sweet melancholy. He writes: —

> Into primordial atoms, we discern,
> All sentient beings, though diverse, return.

Having proceeded at this rate for a hundred lines, he hands the fresh manuscript to his boy. Tom reads the lines respectfully, and declares them fine; but his wise old father sees that they touch no feeling whatever in Tom, except his pride at being consulted. Of course they have not. Who can weep over atoms?

15. Now suppose Master Will Shakspere sitting at New Place, famous and lonely; famous because the queen and all her people like his plays; lonely, too, because remembering his golden-haired boy who lies in the churchyard by the river. How white that face was beneath the golden hair! not like those of the chimneysweeps the poet had seen in London. Shakspere feels a touch of humor at the memory of their impish black, and a touch of pity for their lives. Ah! but it will soon be

with them as it is with the golden head in the churchyard.
The great man picks up his pen and goes on with the
dirge he is writing, to be spoken in his new play of
"Cymbeline": —

> Golden lads and girls all must,
> As chimney-sweepers, come to dust, —

and here, I think, he must have laid the pen down again
and gone out into the green fields; for the poet can write
well of his emotions when he remembers them dimly, but
not when they are choking him again. How did Shak-
spere, unconsciously enough, produce, in those who heard
these two lines next month at the theatre, the mingled
emotions of humor, pity, and sorrow? Merely by trans-
ferring his own emotion through images. He makes us
see the golden hair, the white skin, the impish black faces,
and, lastly, the coffined dust in the churchyard.

16. Let us take another example. Suppose we wish to
convey a sense of the loneliness of a deserted house. If
we write, "There were none of the accustomed sounds of
busy life, and so all the minor noises of the deserted
place were plainly audible," our sentence arouses no emo-
tion. But when Tennyson treats the same subject, he calls
up the sound-images, and produces at once the desired
impression: —

> All day within the dreamy house,
>   The doors upon their hinges creak'd;
> The blue fly sung in the pane; the mouse
>   Behind the mouldering wainscot shriek'd.

17. Sound-images and sight-images are preferred by the
arts, but images of odor, touch, motion, muscular contrac-
tion, etc., are also employed. Images of odor are some-
times very effective in arousing forgotten feelings that once
happened to be associated with the given odor. Thus, the

poet Owen Meredith makes the scent of a jasmine flower
recall to a man his dead sweetheart: —

> Oh, the faint, sweet smell of that jasmine flower!
> It made me start, and it made me cold.

18. If a poet is really great, his work is a tissue of
images, though free from over-decoration. They are not
merely memories of actual sights and sounds, filling his
mind like tiny landscapes in a camera; some are new com-
binations. He sees the sky, and is about to call it "the
starry sky," when it suggests to him a floor inlaid with bits
of gold. Thus he enriches the reader with several impres-
sions instead of one. The resemblances noted by the poet
between different images give rise to "figures." Gazing
upon the waves and listening to them, the poet sees points
of resemblance to various other things: dancing children;
galloping horses; a mass of beautiful hair; tears; a march-
ing army; a turbulent mob; a symphony; laughing or
moaning human voices; molten silver, or emerald, or tur-
quoise (things that he never saw, but that he understood
by combining various images). When he writes of the
"dancing waves," or the "horses of Neptune," or the
" waves of golden hair," or the "emerald depths," he
is making "figures."[1] Figures, then, are compounds of
images, and are made by the rare gift of seeing a resem-
blance where most persons fail to see it. We may call
them a kind of invention.

19. Our definition has now advanced thus far: Litera-
ture is an art which transmits thoughtful emotion by images
and inventions embodied in words. The word *invention*

---

[1] The two most important figures are metaphor and simile. "The wave
is like a dancer " is simile, that is, the explicit statement of a resemblance
between two things unlike in most respects. "The wave dances" and "the
dancing wave" are metaphors. Metaphor *identifies* the two things com-
pared.

ought to include more than figures of speech.   If the artist can invent these, why may he not invent whole landscapes? The painter can take his sketches of different places, his memories of lights and lines, and by combining and rejecting can create a new landscape.   So can the poet.   Dreams sometimes permit ordinary persons to do the same thing, though usually there is not much reason in dream pictures. By observing many persons, the novelist is able to create a character like them all, yet different from any one of them. He wishes to draw a commercial traveller, let us say.   He jots down notes of all the "drummers" he meets; by and by he compares notes and constructs a "type."   What would be the details of dress and manner common to most "drummers"?

20. This making of composite photographs by the inventive imagination is not hard to understand when an imaginary landscape is the product.   It is more difficult to grasp when a real person, not merely a type, seems to be created outright.   The novelist sets his memory whirling, full of memories of a hundred men, and suddenly he hands you out a Crusoe or a Hamlet.   The new character seems truer to life than one's own neighbors.   Jim Hawkins never lived; nor Friday, nor Leatherstocking, nor Ivanhoe, nor Shylock; yet each is a strangely real unity, — entirely alive and responsible for his acts.   It would puzzle Shakspere himself to say how his character Lear came to be.   We can only guess that the same inventive principle which produces figures of speech and composite landscapes is capable of creating Cordelias and Lears.   Somehow that rare gift of seeing resemblances must have done the work.   Newton, says some one, was the first man to see that the earth is like an apple falling toward the sun. Shakspere was the first to see, in supremely beautiful and touching images, that he who is heartlessly self-willed is

very like a madman.   Consequently, Shakspere was the first and only man who could write the tragedy of Lear.

21. Having assured ourselves that literature is an art which transmits thoughtful emotion by language embodying images and inventions, we must ask, Should the images and the language be pleasing?   We did not ask that question about emotion.   We agreed that art may express any emotion, pleasant or not.   We probably agree that we desire just as much beauty of style as the subject will permit.   We know that, when Macbeth comes out from King Duncan's chamber, he comes a murderer; yet we like the excited poetic language in which he says : —

> Here lay Duncan,
> His silver skin laced with his golden blood.

In a later act, Lady Macbeth, walking in her sleep, tries to wash the foul stains of blood from her hands.   This scene rouses an extremely unpleasant feeling, but it is relieved by the beauty of Lady Macbeth's words : —

> Here's the smell of the blood still: all the perfumes of Arabia will not sweeten this little hand.

Here Shakspere has felt that he cannot give us only pleasant images, for he is portraying the mind of a murderess.   He suggests the smell of blood, but tries to relieve it with the odors of Araby the blest.

22. In like manner, the very language of literature should sound as sweet as the emotion to be conveyed will permit.   Without reference to what it means, it should itself be pleasant.   A word like *mellow*, or *golden*, or *shadowy*, is more agreeable than one like *smash, recognize*, or *muggy*.   The first examples are called *euphonious*, or well-sounding words; the second are called *cacophonous*, or ill-sounding.   *Euphonious* is itself rather a pleasant word; *cacophonous* is as harsh as the quality it stands for.

Pick out the euphonious and the cacophonous words in the following list; never mind the meaning: *cragged, perfidious, hesperides, lovely, marble, celestial, glutted, cinnamon, ambrosia, lucent, argosies, Fez, manna, immemorial, litanies, silver, musquash, grate, martlet, tintinnabulation, croaks, billowy, Karshish, Felippa, Hakkadosh, delicate, acoustics, Magdeburg, dulcimer.*

23. Pick out the euphonious and the cacophonous combinations in the following list: *his is; as is the case; owns us as her sons; murmur of doves in immemorial elms; Dirck galloped; showery rain; vesper chime; songless lute; lute unswept; by the mirage is lifted; closing in slumbers the while; stately pleasure dome; white, white violet; silence in the atmosphere; quietly rested; drums and tramplings; molten, golden notes; the rust within their throats.*

24. From such a phrase as "myriad-starred mignonette," there is another pleasure to be had besides the presence of delicate vowels and the absence of harsh consonants. The phrase goes with a tripping rhythm, a lilt. It has four accents: "my'riad star'red mign'onette'." Rhythm is a pleasing thing to the human animal. If one leg had no chance to rest while the other took the step, walking would be as hard as convict labor. We are set to rhythm even in our heart-beats and our breathing. Now, speech depends on breath; and since breath is rhythmical, speech is rhythmical. Curiously enough, the more interested a speaker becomes in his subject the more rhythmical he becomes in speech. Emotion seems to express itself so, even in savage man.

25. The writer too finds rhythm an aid to the expression of feeling. With almost every breath he regularly pauses, thus giving us the line, or verse.[1] And he beats out the

---

[1] *Verse* properly means not stanza, but line. Note the force of the derivation from Latin *vertere*, "to turn," while *prose* is from Latin *prorsus*, "straight on."

line into metre, that is, into a definite number of feet, each consisting of one accented and one or more unaccented syllables. A trochaic foot, or trochee, consists of an accent followed by a rest, thus: *lovely*. If another unaccented syllable is added, we have a dactyl, thus: *merrily*. If, now, the rest precedes the accent, we get an iambus, thus : *above;* and if two unaccented syllables precede, the result is an anapest, thus : *indiscreet.* In English poetry not every line is all composed of one kind of foot, but there is in every poem a predominant foot. According to this we name the metre trochaic, iambic, dactyllic, or anapestic. According to the number of accents in the line — two, three, four, five, six, or seven — we call the metre dimeter, trimeter, tetrameter, pentameter, hexameter, or heptameter. We shall find that each metre has its value; for example, iambic trimeter is a very rapid metre, while trochaic heptameter is a very slow one.

26. Our definition is now fairly complete. Literature is the art which transmits thoughtful emotion by language of pleasant sound, embodying images and inventions as pleasant as the given emotion permits. Poetry, in the ordinary sense, is that form of literature which employs metre.

CHAPTER I

THE NOBILITY OF ANIMALS

SCIENTISTS describe animals and classify them, sometimes cutting them up alive to be perfectly sure as to how their nerves and muscles work; but savages, children, and poets love animals. The savage is near enough to the beast not to think himself so very much the superior creature. Hiawatha talks of squirrels and birds as his brothers. Mr. Kipling's creation, the jungle-child Mowgli, understands what wild creatures say. Children get on famously with cats and dogs that are irritable toward the grown. Great artists find in the higher brutes many manlike qualities. Indeed, there are some animals so human and some men so brutal, that if the poet is properly to honor the former, he must neglect the latter. Animals have been known to die of grief on their master's grave; men have been known to grudge the time they spent at the funeral of a benefactor.

Horses and dogs are by common consent the noblest of the lower creatures, for they enter into the lives of their masters. Robert Browning has a poem which exhibits in a touching way the sympathy between the Arab and his courser. Muléykeh, the Pearl, has never been beaten in speed, even by her sister Buhéyseh. Both horses sleep in their owner's tent. One night the Pearl is stolen by a man who has in vain tried to buy or beg her. Hóseyn sees that the tether is cut which bound her to his ankle, and that the mare is gone. He springs on Buhéyseh and follows like the wind. Now we see the problem: either he must lose

the Pearl or the Pearl must lose her record. Buhéyseh
gains, frantic to beat her sister. The master cannot bear it.
He shouts to the thief to touch the right ear and press the
left flank. The Pearl hears the familiar voice and springs
away beyond hope of recovery. The Arab returns, and is
ridiculed by his friends. Had he kept his mouth shut,
here would have been the Pearl again, the eyed like an
antelope : —

> " And the beaten in speed ! " wept Hóseyn;
> " You have never loved my Pearl."

In reading of famous horseback rides we are often at
loss to know which is the true hero of the hour, — the man
or the animal. In Longfellow's *Ride of Paul Revere* it is
the midnight message which we honor, but the poet cannot
help saying that the spark struck out by that steed in his
flight kindled the land into flame with its heat. In
Buchanan Read's *Sheridan's Ride* the balance of praise is
quite with the galloping black, although the poet hurrahs
for horse and man. In O'Reilly's *Ride of Collins Grave*
we forget all but the errand, — to save a town from death
by flood. After reading the first two poems in this chapter,
decide in each case whether the balance of honor is evenly
divided or whether the horse is the hero.

The first of these two poems is by Mrs. Norton, an Eng-
lish poet of the last generation. The king and his thirty
nobles mount in hot haste, and away they start for the
castle where the king's betrothed lies dying. The nobles
are beaten one by one; only the king and his little fair
page win through. Even the page drops now, and the king
rides in alone. His charger has strained every nerve, but
it is too late. The king comes back into the courtyard.
Choking with grief, he bows his head on the horse's
neck.

The King
of Den-
mark's
Ride,
p. 18.

How they
brought the
Good News
from Ghent
to Aix,
p. 20.

The second poem is by Browning. It tells of a ride made from Ghent, in the Netherlands, to Aix-la-Chapelle, in France, to bring word of the treaty, — a piece of news that, if in time, would save Aix from being burned by her own despairing citizens. Historically there was never such a ride, but the story is so magnificently told that there really ought to have been such an incident. According to Browning there were three messengers, — Joris, Dirck, and the unnamed man who tells the tale. They start at midnight and ride steadily till the next afternoon. They pass town after town, — Lokeren, Boom, Düffeld, Mecheln, Aershot, Hasselt, Looz, Tongres, Dalhem, — Dirck and Joris dropping out by the way, until at last the horse Roland gallops into Aix, and his hatless, bootless, beltless rider knows no more. When he comes to himself he is sitting on the ground, with Roland's head in his lap. He calls for wine to give the horse. Aix has used up her wine in the siege; but somehow a single last precious measure is found, and the burgesses instantly vote that it belongs to Roland.

The dog has fared in poetry almost as well as the horse. Even Homer, whose Greeks are always praising their swift steeds, introduces a dog at one of the most dramatic moments of the "Odyssey." After Ulysses has endured every manner of peril by land and sea, and managed to get back home, no one recognizes him without help except his old dog Argos. "He wagged his tail and dropped both ears, but toward his master had not strength to move." That Shakspere has little to say about dogs is perhaps due to the difficulty of introducing them on the stage. Tennyson has an old Rover — "Owd Roä" — who saves a child's life in the smoke of the burning building, and is in turn saved by his master. Telling his rescued boy how it happened, the old farmer says: —

" Sa I browt tha down, an' I says ' I mun
  Gaw up ageän fur Roä.'
' Gaw up ageän fur the varmint ? '
  I tell'd 'er ' Yeäs I mun goä.' "

Both Tennyson and Browning were bitterly opposed to
vivisection — cutting into a live creature to observe the
effect of drugs upon it, or to settle questions of anatomy.
At times vivisection has furnished knowledge whereby
human life has been saved; at other times it has been a
profitless cruelty. Browning's poem called *Tray* is an Tray, p. 23.
extremely sharp satire on vivisection. The poet represents
himself as asking a group of friends to sing him the story
of some real hero. One begins to recount a deed of Sir
Olaf, the good knight; the poet cuts him short. A second
starts to praise some hero not so righteous as Sir Olaf; the
poet will not listen to him either. A third begins to speak
of a beggar child who fell from a quay into the water. The
poet is interested and attends. The bystanders on the quay
did not come to the child's assistance; their lives were too
precious to their families to be risked. A dog, however,
jumped in, saved the child with difficulty, and then returned
for the little one's doll, much to the amusement of the
rational beings who looked on. Convinced that the second
rescue was an absurd, a merely instinctive act, one by-
stander sent off to catch the animal and have its brain vivi-
sected, to see how dog's brain secretes dog's soul!

Sir Walter Scott was a great lover of animals; a list of
noble dogs and horses could be made from his novels.
The poem called *Helvellyn* concerns the heroism of a little Helvellyn,
terrier. Scott climbed the great mountain Helvellyn, in p. 25.
the English lake region, — how well the present writer re-
members doing the same thing because Sir Walter wrote
this poem, — and saw the place where, in 1805, a young
man perished, and where, three months later, his body

c

was found, guarded by the faithful dog. They have raised a cairn of stones on the spot now; but Wordsworth's poem *Fidelity* and Scott's *Helvellyn* are the lasting memorials of that dumb hero.

THE KING OF DENMARK'S RIDE

CAROLINE ELIZABETH S. NORTON

Word was brought to the Danish king
 (Hurry!)
That the love of his heart lay suffering,
And pin'd for the comfort his voice would bring;
 (Oh! ride as though you were flying!)   5
Better he loves each golden curl
On the brow of that Scandinavian girl
Than his rich crown jewels of ruby and pearl;
 And his rose of the isles is dying!

Thirty nobles saddled with speed,   10
 (Hurry!)
Each one mounting a gallant steed
Which he kept for battle and days of need;
 (Oh! ride as though you were flying!)

2. Does *Hurry* rhyme with any word? Does it increase the speed of the poem? 3. Ordinarily where do you accent *suffering?* What two accents fall on this word in the poem? It is not good poetic art to force an unnatural accent upon a word. 5. This line closes without an accent. Such a line is said to have a feminine ending. In lines 5 and 9 do the feminine endings hasten or retard the motion of the poem? 9. Having read the stanza aloud, do you find the metre rapid enough to suggest a swift ride? 10. Note where the accents fall: Thirty nóbles sáddled with spéed. Let us mark the unaccented syllables thus ˘. Then we have: Thĭrtў nóblĕs sáddlĕd with spéed. Take your pencil and mark all the accented and unaccented syllables in the second stanza. You will find four accents to the line, and will recognize the metre as tetrameter (see page 13).

Spurs were struck in the foaming flank;　　　　15
Worn-out chargers stagger'd and sank;
Bridles were slacken'd, and girths were burst;
But ride as they would, the king rode first,
　　For his rose of the isles lay dying!

His nobles are beaten, one by one;　　　　20
　　(Hurry!)
They have fainted, and falter'd, and homeward gone;
His little fair page now follows alone,
　　For strength and for courage trying.
The king look'd back at that faithful child;　　　　25
Wan was the face that answering smil'd;
They passed the drawbridge with clattering din,
Then he dropp'd; and only the king rode in
　　Where his rose of the isles lay dying!

The king blew a blast on his bugle horn;　　　　30
　　(Silence!)
No answer came; but faint and forlorn
An echo return'd on the cold gray morn,
　　Like the breath of a spirit sighing.
The castle portal stood grimly wide;　　　　35
None welcom'd the king from that weary ride;
For dead, in the light of the dawning day,
The pale sweet form of the welcomer lay,
　　Who had yearn'd for his voice while dying!

The panting steed, with a drooping crest,　　　　40
　　Stood weary.
The king return'd from her chamber of rest,
The thick sobs choking in his breast;
And, that dumb companion eying,

25-26. What trait of the king is suggested?

The tears gush'd forth which he strove to check;   45
He bowed his head on his charger's neck:
"O steed — that every nerve didst strain,
Dear steed, our ride hath been in vain
    To the halls where my love lay dying!"

   45. What trait of the king? In a few words sketch the character of the king as you now know it.
   Has the poem unity — is all about one event? Has it climax — that is, does it become steadily more interesting? Is it clear, easy to understand? Has it a good deal of force — that is, does it stir the feelings? Do you learn anything about the horse except that it was swift and sympathetic?

HOW THEY BROUGHT THE GOOD NEWS FROM GHENT TO AIX

ROBERT BROWNING

I sprang to the stirrup, and Joris, and he;
I galloped, Dirck galloped, we galloped all three;
"Good speed!" cried the watch, as the gate-bolts undrew;
"Speed!" echoed the wall to us galloping through;
Behind shut the postern, the lights sank to rest,   5
And into the midnight we galloped abreast.

Not a word to each other; we kept the great pace
Neck by neck, stride by stride, never changing our place;
I turned in my saddle and made its girths tight,

   1. Name the metre according to the number of accents (see p. 13). 2. Does this line suggest a gallop? Would it be more like a gallop if, instead of *Dirck*, the word were *and?* Mark the accented and unaccented syllables in this line; it begins with an accented syllable. Turn back to the first stanza of Mrs. Norton's poem and see if any lines begin with an unaccented syllable. Which of the two poems is the more suggestive of a gallop? 8. Why is this line difficult to say rapidly? When said rapidly and well, does it help or hinder our getting the poet's thought?

Then shortened each stirrup, and set the pique right,   10
Rebuckled the cheek-strap, chained slacker the bit,
Nor galloped less steadily Roland a whit.

'Twas moonset at starting; but while we drew near
Lokeren, the cocks crew and twilight dawned clear;
At Boom, a great yellow star came out to see;   15
At Düffeld, 'twas morning as plain as could be;
And from Mecheln church-steeple we heard the half-chime,
So, Joris broke silence with, "Yet there is time!"

At Aershot, up leaped of a sudden the sun,
And against him the cattle stood black every one,   20
To stare thro' the mist at us galloping past,
And I saw my stout galloper Roland at last,
With resolute shoulders, each butting away
The haze, as some bluff river headland its spray:

And his low head and crest, just one sharp ear bent back   25
For my voice, and the other pricked out on his track;
And one eye's black intelligence, — ever that glance
O'er its white edge at me, his own master, askance!
And the thick heavy spume-flakes which aye and anon
His fierce lips shook upwards in galloping on.   30

By Hasselt, Dirck groaned; and cried Joris, "Stay spur!
Your Roos galloped bravely, the fault's not in her,
We'll remember at Aix " — for one heard the quick wheeze

11. Hard or easy to pronounce? Was the action itself hard or easy?
12. Hard or easy to pronounce? Do lines 11 and 12 make a good contrast
between the horse's action and the man's? 25–30. Would not these lines
be more pleasant to the ear if there were fewer monosyllables and more
such polysyllables as *steadily, resolute, galloper, galloping, Joris, yellow,
shoulders?*

"' Up he comes with the child, see, tight
In mouth, alive too, clutched from quite
A depth of ten feet — twelve, I bet!
Good dog! What, off again? There's yet   25
Another child to save? All right!

"' How strange we saw no other fall!
It's instinct in the animal.
Good dog! But he's a long while under:
If he got drowned I should not wonder — .   30
Strong current, that against the wall!

"' Here he comes, holds in mouth this time
— What may the thing be? Well, that's prime!
Now, did you ever? Reason reigns
In man alone, since all Tray's pains   35
Have fished — the child's doll from the slime!'

"And so, amid the laughter gay,
Trotted my hero off, — old Tray, —
Till somebody, prerogatived
With reason, reasoned: 'Why he dived,   40
His brain would show us, I should say.

"' John, go and catch — or, if needs be,
Purchase — that animal for me!
By vivisection, at expense
Of half an hour and eighteenpence,   45
How brain secretes dog's soul, we'll see!'"

---

39. *prerogatived with reason* — privileged (to say so and so).

Having read the poem, do you find the metre smooth and flowing, or abrupt and difficult? Name it according to number of accents (see p. 13). Has the poem unity? climax? perfect clearness? force?

HELVELLYN

SIR WALTER SCOTT

I climb'd the dark brow of the mighty Helvellyn,
  Lakes and mountains beneath me gleam'd misty and
    wide;
All was still, save by fits, when the eagle was yelling,
  And starting around me the echoes replied.
On the right, Striden-edge round the Redtarn was bending,
And Catchedicam its left verge was defending.   6
One huge nameless rock in the front was ascending,
  When I mark'd the sad spot where the wanderer had died.

Dark green was that spot 'mid the brown mountain-heather,
  Where the Pilgrim of Nature lay stretch'd in decay,   10
Like the corpse of an outcast abandoned to weather,
  Till the mountain winds wasted the tenantless clay.
Nor yet quite deserted, though lonely extended,
For, faithful in death, his mute favorite attended,
The much-loved remains of her master defended,   15
  And chased the hill-fox and the raven away.

How long didst thou think that his silence was slumber?
  When the wind waved his garment, how oft didst thou
    start?
How many long days and long weeks didst thou number,
  Ere he faded before thee, the friend of thy heart?   20
And oh! was it meet, that — no requiem read o'er him —

1. Trimeter, tetrameter, pentameter, hexameter, or heptameter? 2. Masculine or feminine ending? 3. A very bad rhyme. 5. Masculine or feminine ending? 8. Is the variety of endings in this stanza pleasant? 10. *Pilgrim of Nature* evidently means that the young man who was lost had been in the habit of taking solitary rambles to study nature.

No mother to weep, and no friend to deplore him,
And thou, little guardian, alone stretch'd before him —
Unhonor'd the Pilgrim from life should depart?

When a Prince to the fate of the Peasant has yielded, 25
The tapestry waves dark round the dim-lighted hall;
With scutcheons of silver the coffin is shielded,
And pages stand mute by the canopied pall:
Through the courts, at deep midnight, the torches are
gleaming;
In the proudly-arch'd chapel the banners are beaming, 30
Far adown the long aisle sacred music is streaming,
Lamenting a Chief of the people should fall.

But meeter for thee, gentle lover of nature,
To lay down thy head like the meek mountain lamb,
When, wilder'd, he drops from some cliff huge in stature,
And draws his last sob by the side of his dam. 36
And more stately thy couch by this desert lake lying,
Thy obsequies sung by the gray plover flying,
With one faithful friend but to witness thy dying,
In the arms of Helvellyn and Catchedicam. 40

35. *wilder'd*, bewildered. *Stature, nature*, an imperfect, but not un-
pleasant rhyme.

Enumerate the sounds suggested in this poem. What two pictures
does Scott contrast?

Plan of Summary. — Reviewing the chapter, (1) enumerate the
kinds of metre, naming them merely by the number of accents in the line.
Then (2) say which poem is most noticeable for melody; (3) which
for beauty of suggested sights; (4) which for pleasure of suggested
sounds; (5) which for pleasure of suggested activity; (6) which is
most easily understood; (7) which moves the reader most deeply;
(8) which shows most skill in character drawing; (9) which, your
critical judgment tells you, is the best piece of work; (10) which you
like the best, — without regard to its deserved rank, or its fame.

CHAPTER II

THE HEROISM OF WAR

WHETHER righteous or unrighteous, every war is a terrible thing. The boy dreams of it, is haunted by the thought of it, dreads it. He imagines himself leading forlorn hopes, sustaining hideous wounds, or meeting death with fortitude; but he thanks his stars when he remembers that he is not yet called to arms. It is therefore extraordinary that, when war actually breaks out, boys are not slow to enlist. They become different persons. Reserve powers, that not even they suspected, have been called out. Yesterday they thought death the most horrible thing in the world; to-day they regard it as an incident. Suppose they die; they will do their duty first. If they cannot control death, they will defy him; put them in a hopeless fight, and they will sell their lives as dearly as possible. This defiance of the uncontrollable we call sublimity of character.

Emerson's lines beginning, "In an Age of Fops and Toys," remind us that a possibility of the sublime is in every boy.

> So nigh is grandeur to our dust,
> So near is God to man,
> When Duty whispers low, *Thou must*,
> The Youth replies, *I can*. ,

This was often demonstrated in 1860, in the case of tender boys who, as Emerson elsewhere puts it, " had never encountered any rougher play than a baseball match."

Once in the war, the youth has no lack of chances to live the same first experience over. One day he is a commonplace soldier, the next, a hero. Perhaps he is anything but the educated and refined youth of Emerson's thought, and yet have splendid possibilities. The British soldier, as Mr. Kipling has shown him to us, is rather a rough piece of humanity, even when he is fighting for " The Widow." The first poem in this chapter, by Sir Francis Doyle, exhibits exactly this kind of fellow, poor, reckless, rude, low-born, untaught, who last night jested, quaffed, and swore, but who to-day would not flinch, though torn limb from limb. He dies like a Spartan, for his soul is great.

The Private of the Buffs, p. 34.

He probably would deny that he is brave. Emerson writes as follows in his essay on *Courage*: —

" I knew a young soldier who died in the early campaign, who confided to his sister that he had made up his mind to volunteer for the war. ' I have not,' he said, ' any proper courage, but I shall never let any one find it out.' And he had accustomed himself always to go into whatever place of danger, and do whatever he was afraid to do, setting a dogged resolution to resist this natural infirmity."

If the young soldier must fight, he prefers to charge. When elbow touches elbow in a double-quick, or stirrup grazes stirrup in a gallop, then nobody stops to reckon the chances of coming out alive. Mr. Edmund Clarence Stedman and the late Lord Tennyson have celebrated the glorious rush of the cavalry charge. The incident of the latter's poem is historic, belonging to the Crimean War, where dogged English met savage Russians. Six hundred British horsemen charged what was practically an army ; a few came back.

The Charge of the Light Brigade, p. 36.

The English soldier is good at this kind of thing. He has no serious objection to fighting against a few odds, and he is said not to know when he is beaten. A braver deed than the charge of the light brigade was the attack made by a single English ship, the *Revenge*, on fifty-three galleons of

The *Revenge*, p. 38.

the Spanish Armada.   Sir Walter Raleigh, a cousin of Sir
Richard Grenville, who commanded the *Revenge*, has a
fine prose account of the exploit, and Tennyson, keeping
very close to the facts, has written on the same subject one
of the best of war ballads.   It seems that when the Span-
iards were reported to Sir Richard at Flores, in the Azores,
there were five other English ships with him, under com-
mand of Lord Thomas Howard.   This gentleman had the
reputation of a brave soldier, but he was no Grenville; so
he got away with his five ships, to mend them for a battle.
Grenville, delaying to bring his sick aboard, could not
escape meeting the enemy.   He made straight at the gal-
leons, fought them for a day and a night, sank some and
shattered many, and yielded only when wounded to the
death.

Fighting is not the only duty of war.*   Sometimes it is a
soldier's business to stand very still and be shot at.   Some-
times it is to bear privation or disease gracefully.   Some-
times it is to wait for months for reënforcements, as Gordon
waited at Khartoum, only to lose his life by his govern-
ment's delay.   Waiting to be rescued is not always blessed
by such relief as came to the British soldiers shut up in
Lucknow.   Robert Lowell and Whittier have both sung
that story, with its honorable mention of the Highland girl
whose keen ear caught the sound of the Highland pipes
before any one else in that despairing garrison could hear
them.   Sometimes it is a soldier's business to die as those
of the *Birkenhead* died, whom Sir Francis Doyle has com-
memorated.   The *Birkenhead* went on the rocks of the
African coast, in 1852.   Five hundred persons — soldiers
and their families — were on board, besides the crew.   The
water was full of sharks.   The soldiers were marshalled on
deck and stood at attention while the women and children
were carried ashore in the boats.   The ship did not hold

The Loss of
the *Birken-
head*, p. 45.

together long, but when she keeled over and went down, nearly all the soldiers were still standing at attention.

This "disciplined heroism," as Lowell termed it, has come to be called "the Birkenhead drill." When the magnificent new battleship *Victoria* capsized, a few years ago, the Birkenhead drill was easily enforced. Admiral, officers, and marines went down together. Mr. Kipling wrote a dialect poem celebrating the behavior of the marines on this occasion, and Mr. Watts-Dunton made a noble sonnet on the conduct of two officers, one of the highest rank in the service, the other of the lowest, who stood shoulder to shoulder at the wheel.

Soldier and Sailor Too, p. 47.

Midshipman Lanyon, p. 48.

Such deeds as these tax the courage of the bravest, but it must be remembered that one ship is not one man. Courage is contagious. Probably it is easier to die with many than venture alone against a few. Even the superb exploit of rallying an army by the sound of fife and drum, an exploit achieved by the two boys in Mr. Kipling's story, would hardly have been dared by one alone. There is nothing in fiction more stirring than the account of how these fourteen-year-old gamins, the very scourings of the street, watched with disgust the flight of their regiment before the terrible Afghan knives, and then sallied out across an exposed valley, within easy range of hundreds of Martinis, to see if their discordant little strains of music might not save the day. That music did save the day, though both drummers had to seal the bargain with their lives. Into this act there entered several elements: first, the inborn heroic courage which distinguished these little martyrs; then the pride and confidence that grows out of comradeship; and lastly, I regret to say, the fumes of a certain amount of canteen rum. Lonely and fine as this bravery was, Browning's *Incident of the French Camp* exploits a lonelier and finer bravery as it appeared in a boy of the

The Drums of the Fore and Aft, p. 49.

Incident of the French Camp, p. 81.

Napoleonic wars. He rode alone on a dangerous mission to acquaint the emperor with the fall of Ratisbon, an important post of the enemy. He made his report in erect military fashion, and the despondent Napoleon was instantly encouraged in his plans — they soared up again like fire. But presently the keen eye of the great man perceived that the lad ·was hurt. "You're wounded!" "Nay, I'm killed, sire," replied the proud boy, as he fell at his emperor's feet.

The last poem by Browning in this chapter indicates the worth of the unassuming hero, and the many kinds of skilful individual service required in war. In the English war with the French, 1692, a French squadron was almost chased ashore at Saint-Malo. It begged for harbor, but the pilots of the place declared that ships of such burthen could not clear the rocks at the narrow river mouth. In this dilemma a simple Breton sailor, Hervé Riel, offered to get the squadron safely in or forfeit his head. The commander, Damfreville, let him try. Riel saved the twenty-two ships, and would take no other reward than release from the service for the rest of his life. Browning, who likes to sharpen dramatic effects, makes him ask and get nothing but a single holiday. Hervé Riel, p. 83.

It is fine to see what a high sense of loyalty is developed in war. At the very time when camp and field are ruining many of the soldiers, turning them into cruel, profane, and drunken brutes, the sense of duty to the flag is the last quality of character to degenerate. A deserter is a rare thing, whether in an Anglo-Saxon or in a Spanish army. Mr. Gerald Massey makes use of the soldier's hatred for desertion to exhibit the detestable quality of a deserter from any cause. The Deserter from the Cause, p. 89.

In the account of the Birkenhead we had a story of passive heroism, noble endurance. Two poems in this chapter exhibit endurance unhelped by the stimulus of comradeship.

Heather Ale, p. 90. The old man in Stevenson's ballad refuses to disclose to the enemy the secret of the famous ale, though they slay his son and torture him. Pretending that he hesitates to debase himself before his son by treacherously giving up the secret, he advises the enemy to drown the boy. When this is done he stifles his paternal anguish, and declares that he feared the boy's ability to keep the secret. The child is silent forever, and torture of the father will be in

Adam of Gordon, p. 93. vain. Adam Gordon's lady, in the folk ballad, gives her own life and those of her bairns rather than surrender the castle to her husband's enemy. The passive heroism of woman is greater than that of man. Woman is timid in little matters, but intrepid in great.[1]

A Plantation Heroine, p. 96. Women are as brave in war time in our own century as they ever were in the past. Mr. Eggleston, once a Confederate soldier, tells how women starved themselves to furnish food for the Confederate army. Mr. Higginson,

Decoration, p. 103. once a Union soldier, declares that she who, staying uncomplainingly at home, sent her husband and sons to war, was the bravest of the brave. The courage of the army nurse, who faces pestilence and death, has been sung again and again. Longfellow, among other poets, wrote of Florence Nightingale, whose shadow the soldiers kissed. Whittier sang of the Mexican women who worked on the field of Buena Vista. In his note on the subject he says:

The Angels of Buena Vista, p. 98. "A letter-writer from Mexico states that, at the terrible fight of Buena Vista, Mexican women were seen hovering near the field of death, for the purpose of giving aid and

---

[1] When the ill-fated French liner, the *Bourgogne*, went down, July 4, 1898, one woman was saved; nearly two hundred men saved themselves. Of the scores of women who were left to drown, two were members of the Lewis Institute, — Miss Evelyn Reeves, one of the faculty, and Miss Frances Hess, a student-teacher. All the survivors admitted that the women behaved very calmly and bravely.

succor to the wounded. One poor woman was found sur-
rounded by the maimed and suffering of both armies, min-
istering to the wants of Americans as well as Mexicans,
with impartial tenderness."

There is something inexpressibly sad in a soldier's burial
in a foreign land. He has fought for his country and his
family, but these are denied the consolation of burying
him. Tennyson, grieving for his friend Arthur Hallam,
the wonderful youth who died at twenty-three, is partly
consoled when the ship brings Arthur home : —

> 'Tis well; 'tis something; we may stand
> Where he in English earth is laid,
> And from his ashes may be made
> The violet of his native land.

But it is rarely thus with the soldier or the sailor. The one, The Burial
like Sir John Moore, of whose sad fate in Spain Charles of Sir John Moore,
Wolfe wrote, is buried darkly at dead of night, and left p. 104.
alone, afar. The other's

> heavy-shotted hammock-shroud
> Drops in his vast and wandering grave.

Tears for such a death cannot be too bitter if the cause
the soldier fought for was unrighteous. But the soldier of
a good cause cannot be killed. His body may moulder,
but his soul goes marching on. A thousand will rally to
the flag he tried to protect. When America was forced to
free herself from England, there were two Englands, one
of George the Third and one of Chatham. The second of The
these was the sane England, and Chatham told the truth American Revolution,
when he shouted, "You cannot, my lords, you *cannot* con- p. 105.
quer America." It is a pity that the British regulars had
to die for the first of these two Englands. Lowell, standing
beside the grave of a British soldier, at Concord, reflects
thus : —

D

These men were brave enough, and true
To the hired soldier's bull-dog creed;
What brought them here they never knew,
They fought as suits the English breed;
They came three thousand miles, and died,
To keep the Past upon its throne;
Unheard, beyond the ocean tide,
Their English mother made her moan.

Concord
Hymn,
p. 107.
But the king and Lord North did not hear the shot, which, Emerson tells us, was heard round the world. They did not understand that embattled farmers, fighting anywhere for their homes and justice, will dare to die and leave their children free. Strangely enough, the English whose grandfathers belonged to the side of Lord North could not understand, before 1865, that Americans have something more than dollars to fight for. Says Lowell, in his delightful essay, *On a Certain Condescension in Foreigners:* "Till after our Civil War it never seemed to enter the head of any foreigner, especially of an Englishman, that an American had what could be called a country, except as a place to eat, sleep, and trade in. Then it seemed to strike them suddenly. 'By Jove, you know, fellahs don't fight like that for a shop-till!' No, I rather think not."

THE PRIVATE OF THE BUFFS

SIR FRANCIS HASTINGS DOYLE

Last night, among his fellow-roughs,
    He jested, quaff'd, and swore :
A drunken private of the Buffs,
    Who never look'd before.

To-day, beneath the foeman's frown,   5
    He stands in Elgin's place,
Ambassador from Britain's crown,
    And type of all her race.

Poor, reckless, rude, low-born, untaught,
    Bewilder'd, and alone,   10
A heart, with English instinct fraught,
    He yet can call his own.
Ay, tear his body limb from limb,
    Bring cord, or axe, or flame ;
He only knows, that not through him   15
    Shall England come to shame.

Far Kentish hop-fields round him seem'd,
    Like dreams, to come and go ;
Bright leagues of cherry-blossom gleam'd,
    One sheet of living snow ;   20
The smoke, above his father's door,
    In gray soft eddyings hung :
Must he then watch it rise no more,
    Doom'd by himself, so young?

Yes, honor calls ! — with strength like steel   25
    He put the vision by.
Let dusky Indians whine and kneel ;
    An English lad must die.

Note the metre : there are eight syllables in the line, with four accents. That gives four feet, thus : ∪′ | ∪′ | ∪′ | ∪′ | . In each foot the unaccented syllable comes first, and the foot is therefore an iambus (see p. 13). The verses are alternately iambic tetrameter and iambic trimeter.

Note the rhyme-scheme ; it may be marked algebraically thus : a b a b, c d c d.

6. Lord Elgin (the *g* is hard) was a famous English ambassador. 16. In a few words describe the physical appearance and bearing of the hero from what you have thus far read. 24. Does this third stanza contain any suggestion of sounds? What colors are there in the soft Kentish landscape?

And thus, with eyes that would not shrink,
  With knee to man unbent,   30
Unfaltering on its dreadful brink,
  To his red grave he went.

Vain, mightiest fleets, of iron fram'd;
  Vain, those all-shattering guns;
Unless proud England keep, untam'd,   35
  The strong heart of her sons.
So, let his name through Europe ring —
  A man of mean estate,
Who died, as firm as Sparta's king,
  Because his soul was great.   40

32. What is the strongest adjective in the fourth stanza ?
Select from the entire poem all the words that appeal to the sense of muscular tension. Which of the following adjectives best describes the tone of the poem — vigorous, pleasing, rugged, stirring, charming ?

THE CHARGE OF THE LIGHT BRIGADE

ALFRED, LORD TENNYSON

Half a league, half a league,
  Half a league onward,
All in the valley of Death
  Rode the six hundred.
"Forward, the Light Brigade !   5
Charge for the guns !" he said:
Into the valley of Death
  Rode the six hundred.

1. Dimeter, trimeter, tetrameter, pentameter, hexameter, or heptameter?
Trochaic or dactyllic?   (See p. 13.)

" Forward, the Light Brigade ! "
Was there a man dismay'd?   10
Not tho' the soldier knew
   Some one had blunder'd:
Theirs not to make reply,
Theirs not to reason why,
Theirs but to do and die: 15
Into the valley of Death
   Rode the six hundred.

Cannon to right of them,
Cannon to left of them,
Cannon in front of them   20
   Volley'd and thunder'd;
Storm'd at with shot and shell,
Boldly they rode and well,
Into the jaws of Death,
Into the mouth of Hell   25
   Rode the six hundred.

Flash'd all their sabres bare,
Flash'd as they turn'd in air
Sabring the gunners there,
Charging an army, while   30
   All the world wonder'd:
Plunged in the battery-smoke
Right thro' the line they broke;
Cossack and Russian
Reel'd from the sabre-stroke   35
   Shatter'd and sunder'd.
Then they rode back, but not —
   Not the six hundred.

14–16, 19–21, 27–29, 39–41, 53–54. Are the repetitions pleasing? Do they hasten the movement? 34–36. Why does this stanza have extra lines?

Cannon to right of them,
Cannon to left of them,   40
Cannon behind them
   Volley'd and thunder'd;
Storm'd at with shot and shell,
While horse and hero fell,
They that had fought so well   45
Came thro' the jaws of Death,
Back from the mouth of Hell,
All that was left of them,
   Left of six hundred.

When can their glory fade?   50
O the wild charge they made!
   All the world wonder'd.
Honor the charge they made!
Honor the Light Brigade,
   Noble six hundred.   55

THE *REVENGE*

A BALLAD OF THE FLEET

ALFRED, LORD TENNYSON

I

At Flores in the Azores Sir Richard Grenville lay,
And a pinnace, like a flutter'd bird, came flying from far
    away:
"Spanish ships of war at sea! we have sighted fifty-three!"

1. Dimeter, trimeter, tetrameter, pentameter, hexameter, or heptameter?
What is the predominant foot? (See p. 13.) 1. *Flores* has two syllables.
2. *Pinnace*, here a sailboat. 3, 4, 5, 6, etc. Note the rhyme in the middle
of the line — medial rhyme. In reading, pause a bit after each rhyme.
What unpleasant effect would be given if the half-lines were printed as
lines? Note that we enjoy these rhymes in poetry, though spoken by sailors,
whereas we should laugh at them in real conversation.

Then sware Lord Thomas Howard: "'Fore God I am no
    coward;
But I can not meet them here, for my ships are out of
    gear,   5
And the half my men are sick.   I must fly, but follow quick.
We are six ships of the line; can we fight with fifty-three?"

II

Then spake Sir Richard Grenville: "I know you are no
    coward;
You fly them for a moment to fight with them again.
But I've ninety men and more that are lying sick ashore.   10
I should count myself the coward if I left them, my Lord
    Howard,
To these Inquisition dogs and the devildoms of Spain."

III

So Lord Howard past away with five ships of war that day,
Till he melted like a cloud in the silent summer heaven;
But Sir Richard bore in hand all his sick men from the
    land   15
Very carefully and slow,
Men of Bideford in Devon,
And we laid them on the ballast down below;
For we brought them all aboard,
And they blest him in their pain, that they were not left
    to Spain,   20
To the thumbscrew and the stake, for the glory of the Lord.

7. *Ships of the line*, warships large enough for the line of battle.
12. *Inquisition:* the Spanish Inquisition was a Roman Catholic tribunal for
punishing heretics. *Devildoms* seems to be a vague uncomplimentary
name for Spanish localities. 16–17. Why are these lines short? 17. *Devon*
has a short ĕ. 20–21. Why are the lines long, as before?

IV

He had only a hundred seamen to work the ship and to
     fight,

And he sail'd away from Flores till the Spaniard came in
     sight,

With his huge sea-castles heaving upon the weather bow.

"Shall we fight or shall we fly?   25

Good Sir Richard, tell us now,

For to fight is but to die!

There'll be little of us left by the time this sun be set."

And Sir Richard said again: "We be all good English men.

Let us bang these dogs of Seville, the children of the
     devil,   30

For I never turn'd my back upon Don or devil yet."

V

Sir Richard spoke and he laugh'd, and we roar'd a hurrah,
     and so

The little *Revenge* ran on sheer into the heart of the foe,

With her hundred fighters on deck, and her ninety sick
     below;

For half of their fleet to the right and half to the left were
     seen,   35

And the little *Revenge* ran on thro' the long sea-lane between.

VI

Thousands of their soldiers look'd down from their decks
     and laugh'd,

Thousands of their seamen made mock at the mad little
     craft

Running on and on, till delay'd

24. *Weather bow* means the side toward the wind. 25–27. Why are
these lines short? 30. *Seville* always rhymes with *devil*. 31. *Don*, a
Spanish nobleman. 36. Why are there no short lines in this stanza?
39. Why a short line?

By their mountain-like *San Philip* that, of fifteen hundred
    tons,   40
And up-shadowing high above us with her yawning tiers of
    guns,
Took the breath from our sails, and we stay'd.

VII

And while now the great *San Philip* hung above us like a
    cloud
Whence the thunderbolt will fall
Long and loud,   45
Four galleons drew away
From the Spanish fleet that day,
And two upon the larboard and two upon the starboard lay,
And the battle-thunder broke from them all.

VIII

But anon the great *San Philip*, she bethought herself and
    went   50
Having that within her womb that had left her ill content;
And the rest they came aboard us, and they fought us hand
    to hand,
For a dozen times they came with their pikes and musketeers,
And a dozen times we shook 'em off as a dog that shakes
    his ears
When he leaps from the water to the land.   55

IX

And the sun went down, and the stars came out far over the
    summer sea,
But never a moment ceased the fight of the one and the
    fifty-three.

44–45. Why short lines? 46. *Galleons*, large Spanish ships. 46–47. Do
these short lines suggest the gradual process of drawing away?

Ship after ship, the whole night long, their high-built
    galleons came,
Ship after ship, the whole night long, with her battle-
    thunder and flame;
Ship after ship, the whole night long, drew back with
    her dead and her shame.   60
For some were sunk and many were shatter'd, and so could
    fight us no more —
God of battles, was ever a battle like this in the world
    before?

x

For he said "Fight on! fight on!"
Tho' his vessel was all but a wreck;
And it chanced that, when half of the short summer night
    was gone,   65
With a grisly wound to be drest he had left the deck,
But a bullet struck him that was dressing it suddenly dead,
And himself he was wounded again in the side and the
    head,
And he said "Fight on! fight on!"

XI

And the night went down, and the sun smiled out far over
    the summer sea,   70
And the Spanish fleet with broken sides lay round us all in
    a ring;
But they dared not touch us again, for they fear'd that we
    still could sting,
So they watch'd what the end would be.
And we had not fought them in vain,
But in perilous plight were we,   75
Seeing forty of our poor hundred were slain,
And half of the rest of us maim'd for life

In the crash of the cannonades and the desperate strife;
And the sick men down in the hold were most of them stark
    and cold,
And the pikes were all broken or bent, and the powder
    was all of it spent;   .   80
And the masts and the rigging were lying over the side;
But Sir Richard cried in his English pride,
"We have fought such a fight for a day and a night
As may never be fought again!
We have won great glory, my men!   85
And a day less or more
At sea or ashore,
We die — does it matter when?
Sink me the ship, Master Gunner — sink her, split her in
    twain!
Fall into the hands of God, not into the hands of Spain!" 90

XII

And the gunner said "Ay, ay," but the seamen made reply:
"We have children, we have wives,
And the Lord hath spared our lives.
We will make the Spanish promise, if we yield, to let us go;
We shall live to fight again and to strike another blow." 95
And the lion there lay dying, and they yielded to the foe.

XIII

And the stately Spanish men to their flagship bore him
    then,
Where they laid him by the mast, old Sir Richard caught
    at last,
And they praised him to his face with their courtly foreign
    grace;
But he rose upon their decks, and he cried: 100

"I have fought for Queen and Faith like a valiant man and
    true;
I have only done my duty as a man is bound to do:
With a joyful spirit I Sir Richard Grenville die!"
And he fell upon their decks, and he died.

XIV   .

And they stared at the dead that had been so valiant
    and true   105
And had holden the power and glory of Spain so cheap
That he dared her with one little ship and his English few;
Was he devil or man?   He was devil for aught they knew,
But they sank his body with honor down into the deep,
And they mann'd the *Revenge* with a swarthier alien
    crew,   110
And away she sail'd with her loss and long'd for her own;
When a wind from the lands they had ruin'd awoke from
    sleep,
And the water began to heave and the weather to moan,
And or ever that evening ended a great gale blew,
And a wave like the wave that is raised by an earth-
    quake grew,   115
Till it smote on their hulls and their sails and their masts
    and their flags,
And the whole sea plunged and fell on the shot-shatter'd
    navy of Spain,
And the little *Revenge* herself went down by the island
    crags
To be lost evermore in the main.

---

119. Which of the following adjectives and phrases may properly
be applied to this poem: slow, simple in rhythm, complex in rhythm, swift,
rushing, impetuous, swinging, heroic, stirring, pretty, dramatic, pleasing,
thrilling?

THE LOSS OF THE *BIRKENHEAD*

SUPPOSED TO BE NARRATED BY A SOLDIER WHO SURVIVED

SIR FRANCIS HASTINGS DOYLE

Right on our flank the crimson sun went down,
  The deep sea rolled around in dark repose,
When, like the wild shriek from some captured town,
    A cry of women rose.

The stout ship *Birkenhead* lay hard and fast,   5
  Caught, without hope, upon a hidden rock;
Her timbers thrilled as nerves, when through them passed
    The spirit of that shock.

And ever like base cowards, who leave their ranks
  In danger's hour, before the rush of steel,   10
Drifted away, disorderly, the planks
    From underneath her keel.

Confusion spread, for, though the coast seemed near,
  Sharks hovered thick along that white sea-brink.
The boats could hold? — not all; and it was clear   15
    She was about to sink.

"Out with those boats, and let us haste away,"
  Cried one, "ere yet yon sea the bark devours."
The man thus clamoring was, I scarce need say,
    No officer of ours.   20

We knew our duty better than to care
  For such loose babblers, and made no reply,
Till our good colonel gave the word, and there
    Formed us in line to die.

There rose no murmur from the ranks, no thought,　　25
　　By shameful strength, unhonored life to seek;
Our post to quit we were not trained, nor taught
　　　　To trample down the weak.

So we made women with their children go,
　　The oars ply back again, and yet again;　　30
Whilst, inch by inch, the drowning ship sank low,
　　　　Still under steadfast men.

What follows, why recall?　The brave who died,
　　Died without flinching in the bloody surf;
They sleep as well, beneath that purple tide,　　35
　　　　As others, under turf; —

They sleep as well, and, roused from their wild grave,
　　Wearing their wounds like stars, shall rise again,
Joint-heirs with Christ, because they bled to save
　　　　His weak ones, not in vain.　　40

If that day's work no clasp or medal mark,
　　If each proud heart no cross of bronze may press,
Nor cannon thunder loud from Tower and Park,
　　　　This feel we, none the less:

That those whom God's high grace there saved from ill — 45
　　Those also, left His martyrs in the bay —
Though not by siege, though not in battle, still
　　　　Full well have earned their pay.

---

43. London Tower and Hyde Park.
　　Is the diction of this poem plainer, or more elaborate, than that of Tenny-
son's *The Revenge?*　Note the short closing line of each stanza.　Exam-
ine each to see whether some emphatic thought is thus expressed, or whether
the line is a mere "tag" to the stanza.　Is the poem calm in tone?　Should
its tone have been other than it is?

SOLDIER AND SAILOR TOO [1]

RUDYARD KIPLING

. . . They came of our lot, they was brothers to us; they
    was beggars we'd met and knew;
Yes, barrin' an inch in the chest and the arms, they was
    doubles o' me and you;
For they weren't no special chrysanthemums — soldier an'
    sailor too!

. . . We're most of us liars, we're 'arf of us thieves, an' the
    rest are as rank as can be,
But once in a while we can finish in style (which I 'ope
    it won't 'appen to me).   5
But it makes you think better o' you an' your friends, an'
    the work you may 'ave to do,
When you think o' the sinkin' *Victorier's* Jollies — soldier
    an' sailor too!
Now there isn't no room for to say ye don't know — they
    'ave proved it plain and true —
That whether it's Widow, or whether it's ship, Victorier's
    work is to do.
An' they done it, the Jollies — 'Er Majesty's Jollies —
    soldier and sailor too.   10

---

[1] From *The Seven Seas*, Copyright, 1896, by Rudyard Kipling. Quoted
by special permission of the author and of the publishers, D. Appleton and
Co.

MIDSHIPMAN LANYON [1]

THEODORE WATTS-DUNTON

"Midshipman Lanyon refused to leave the Admiral and perished." — *Times*, June 30, 1893.

Our tears are tears of pride who see thee stand,
    Watching the great bows dip, the stern uprear,
    Beside thy chief, whose hope was still to steer,
Though Fate had said, "Ye shall not win the land!"
What joy was thine to answer each command   5
    From him calamity had made more dear,
    Save that which bade thee part when Death drew near,
Till Tryon sank with Lanyon at his hand!
Death only and doom are sure: they come, they rend,
    But still the fight we make can crown us great: 10
    Life hath no joy like his who fights with Fate
Shoulder to shoulder with a stricken friend:
    Proud are our tears for thee, most fortunate,
Whose day, so brief, had such heroic end.

---

[1] Reprinted from "The Coming of Love, and Other Poems," by permission of Mr. John Lane.

How many lines has this poem? Notice the curious rhyme-scheme: *stand uprear steer land, command dear near hand; rend great fate, friend fortunate end.* Express it thus: a b b a, a b b a; c d d, c d c. A poem of fourteen lines rhyming thus is called a sonnet. A sonnet may rhyme in several other ways, but must consist of fourteen lines. Notice that the first eight lines are really complete in themselves (telling the story); the first eight lines of a typical sonnet are called the *octave*. Notice that the last six lines are in a sense complete in themselves (dealing with a general thought suggested by Lanyon's fate); the last six lines of a typical sonnet are called the *sestet*.

THE DRUMS OF THE FORE AND AFT[1]

RUDYARD KIPLING

In the Army List they still stand as " The Fore and Fit Princess Hohenzollern-Sigmaringen-Auspach's Merthyr-Tydfilshire Own Royal Loyal Light Infantry, Regimental District 329A," but the Army through all its barracks and canteens knows them now as the " Fore and Aft." They 5 may in time do something that shall make their new title honorable, but at present they are bitterly ashamed, and the man who calls them " Fore and Aft " does so at the risk of the head which is on his shoulders.

Two words breathed into the stables of a certain Cav- 10 alry Regiment will bring the men out into the streets with belts and mops and bad language ; but a whisper of " Fore and Aft " will bring out this regiment with rifles.

Their one excuse is that they came again and did their best to finish the job in style. But for a time all their 15 world knows that they were openly beaten, whipped, dumb-cowed, shaking, and afraid. The men know it ; their officers know it ; the Horse Guards know it, and when the next war comes the enemy will know it also. There are two or three regiments of the Line that have 20 a black mark against their name which they will then wipe out ; and it will be excessively inconvenient for the troops upon whom they do their wiping.

The courage of the British soldier is officially supposed to be above proof, and, as a general rule, it is so. The 25

---

[1] Mr. Kipling's style is somewhat elliptical, that is, takes a good deal of knowledge on the reader's part for granted ; hence it must be read slowly. The necessity of abridging the piece somewhat (and of omitting here and there rough expressions of army life) makes it no easier for the reader to keep the thread of the story.

E

exceptions are decently shovelled out of sight, only to be
referred to in the freshest of unguarded talk that occa-
sionally swamps a Mess-table at midnight.   Then one
hears strange and horrible stories of men not following
their officers, of orders being given by those who had no 30
right to give them, and of disgrace that, but for the stand-
ing luck of the British Army, might have ended in brilliant
disaster.   These are unpleasant stories to listen to, and
the Messes tell them under their breath, sitting by the big
wood fires; and the young officer bows his head and 35
thinks to himself, please God, his men shall never behave
unhandily.

The British soldier is not altogether to be blamed for
occasional lapses; but this verdict he should not know.
A moderately intelligent General will waste six months 40
in mastering the craft of the particular war that he may
be waging; a Colonel may utterly misunderstand the
capacity of his regiment for three months after it has
taken the field; and even a Company Commander may
err and be deceived as to the temper and temperament 45
of his own handful: wherefore the soldier, and the soldier
of to-day more particularly, should not be blamed for
falling back.   He should be shot or hanged afterwards
— to encourage the others; but he should not be vilified
in newspapers, for that is want of tact and waste of space. 50

He has, let us say, been in the service of the Empress
for, perhaps, four years.   He will leave in another two
years.   He has no inherited morals, and four years are
not sufficient to drive toughness into his fibre, or to teach
him how holy a thing is his Regiment.   He wants to 55
drink, he wants to enjoy himself — in India he wants to
save money — and he does not in the least like getting
hurt.   He has received just sufficient education to make
him understand half the purport of the orders he receives,

and to speculate on the nature of clean, incised, and 60
shattering wounds. Thus, if he is told to deploy under
fire preparatory to an attack, he knows that he runs a
very great risk of being killed while he is deploying, and
suspects that he is being thrown away to gain ten min-
utes' time. He may either deploy with desperate swift- 65
ness, or he may shuffle, or bunch, or break, according
to the discipline under which he has lain for four years.

Armed with imperfect knowledge, cursed with the
rudiments of an imagination, hampered by the intense
selfishness of the lower classes, and unsupported by any 70
regimental associations, this young man is suddenly in-
troduced to an enemy who in eastern lands is always
ugly, generally tall and hairy, and frequently noisy. If
he looks to the right and the left and sees old soldiers
— men of twelve years' service, who, he knows, know 75
what they are about — taking a charge, rush, or demon-
stration without embarrassment, he is consoled and
applies his shoulder to the butt of his rifle with a stout
heart. His peace is the greater if he hears a senior,
who has taught him his soldiering and broken his head 80
on occasion, whispering: "They'll shout and carry on
like this for five minutes. Then they'll rush in, and
then we've got 'em by the short hairs!"

But, on the other hand, if he sees only men of his
own term of service, turning white and playing with 85
their triggers and saying, "What's up now?" while the
Company Commanders are sweating into their sword-
hilts and shouting: "Front-rank, fix bayonets. Steady
there — steady! Sight for three hundred — no, for five!
Lie down, all! Steady! Front-rank, kneel!" and so 90
forth, he becomes unhappy; and grows acutely miserable
when he hears a comrade turn over with the rattle of
fire-irons falling into the fender, and the grunt of a

pole-axed ox. If he can be moved about a little and
allowed to watch the effect of his own fire on the enemy 95
he feels merrier, and may be then worked up to the
blind passion of fighting, which is, contrary to general
belief, controlled by a chilly Devil and shakes men like
ague. If he is not moved about, and begins to feel cold
at the pit of the stomach, and in that crisis is badly 100
mauled and hears orders that were never given, he will
break, and he will break badly; and of all things under
the light of the Sun there is nothing more terrible than
a broken British regiment. When the worst comes to
the worst and the panic is really epidemic, the men must 105
be e'en let go, and the Company Commanders had
better escape to the enemy and stay there for safety's
sake. If they can be made to come again they are not
pleasant men to meet; because they will not break twice.

About thirty years from this date, when we have suc- 110
ceeded in half-educating everything that wears trousers,
our Army will be a beautifully unreliable machine. It
will know too much and it will do too little. Later
still, when all men are at the mental level of the officer
of to-day, it will sweep the earth. Speaking roughly, 115
you must employ either blackguards or gentlemen, or,
best of all, blackguards commanded by gentlemen, to
do butcher's work with efficiency and despatch. The
ideal soldier should, of course, think for himself — the
Pocket-book says so. Unfortunately, to attain this virtue 120
he has to pass through the phrase of thinking of himself,
and that is misdirected genius. A blackguard may be
slow to think for himself, but he is genuinely anxious to
kill, and a little punishment teaches him how to guard
his own skin and perforate another's. A powerfully 125
prayerful Highland Regiment, officered by rank Presby-
terians, is, perhaps, one degree more terrible in action

than a hard-bitted thousand of irresponsible Irish ruffians
led by most improper young unbelievers. But these
things prove the rule — which is that the midway men 130
are not to be trusted alone. They have ideas about the
value of life and an up-bringing that has not taught them
to go on and take the chances. They are carefully un-
provided with a backing of comrades who have been shot
over, and until that backing is re-introduced, as a great 135
many Regimental Commanders intend it shall be, they
are more liable to disgrace themselves than the size of
the Empire or the dignity of the Army allows. Their
officers are as good as good can be, because their train-
ing begins early, and God has arranged that a clean-run 140
youth of the British middle classes shall, in the matter
of backbone and brains, surpass all other youths. For
this reason a child of eighteen will stand up, doing
nothing, with a tin sword in his hand and joy in his
heart until he is dropped. If he dies, he dies like a 145
gentleman. If he lives, he writes Home that he has
been "potted," "sniped," "chipped," or "cut over,"
and sits down to besiege Government for a wound-
gratuity until the next little war breaks out, when he
perjures himself before a Medical Board, blarneys his 150
Colonel, burns incense round his Adjutant, and is
allowed to go to the Front once more.

Which homily brings me directly to a brace of the
most finished little fiends that ever banged drum or
tootled fife in the Band of a British Regiment. They 155
ended their sinful career by open and flagrant mutiny
and were shot for it. Their names were Jakin and Lew
— Piggy Lew — and they were bold, bad drummer-boys,
both of them frequently birched by the Drum-Major of
the Fore and Aft. 160

Jakin was a stunted child of fourteen, and Lew was

about the same age. When not looked after, they smoked and drank. They swore habitually after the manner of the Barrack-room, which is cold-swearing and comes from between clinched teeth; and they fought 165 religiously once a week. Jakin had sprung from some London gutter, and may or may not have passed through Dr. Barnardo's hands ere he arrived at the dignity of drummer-boy. Lew could remember nothing except the Regiment and the delight of listening to the Band from 170 his earliest years. He hid somewhere in his grimy little soul a genuine love for music, and was most mistakenly furnished with the head of a cherub: insomuch that beautiful ladies who watched the Regiment in church were wont to speak of him as a "darling." They never 175 heard his vitriolic comments on their manners and morals, as he walked back to barracks with the Band and matured fresh causes of offence against Jakin.

The other drummer-boys hated both lads on account of their illogical conduct. Jakin might be pounding 180 Lew, or Lew be rubbing Jakin's head in the dirt, but any attempt at aggression on the part of an outsider was met by the combined forces of Lew and Jakin; and the consequences were painful. The boys were the Ishmaels of the corps, but wealthy Ishmaels, for they sold battles 185 in alternate weeks for the sport of the barracks when they were not pitted against other boys; and thus amassed money.

On this particular day there was dissension in the camp. They had just been convicted afresh of smoking, 190 which is bad for little boys who use plug-tobacco, and Lew's contention was that Jakin had "stunk so 'orrid bad from keepin' the pipe in pocket," that he and he alone was responsible for the birching they were both tingling under. . . . They [the regiment] wanted to go 195 to the Front — they were enthusiastically anxious to go — but they had no knowledge of what war meant, and there was none to tell them. They were an educated regiment, the percentage of school-certificates in their ranks was high, and most of the men could do more than 200 read and write. They had been recruited in loyal observance of the territorial idea; but they themselves had no notion of that idea. They were made up of drafts from an over-populated manufacturing district. The system had put flesh and muscle upon their small bones, 205 but it could not put heart into the sons of those who for generations had done over-much work for over-scanty pay, had sweated in drying-rooms, stooped over looms, coughed among white-lead, and shivered on lime-barges. The men had found food and rest in the Army, and now 210 they were going to fight "niggers" — people who ran away if you shook a stick at them. Wherefore they cheered lustily when the rumor ran, and the shrewd, clerkly, non-commissioned officers speculated on the chances of battle and of saving their pay. At Head- 215 quarters men said: "The Fore and Fit have never been under fire within the last generation. Let us, therefore, break them in easily by setting them to guard lines of communication." And this would have been done but for the fact that British Regiments were wanted — badly 220 wanted — at the Front, and there were doubtful Native Regiments that could fill the minor duties. "Brigade 'em with two strong Regiments," said Headquarters. "They may be knocked about a bit, though they'll learn their business before they come through. Nothing like 225 a night-alarm and a little cutting up of stragglers to make a Regiment smart in the field. Wait till they've had half-a-dozen sentries' throats cut."

The Colonel wrote with delight that the temper of his

men was excellent, that the Regiment was all that could 230
be wished and as sound as a bell. The Majors smiled
with a sober joy, and the subalterns waltzed in pairs
down the Mess-room after dinner, and nearly shot them-
selves at revolver-practice. But there was consternation
in the hearts of Jakin and Lew. What was to be done 235
with the Drums? Would the Band go to the Front?
How many of the Drums would accompany the Regi-
ment?

They took counsel together, sitting in a tree and
smoking. 240

"It's more than a bloomin' toss-up they'll leave us
be'ind at the Depot with the women. You'll like that,"
said Jakin, sarcastically.

"'Cause o' Cris, y' mean? Wot's a woman, or a
'ole bloomin' depot o' women, 'longside o' the chanst 245
of field-service? You know I'm as keen on goin' as
you," said Lew.

"Wish I was a bloomin' bugler," said Jakin, sadly.
"They'll take Tom Kidd along, that I can plaster a wall
with, an' like as not they won't take us." 250

"Then let's go an' make Tom Kidd so bloomin' sick
'e can't bugle no more. You 'old 'is 'ands an' I'll kick
him," said Lew, wriggling on the branch.

"That ain't no good neither. We ain't the sort o'
characters to presoom on our rep'tations — they're bad. 255
If they leave the Band at the Depot we don't go, and no
error *there*. If they take the Band we may get cast for
medical unfitness. Are you medical fit, Piggy?" said
Jakin, digging Lew in the ribs with force.

"Yus," said Lew with an oath. "The Doctor says 260
your 'eart's weak through smokin' on an empty stum-
mick. Throw a chest an' I'll try yer."

Jakin threw out his chest, which Lew smote with all

his might. Jakin turned very pale, gasped, crowed, screwed up his eyes, and said — "That's all right." 265

"You'll do," said Lew. "I've 'eard o' men dyin' when you 'it 'em fair on the breastbone."

"Don't bring us no nearer goin', though," said Jakin. "Do you know where we're ordered?"

"Somewheres up to the Front to kill Paythans — hairy 270 big beggars that turn you inside out if they get 'old o' you."

"Any loot?" asked the abandoned Jakin.

"Not a bloomin' anna, they say, unless you dig up the ground an' see what the niggers 'ave 'id. They're 275 a poor lot." Jakin stood upright on the branch and gazed across the plain.

"Lew," said he, "there's the Colonel coming. 'Colonel's a good old beggar. Let's go an' talk to 'im."

Lew nearly fell out of the tree at the audacity of the 280 suggestion. Like Jakin he feared not God, neither regarded he Man, but there are limits even to the audacity of a drummer-boy, and to speak to a Colonel was —

But Jakin had slid down the trunk and doubled in the direction of the Colonel. That officer was walking 285 wrapped in thought and visions of a C.B.[1] — yes, even a K.C.B., for had he not at command one of the best Regiments of the Line — the Fore and Fit? And he was aware of two small boys charging down upon him. Once before it had been solemnly reported to him that 290 "the Drums were in a state of mutiny," Jakin and Lew being the ringleaders. This looked like an organized conspiracy.

The boys halted at twenty yards, walked to the regu-

---

[1] C. B., Companion of the Bath; K. C. B., Knight Commander of the Bath — two titles much prized as rewards of distinguished service in the British army.

lation four paces, and saluted together, each as well-set- 295 up as a ramrod and little taller.

The Colonel was in a genial mood; the boys appeared very forlorn and unprotected on the desolate plain, and one of them was handsome.

"Well!" said the Colonel, recognizing them. "Are 300 you going to pull me down in the open? I'm sure I never interfere with you, even though" — he sniffed suspiciously — "you have been smoking."

It was time to strike while the iron was hot. Their hearts beat tumultuously. 305

"Beg y' pardon, Sir," began Jakin. "The Reg'-ment's ordered on active service, Sir?"

"So I believe," said the Colonel, courteously.

"Is the Band goin', Sir?" said both together. Then, without pause, "We're goin', Sir, ain't we?" 310

"You!" said the Colonel, stepping back the more fully to take in the two small figures. "You! You'd die in the first march."

"No, we wouldn't, Sir. We can march with the Reg'ment anywheres — p'rade an' anywhere else," said 315 Jakin.

"If Tom Kidd goes 'e'll shut up like a clasp-knife," said Lew. "Tom 'as very-close veins[1] in both 'is legs, Sir."

"Very how much?" 320

"Very-close veins, Sir. That's why they swells after long p'rade, Sir. If 'e can go, we can go, Sir."

Again the Colonel looked at them long and intently.

"Yes, the Band is going," he said as gravely as though he had been addressing a brother officer. "Have you 325 any parents, either of you two?"

"No, Sir," rejoicingly from Lew and Jakin. "We're

---

[1] Lew means *varicose*, i.e. swollen.

both orphans, Sir. There's no one to be considered of
on our account, Sir."

"You poor little sprats, and you want to go up to the
Front with the Regiment, do you? Why?"

"I've wore the Queen's Uniform for two years," said
Jakin. "It's very 'ard, Sir, that a man don't get no
recompense for doin' of 'is dooty, Sir."

"An' — an' if I don't go, Sir," interrupted Lew, "the
Bandmaster 'e says 'e'll catch an' make a bloo — a
blessed musician o' me, Sir. Before I've seen any
service, Sir."

The Colonel made no answer for a long time. Then
he said quietly: "If you're passed by the Doctor I
daresay you can go. I shouldn't smoke if I were you."

The boys saluted and disappeared. The Colonel
walked home and told the story to his wife, who nearly
cried over it. The Colonel was well pleased. If that
was the temper of the children, what would not the
men do?

Jakin and Lew entered the boys' barrack-room with
great stateliness, and refused to hold any conversation
with their comrades for at least ten minutes. Then,
bursting with pride, Jakin drawled: "I've bin intervooin'
the Colonel. Good old beggar is the Colonel. Says I
to 'im, 'Colonel,' says I, 'let me go to the Front, along
o' the Reg'ment.' — 'To the Front you shall go,' says
'e, 'an' I only wish there was more like you among the
dirty little devils that bang the bloomin' drums.' Kidd,
if you throw your 'courtrements¹ at me for tellin' you
the truth to your own advantage, your legs'll swell." . . .

Public feeling among the drummer-boys rose to fever
pitch and the lives of Jakin and Lew became unenviable.
Not only had they been permitted to enlist two years

¹ Accoutrements.

before the regulation boy's age — fourteen — but, by
virtue, it seemed, of their extreme youth, they were al-
lowed to go to the Front — which thing had not happened
to acting-drummers within the knowledge of boy.   The
Band which was to accompany the Regiment had been 365
cut down to the regulation twenty men, the surplus re-
turning to the ranks.   Jakin and Lew were attached to
the Band as supernumeraries, though they would much
have preferred being Company buglers.

"'Don't matter much," said Jakin after the medical 370
inspection.   "Be thankful that we're 'lowed to go at
all.   The Doctor 'e said that if we could stand what we
took from the Bazar-Sergeant's son we'd stand pretty
nigh anything."

"Which we will," said Lew, looking tenderly at the 375
ragged and ill-made housewife that Cris [the Color-
Sergeant's little girl] had given him, with a lock of her
hair worked into a sprawling "L" upon the cover.

"It was the best I could," she sobbed.   "I wouldn't
let mother nor the Sergeants' tailor 'elp me.   Keep it 380
always, Piggy, an' remember I love you true."

They marched to the railway station, nine hundred
and sixty strong, and every soul in cantonments turned
out to see them go.   The drummers gnashed their teeth
at Jakin and Lew marching with the Band, the married 385
women wept upon the platform, and the Regiment
cheered its noble self black in the face.

"A nice level lot," said the Colonel to the Second-in-
Command as they watched the first four companies
entraining.   390

"Fit to do anything," said the Second-in-Command,
enthusiastically.   "But it seems to me they're a thought
too young and tender for the work in hand.   It's bitter
cold up at the Front now."

"They're sound enough," said the Colonel. "We 395 must take our chance of sick casualties."

So they went northward, ever northward, past droves and droves of camels, armies of camp followers, and legions of laden mules, the throng thickening day by day, till with a shriek the train pulled up at a hopelessly 400 congested junction where six lines of temporary track accommodated six forty-wagon trains; where whistles blew, Babus sweated, and Commissariat officers swore from dawn till far into the night amid the wind-driven chaff of the fodder-bales and the lowing of a thousand 405 steers.

"Hurry up — you're badly wanted at the Front," was the message that greeted the Fore and Aft, and the occupants of the Red Cross carriages told the same tale.

"'Tisn't so much the bloomin' fightin'," gasped a 410 trooper of Hussars to a knot of admiring Fore and Afts. "'Tisn't so much the bloomin' fightin', though there's enough o' that. It's the bloomin' food an' the bloomin' climate. Frost all night 'cept when it hails, and biling sun all day, and the water stinks fit to knock you down. 415 I got my 'ead chipped like a egg; I've got pneumonia too. 'Tain't no bloomin' picnic in those parts, I can tell you."

"Wot are the niggers like?" demanded a private.

"There's some prisoners in that train yonder. Go 420 an' look at 'em. They're the aristocracy o' the country. The common folk are a sight uglier. If you want to know what they fight with, reach under my seat an' pull out the long knife that's there."

They dragged out and beheld for the first time the 425 grim, bone-handled, triangular Afghan knife. It was almost as long as Lew.

"That's the thing to jint ye," said the trooper, feebly.

"It can take off a man's arm at the shoulder as easy as slicing butter. I halved the beggar that used that 'un, 430 but there's more of his likes up above."

The men strolled across the tracks to inspect the Afghan prisoners. They were unlike any "niggers" that the Fore and Aft had ever met — these huge, black-haired, scowling sons of the Beni-Israel. As the men 435 stared, the Afghans spat freely and muttered one to another with lowered eyes.

"My eyes! Wot awful swine!" said Jakin, who was in the rear of the procession. The tallest of the company turned, his leg-irons clanking at the movement, 440 and stared at the boy. "See!" he cried to his fellows in Pushto. "They send children against us. What a people, and what fools!"

"*Hya !*" said Jakin, nodding his head cheerily. . . . Good-by, ole man. Take care o' your beautiful 445 figure-'ed."

The men laughed and fell in for their first march, when they began to realize that a soldier's life was not all beer and skittles. They were much impressed with the size and bestial ferocity of the niggers whom they 450 had now learned to call "Paythans," and more with the exceeding discomfort of their own surroundings. Twenty old soldiers in the corps would have taught them how to make themselves moderately snug at night, but they had no old soldiers, and, as the troops on the line 455 of march said, "they lived like pigs." . . .

At the end of their third march they were disagreeably surprised by the arrival in their camp of a hammered iron slug which, fired from a steady rest at seven hundred yards, flicked out the brains of a private seated by the 460 fire. This robbed them of their peace for a night, and was the beginning of a long-range fire carefully calcu-

lated to that end. In the daytime they saw nothing ex-
cept an unpleasant puff of smoke from a crag above the
line of march. At night there were distant spurts of 465
flame and occasional casualties, which set the whole
camp blazing into the gloom and, occasionally, into
opposite tents. Then they swore vehemently and vowed
that this was magnificent, but not war.

Indeed it was not. The Regiment could not halt for 470
reprisals against the sharpshooters of the country-side.
Its duty was to go forward and make connection with
the Scotch and Gurkha troops with which it was brigaded.
The Afghans knew this, and knew too, after their first
tentative shots, that they were dealing with a raw regi- 475
ment. Thereafter they devoted themselves to the task
of keeping the Fore and Aft on the strain. Not for
anything would they have taken equal liberties with a
seasoned corps — with the wicked little Gurkhas, whose
delight it was to lie out in the open on a dark night and 480
stalk their stalkers, — with the terrible big men dressed
in women's clothes, who could be heard praying to their
God in the night-watches, and whose peace of mind no
amount of "sniping" could shake; — or with those vile
Sikhs, who marched so ostentatiously unprepared and 485
who dealt out such grim reward to those who tried to
profit by that unpreparedness. This white regiment was
different — quite different. It slept like a hog, and,
like a hog, charged in every direction when it was
roused. Its sentries walked with a footfall that could 490
be heard for a quarter of a mile; would fire at anything
that moved — even a driven donkey — and when they
had once fired, could be scientifically "rushed" and laid
out a horror and an offence against the morning sun.
Then there were camp-followers who straggled and could 495
be cut up without fear. Their shrieks would disturb the

white boys, and the loss of their services would incon-
venience them sorely.

Thus, at every march, the hidden enemy became
bolder and the regiment writhed and twisted under 500
attacks it could not avenge. The crowning triumph
was a sudden night-rush ending in the cutting of many
tent-ropes, the collapse of the sodden canvas, and a
glorious knifing of the men who struggled and kicked
below. It was a great deed, neatly carried out, and it 505
shook the already shaken nerves of the Fore and Aft.
All the courage that they had been required to exercise
up to this point was the "two o'clock in the morning
courage"; and, so far, they had only succeeded in
shooting their comrades and losing their sleep.   510

Sullen, discontented, cold, savage, sick, with their
uniforms dulled and unclean, the Fore and Aft joined
their Brigade.

"I hear you had a tough time of it coming up," said
the Brigadier. But when he saw the hospital-sheets his 515
face fell.

"This is bad," said he to himself. . . . And aloud
to the Colonel — "I'm afraid we can't spare you just
yet. We want all we have, else I should have given you
ten days to recover in."   520

The Colonel winced. "On my honor, Sir," he re-
turned, "there is not the least necessity to think of
sparing us. My men have been rather mauled and upset
without a fair return. They only want to go in some-
where where they can see what's before them."   525

"Can't say I think much of the Fore and Fit," said the
Brigadier in confidence to his Brigade-Major. "They've .
lost all their soldiering, and, by the trim of them, might
have marched through the country from the other side.
A more fagged-out set of men I never put eyes on."   530

"Oh, they'll improve as the work goes on. The parade gloss has been rubbed off a little, but they'll put on field polish before long," said the Brigade-Major. "They've been mauled, and they don't quite understand it." 535

They did not. All the hitting was on one side, and it was cruelly hard hitting, with accessories that made them sick. There was also the real sickness that laid hold of a strong man and dragged him howling to the grave. Worst of all, their officers knew just as little of 540 the country as the men themselves, and looked as if they did. The Fore and Aft were in a thoroughly unsatisfactory condition, but they believed that all would be well if they could once get a fair go-in at the enemy. Pot-shots up and down the valleys were unsatisfactory, 545 and the bayonet never seemed to get a chance. Perhaps it was as well, for a long-limbed Afghan with a knife had a reach of eight feet, and could carry away lead that would disable three Englishmen.

The Fore and Fit would like some rifle-practice at 550 the enemy — all seven hundred rifles blazing together. That wish showed the mood of the men.

The Gurkhas walked into their camp, and in broken, barrack-room English strove to fraternize with them; offered them pipes of tobacco and stood them treat at 555 the canteen. But the Fore and Aft, not knowing much of the nature of the Gurkhas, treated them as they would treat any other "niggers," and the little men in green trotted back to their firm friends the Highlanders, and with many grins confided to them: "That white regi- 560 ment no use. Sulky — ugh! Dirty — ugh! Hya, any tot for Johnny?" Whereat the Highlanders smote the Gurkhas as to the head, and told them not to vilify a British Regiment, and the Gurkhas grinned cavernously,

F

for the Highlanders were their elder brothers and en- 565
titled to the privileges of kinship. The common soldier
who touches a Gurkha is more than likely to have his
head sliced open.

Three days later the Brigadier arranged a battle ac-
cording to the rules of war and the peculiarity of the 570
Afghan temperament. The enemy were massing in in-
convenient strength among the hills, and the moving of
many green standards warned him that the tribes were
" up " in aid of the Afghan regular troops. A squadron
and a half of Bengal Lancers represented the available 575
Cavalry, and two screw-guns borrowed from a column
thirty miles away the Artillery at the General's disposal.

" If they stand, as I've a very strong notion that they
will, I fancy we shall see an infantry fight that will be
worth watching," said the Brigadier. " We'll do it in 580
style. Each regiment shall be played into action by its
Band, and we'll hold the Cavalry in reserve."

" For *all* the reserve ? " somebody asked.

" For all the reserve ; because we're going to crumple
them up," said the Brigadier, who was an extraordinary 585
Brigadier, and did not believe in the value of a reserve
when dealing with Asiatics. Indeed, when you come
to think of it, had the British Army consistently waited
for reserves in all its little affairs, the boundaries of Our
Empire would have stopped at Brighton beach.   590

That battle was to be a glorious battle.

The three regiments debouching from three separate
gorges, after duly crowning the heights above, were to
converge from the centre, left, and right upon what we
will call the Afghan army, then stationed toward the 595
lower extremity of a flat-bottomed valley. Thus it will
be seen that three sides of the valley practically be-
longed to the English, while the fourth was strictly

Afghan property. In the event of defeat the Afghans had the rocky hills to fly to, where the fire from the 600 guerilla tribes in aid would cover their retreat. In the event of victory these same tribes would rush down and lend their weight to the rout of the British.

The screw-guns were to shell the head of each Afghan rush that was made in close formation, and the Cavalry, 605 held in reserve in the right valley, were to gently stimulate the break-up which would follow on the combined attack. The Brigadier, sitting upon a rock overlooking the valley, would watch the battle unrolled at his feet. The Fore and Aft would debouch from the central gorge, 610 the Gurkhas from the left, and the Highlanders from the right, for the reason that the left flank of the enemy seemed as though it required the most hammering. It was not every day that an Afghan force would take ground in the open, and the Brigadier was resolved to 615 make the most of it.

"If we only had a few more men," he said plaintively, "we could surround the creatures and crumple 'em up thoroughly. As it is, I'm afraid we can only cut them up as they run. It's a great pity." 620

The Fore and Aft had enjoyed unbroken peace for five days, and were beginning, in spite of dysentery, to recover their nerve. But they were not happy, for they did not know the work in hand, and had they known, would not have known how to do it. Throughout those 625 five days in which old soldiers might have taught them the craft of the game, they discussed together their misadventures in the past — how such an one was alive at dawn and dead ere the dusk, and with what shrieks and struggles such another had given up his soul under the 630 Afghan knife. Death was a new and horrible thing to the sons of mechanics who were used to die decently of

zymotic disease; and their careful conservation in bar-
racks had done nothing to make them look upon it with
less dread.   635

Very early in the dawn the bugles began to blow, and
the Fore and Aft, filled with a misguided enthusiasm,
turned out without waiting for a cup of coffee and a bis-
cuit; and were rewarded by being kept under arms in
the cold while the other regiments leisurely prepared for 640
the fray. All the world knows that it is ill taking the
breeks off a Highlander. It is much iller to try to make
him stir unless he is convinced of the necessity for haste.

The Fore and Aft waited, leaning upon their rifles
and listening to the protests of their empty stomachs. 645
The Colonel did his best to remedy the default of lining
as soon as it was borne in upon him that the affair would
not begin at once, and so well did he succeed that the
coffee was just ready when — the men moved off, their
Band leading. Even then there had been a mistake in 650
time, and the Fore and Aft came out into the valley ten
minutes before the proper hour. Their Band wheeled
to the right after reaching the open, and retired behind
a little rocky knoll, still playing while the regiment went
past.   655

It was not a pleasant sight that opened on the unin-
structed view, for the lower end of the valley appeared
to be filled by an army in position — real and actual
regiments attired in red coats, and — of this there was
no doubt — firing Martini-Henry bullets which cut up 660
the ground a hundred yards in front of the leading com-
pany. Over that pock-marked ground the regiment had
to pass, and it opened the ball with a general and pro-
found courtesy to the piping pickets; ducking in perfect
time, as though it had been brazed on a rod. Being 665
half-capable of thinking for itself, it fired a volley by the

simple process of pitching its rifle into its shoulder and
pulling the trigger. The bullets may have accounted for
some of the watchers on the hillside, but they certainly
did not affect the mass of enemy in front, while the 670
noise of the rifles drowned any orders that might have
been given. . . .

The Fore and Aft continued to go forward, but with
shortened stride. Where were the other regiments, and
why did these niggers use Martinis? They took open 675
order instinctively, lying down and firing at random,
rushing a few paces forward and lying down again, ac-
cording to the regulations. Once in this formation,
each man felt himself desperately alone, and edged in
toward his fellow for comfort's sake. 680

Then the crack of his neighbor's rifle at his ear led
him to fire as rapidly as he could — again for the sake
of the comfort of the noise. The reward was not long
delayed. Five volleys plunged the files in banked smoke
impenetrable to the eye, and the bullets began to take 685
ground twenty or thirty yards in front of the firers, as
the weight of the bayonet dragged down and to the right
arms wearied with holding the kick of the leaping Mar-
tini. The Company Commanders peered helplessly
through the smoke, the more nervous mechanically trying 690
to fan it away with their helmets.

"High and to the left!" bawled a Captain till he was
hoarse. "No good! Cease firing, and let it drift away
a bit."

Three and four times the bugles shrieked the order, 695
and when it was obeyed the Fore and Aft looked that
their foe should be lying before them in mown swaths of
men. A light wind drove the smoke to leeward, and
showed the enemy still in position and apparently
unaffected. A quarter of a ton of lead had been 700

buried a furlong in front of them, as the ragged earth
attested.

That was not demoralizing to the Afghans, who have
not European nerves. They were waiting for the mad
riot to die down, and were firing quietly into the heart 705
of the smoke. A private of the Fore and Aft spun up
his company shrieking with agony, another was kicking
the earth and gasping, and a third . . . was calling
aloud on his comrades to put him out of his pain.
These were the casualties, and they were not soothing 710
to hear or see. The smoke cleared to a dull haze.

Then the foe began to shout with a great shouting,
and a mass — a black mass — detached itself from the
main body, and rolled over the ground at horrid speed.
It was composed of, perhaps, three hundred men, who 715
would shout and fire and slash if the rush of their fifty
comrades who were determined to die carried home.
The fifty were Ghazis, half-maddened with drugs and
wholly mad with religious fanaticism. When they
rushed the British fire ceased, and in the lull the order 720
was given to close ranks and meet them with the
bayonet.

Any one who knew the business could have told the
Fore and Aft that the only way of dealing with a Ghazi
rush is by volleys at long ranges; because a man who 725
means to die, who desires to die, who will gain heaven
by dying, must, in nine cases out of ten, kill a man who
has a lingering prejudice in favor of life. Where they
should have closed and gone forward, the Fore and Aft
opened out and skirmished, and where they should have 730
opened out and fired, they closed and waited.

A man dragged from his blankets half awake and
unfed is never in a pleasant frame of mind. Nor does
his happiness increase when he watches the whites of

the eyes of three hundred six-foot fiends upon whose 735
beards the foam is lying, upon whose tongues is a roar
of wrath, and in whose hands are yard-long knives.

The Fore and Aft heard the Gurkha bugles bringing
that regiment forward at the double, while the neighing
of the Highland pipes came from the left. They strove 740
to stay where they were, though the bayonets wavered
down the line like the oars of a ragged boat. Then they
felt body to body the amazing physical strength of their
foes; a shriek of pain ended the rush, and the knives
fell amid scenes not to be told. The men clubbed 745
together and smote blindly — as often as not at their
own fellows. Their front crumpled like paper, and the
fifty Ghazis passed on; their backers, now drunk with
success, fighting as madly as they.

Then the rear-ranks were bidden to close up, and the 750
subalterns dashed into the stew — alone. For the rear-
rank had heard the clamor in front, the yells and the
howls of pain, and had seen the dark stale blood that
makes afraid. They were not going to stay. It was the
rushing of the camps over again. . . .   755

"Come on!" shrieked the subalterns, and their men,
cursing them, drew back, each closing into his neighbor
and wheeling round.

Charteris and Devlin, subalterns of the last company,
faced their death alone in the belief that their men 760
would follow.

"You've killed me, you cowards," sobbed Devlin and
dropped, cut from the shoulder-strap to the centre of
the chest, and a fresh detachment of his men retreating,
always retreating, trampled him under foot as they made 765
for the pass whence they had emerged. . . .

The Gurkhas were pouring through the left gorge and
over the heights at the double to the invitation of their

Regimental Quick-step. The black rocks were crowned with dark green spiders as the bugles gave tongue 770 jubilantly : —

> In the morning! In the morning *by* the bright light!
> When Gabriel blows his trumpet in the morning!

The Gurkha rear-companies tripped and blundered over loose stones. The front-files halted for a moment 775 to take stock of the valley and to settle stray boot-laces. Then a happy little sigh of contentment soughed down the ranks, and it was as though the land smiled, for behold there below was the enemy, and it was to meet them that the Gurkhas had doubled so hastily. There 780 was much enemy. There would be amusement. The little men hitched their *kukris* well to hand, and gaped expectantly at their officers as terriers grin ere the stone is cast for them to fetch. The Gurkhas' ground sloped downward to the valley, and they enjoyed a fair 785 view of the proceedings. They sat upon the boulders to watch, for their officers were not going to waste their wind in assisting to repulse a Ghazi rush more than half a mile away. Let the white men look to their own front. . . . 790

Horrified, amused, and indignant, the Gurkhas beheld the retirement of the Fore and Aft with a running chorus of oaths and commentaries.

"They run! The white men run! Colonel Sahib,[1] may *we* also do a little running?" murmured Runbir 795 Thappa, the Senior Jemadar.

But the Colonel would have none of it. "Let the beggars be cut up a little," said he, wrathfully. "'Serves 'em right. They'll be prodded into facing

---

. [1] Sahib is a Hindoo form of respectful address — "Master."

round in a minute." He looked through his field- 800
glasses, and caught the glint of an officer's sword.

"Beating 'em with the flat[1]! How the Ghazis are
walking into them!" said he.

The Fore and Aft, heading back, bore with them their
officers. The narrowness of the pass forced the mob 805
into solid formation, and the rear-rank delivered some
sort of a wavering volley. The Ghazis drew off, for they
did not know what reserves the gorge might hide.
Moreover, it was never wise to chase white men too far.
They returned as wolves return to cover, satisfied with 810
the slaughter that they had done, and only stopping to
slash at the wounded on the ground. A quarter of a
mile had the Fore and Aft retreated, and now, jammed
in the pass, was quivering with pain, shaken and de-
moralized with fear, while the officers, maddened beyond 815
control, smote the men with the hilts and the flats of
their swords.

"Get back! Get back, you cowards — you women!
Right about face — column of companies, form — you
hounds!" shouted the Colonel, and the subalterns swore 820
aloud. But the Regiment wanted to go — to go any-
where out of the range of those merciless knives. It
swayed to and fro irresolutely with shouts and outcries,
while from the right the Gurkhas dropped volley after
volley of cripple-stopper Snider bullets at long range into 825
the mob of the Ghazis returning to their own troops.

The Fore and Aft Band, though protected from direct
fire by the rocky knoll under which it had sat down, fled
at the first rush. Jakin and Lew would have fled also,
but their short legs left them fifty yards in the rear, and 830
by the time the Band had mixed with the regiment, they

---

[1] Of the sword.

were painfully aware that they would have to close in
alone and unsupported.

"Get back to that rock," gasped Jakin. "They won't
see us there."   835

And they returned to the scattered instruments of the
Band, their hearts nearly bursting their ribs.

"Here's a nice show for *us*," said Jakin, throwing
himself full length on the ground. "A bloomin' fine
show for British Infantry! They've gone an' left us 840
alone here! Wot'll we do?"

Lew took possession of a cast-off water bottle, which
naturally was full of canteen rum, and drank till he
coughed again.

"Drink," said he, shortly. "They'll come back in a 845
minute or two — you see."

Jakin drank, but there was no sign of the Regiment's
return. They could hear a dull clamor from the head
of the valley of retreat, and saw the Ghazis slink back,
quickening their pace as the Gurkhas fired at them.   850

"We're all that's left of the Band, an' we'll be cut up
as sure as death," said Jakin.

"I'll die game, then," said Lew, thickly, fumbling
with his tiny drummer's sword. The drink was working
on his brain as it was on Jakin's.   855

"'Old on! I know something better than fightin',"
said Jakin, "stung by the splendor of a sudden thought"
due chiefly to rum. "Tip our bloomin' cowards yonder
the word to come back. The Paythan beggars are well
away. Come on, Lew! We won't get hurt. Take the 860
fife and give me the drum. . . . There's a few of our
men coming back now. Stand up, ye drunken little
defaulter. By your right — quick march!"

He slipped the drum-sling over his shoulder, thrust
the fife into Lew's hand, and the two boys marched out 865

of the cover of the rock into the open, making a hideous hash of the first bars of the *British Grenadiers*.

As Jakin had said, a few of the Fore and Aft were coming back sullenly and shamefacedly under the stimulus of blows and abuse; their red coats shone at the head of the valley, and behind them were wavering bayonets. But between this shattered line and the enemy, who with Afghan suspicion feared that the hasty retreat meant an ambush, and had not moved therefore, lay half a mile of level ground dotted only by the wounded.

The tune settled into full swing and the boys kept . shoulder to shoulder, Jakin banging the drum as one possessed. The one fife made a thin and pitiful squeaking, but the tune carried far, even to the Gurkhas.

"Come on, you dogs!" muttered Jakin to himself. "Are we to play for hever?" Lew was staring straight in front of him and marching more stiffly than ever he had done on parade.

And in bitter mockery of the distant mob, the old tune of the Old Line shrilled and rattled: —

> Some talk of Alexander,
>   And some of Hercules;
> Of Hector and Lysander,
>   And such great names as these!

There was a far-off clapping of hands from the Gurkhas, and a roar from the Highlanders in the distance, but never a shot was fired by British or Afghan. The two little red dots moved forward in the open parallel to the enemy's front.

> But of all the world's great heroes
>   There's none that can compare,
> With a tow-row-row-row-row-row,
>   To the British Grenadier!

The men of the Fore and Aft were gathering thick at the entrance to the plain.   The Brigadier on the heights ₉₀₀ far above was speechless with rage.   Still no movement from the enemy.   The day stayed to watch the children.

Jakin halted and beat the long roll of the Assembly, while the fife squealed despairingly.

"Right about face!   Hold up, Lew, you're drunk," ₉₀₅ said Jakin.   They wheeled and marched back: —

> Those heroes of antiquity
> Ne'er saw a cannon-ball,
> Nor knew the force o' powder,

"Here they come!" said Jakin.   "Go on, Lew": — ₉₁₀

> To scare their foes withal!

The Fore and Aft were pouring out of the valley. What officers had said to men in that time of shame and humiliation will never be known; for neither officers nor men speak of it now.   ₉₁₅

"They are coming anew!" shouted a priest among the Afghans.   "Do not kill the boys!   Take them alive and they shall be of our faith."

But the first volley had been fired, and Lew dropped on his face.   Jakin stood for a minute, spun round and ₉₂₀ collapsed, as the Fore and Aft came forward, the curses of their officers in their ears, and in their hearts the shame of open shame.

Half the men had seen the drummers die, and they made no sign.   They did not even shout.   They doubled ₉₂₅ out straight across the plain in open order, and they did not fire.

"This," said the Colonel of Gurkhas, softly, "is the real attack, as it should have been delivered.   Come on, my children."   ₉₃₀

"Ulu-lu-lu-lu!" squealed the Gurkhas, and came

down with a joyful clicking of *kukris* — those vicious
Gurkha knives.

On the right there was no rush. The Highlanders,
cannily commending their souls to God, . . . opened 935
out and fired according to their custom, that is to say
without heat and without intervals, while the screw-guns,
having disposed of the impertinent mud fort aforemen-
tioned, dropped shell after shell into the clusters round
the flickering green standards on the heights.   940

"Charrging is an unfortunate necessity," murmured
the Color-Sergeant of the right company of the High-
landers. "It makes the men sweer so, but I am thinkin'
that it will come to a charrge if these black devils stand
much longer. Stewarrt, man, you're firing into the eye 945
of the sun, and e'll not take any harm for Government
ammuneetion. A foot lower and a great deal slower!
What are the English doing? They're very quiet there
in the centre. Running again?"

The English were not running. They were hacking 950
and hewing and stabbing, for though one white man is
seldom physically a match for an Afghan in a sheepskin
or wadded coat, yet, through the pressure of many
white men behind, and a certain thirst for revenge in
his heart, he becomes capable of doing much with both 955
ends of his rifle. The Fore and Aft held their fire till
one bullet could drive through five or six men, and the
front of the Afghan force gave on the volley. They then
selected their men, and slew them with deep gasps and
short hacking coughs, and groanings of leather belts 960
against strained bodies, and realized for the first time
that an Afghan attacked is far less formidable than an
Afghan attacking: which fact old soldiers might have
told them.

But they had no old soldiers in their ranks. . . .   965

As the Afghans wavered, the green standards on the
mountain moved down to assist them in a last rally.
This was unwise.   The Lancers chafing in the right gorge
had thrice despatched their only subaltern as galloper to
report on the progress of affairs.   On the third occasion 970
he returned, with a bullet-graze on his knee, swearing
strange oaths in Hindustani, and saying that all things
were ready.   So that Squadron swung round the right of
the Highlanders with a wicked whistling of wind in the
pennons of its lances, and fell upon the remnant just 975
when, according to all the rules of war, it should have
waited for the foe to show more signs of wavering.

But it was a dainty charge, deftly delivered, and it
ended by the Cavalry finding itself at the head of the
pass by which the Afghans intended to retreat; and down 980
the track that the lances had made streamed two com-
panies of the Highlanders, which was never intended by
the Brigadier.   The new development was successful.
It detached the enemy from his base as a sponge is torn
from a rock, and left him ringed about with fire in that 985
pitiless plain.   And as a sponge is chased round the
bath-tub by the hand of the bather, so were the Afghans
chased till they broke into little detachments much more
difficult to dispose of than large masses.

"See!" quoth the Brigadier.   "Everything has come 990
as I arranged.   We've cut their base, and now we'll
bucket 'em to pieces."

A direct hammering was all that the Brigadier had
dared to hope for, considering the size of the force at
his disposal; but men who stand or fall by the errors of 995
their opponents may be forgiven for turning Chance into
Design.   The bucketing went forward merrily.   The
Afghan forces were upon the run — the run of wearied
wolves who snarl and bite over their shoulders.   The

red lances dipped by twos and threes, and, with a shriek, 1000
up rose the lance-butt, like a spar on a stormy sea, as
the trooper cantering forward cleared his point. The
Lancers kept between their prey and the steep hills, for
all who could were trying to escape from the valley of
death. The Highlanders gave the fugitives two hundred 1005
yards' law, and then brought them down, gasping and
choking ere they could reach the protection of the
boulders above. The Gurkhas followed suit; but the
Fore and Aft were killing on their own account, for they
had penned a mass of men between their bayonets and a 1010
wall of rock, and the flash of the rifles was lighting the
wadded coats.

"We cannot hold them, Captain Sahib!" panted a
Ressaidar of Lancers. "Let us try the carbine. The
lance is good, but it wastes time." 1015

They tried the carbine, and still the enemy melted
away — fled up the hills by hundreds when there were
only twenty bullets to stop them. On the heights the
screw-guns ceased firing — they had run out of ammuni-
tion — and the Brigadier groaned, for the musketry fire 1020
could not sufficiently smash the retreat. Long before
the last volleys were fired, the doolies were out in force
looking for the wounded. The battle was over, and, but
for want of fresh troops, the Afghans would have been
wiped off the earth. As it was they counted their dead 1025
by hundreds, and nowhere were the dead thicker than
in the track of the Fore and Aft.

But the Regiment did not cheer with the Highlanders,
nor did they dance uncouth dances with the Gurkhas
among the dead. They looked under their brows at the 1030
Colonel as they leaned upon their rifles and panted.

"Get back to camp, you. Haven't you disgraced
yourself enough for one day! Go and look to the

wounded. It's all you're fit for," said the Colonel.
Yet for the past hour the Fore and Aft had been doing 1035
all that mortal commander could expect. They had lost
heavily because they did not know how to set about their
business with proper skill, but they had borne them-
selves gallantly, and this was their reward.

A young and sprightly Color-Sergeant, who had begun 1040
to imagine himself a hero, offered his water-bottle to a
Highlander, whose tongue was black with thirst. "I
drink with no cowards," answered the youngster, huskily,
and, turning to a Gurkha, said, "Hya, Johnny! Drink
water got it?" The Gurkha grinned and passed his 1045
bottle. The Fore and Aft said no word.

They went back to camp when the field of strife had
been a little mopped up and made presentable, and the
Brigadier, who saw himself a Knight in three months,
was the only soul who was complimentary to them. The 1050
Colonel was heart-broken, and the officers were savage
and sullen.

"Well," said the Brigadier, "they are young troops of
course, and it was not unnatural that they should retire
in disorder for a bit."　　　　　．　　　　　1055

"Oh, my only Aunt Maria!" murmured a junior Staff
Officer. "Retire in disorder! It was a bally run!"

"But they came again, as we all know," cooed the
Brigadier, the Colonel's ashy-white face before him,
"and they behaved as well as could possibly be expected. 1060
Behaved beautifully, indeed. I was watching them.
It's not a matter to take to heart, Colonel. As some
German General said of his men, they wanted to be
shooted over a little, that was all." To himself he said
— "Now they're blooded I can give 'em responsible 1065
work. It's as well that they got what they did. 'Teach
'em more than half a dozen rifle flirtations, that will

— later — run alone and bite. Poor old Colonel, though."

All that afternoon the heliograph winked and flickered 1070 on the hills, striving to tell the good news to a mountain forty miles away. And in the evening there arrived, dusty, sweating, and sore, a misguided Correspondent, who had gone out to assist at a trumpery village-burning, and who had read off the message from afar, cursing 1075 his luck the while.

"Let's have the details somehow — as full as ever you can, please. It's the first time I've ever been left this campaign," said the Correspondent to the Brigadier; and the Brigadier, nothing loath, told him how an Army 1080 of Communication had been crumpled up, destroyed, and all but annihilated, by the craft, strategy, wisdom, and foresight of the Brigadier.

But some say, and among these be the Gurkhas who watched on the hillside, that that battle was won by 1085 Jakin and Lew, whose little bodies were borne up just in time to fit two gaps at the head of the big ditch-grave for the dead under the heights of Jagai.

Are the drummer-boys mere types, or are they real characters, mixtures of bad and good? Read over the General Introduction, §§ 19, 20. Describe their personal appearance and their characters. Is the story powerful? graphic? true to human nature? Would it have been a better story if the author had been able to arouse the same emotions of admiration and pity without the use of slang?

INCIDENT OF THE FRENCH CAMP

ROBERT BROWNING

You know, we French stormed Ratisbon:
    A mile or so away,
On a little mound, Napoleon
    Stood on our storming-day;

1. The metre is tetrameter. Is it iambic tetrameter, or trochaic tetrameter ?

G

With neck out-thrust, you fancy how,   5
  Legs wide, arms locked behind,
As if to balance the prone brow
  Oppressive with its mind.

Just as perhaps he mused "My plans
  That soar, to earth may fall,   10
Let once my army-leader Lannes
  Waver at yonder wall," —
Out 'twixt the battery-smokes there flew
  A rider, bound on bound
Full-galloping; nor bridle drew   15
  Until he reached the mound.

Then off there flung in smiling joy,
  And held himself erect
By just his horse's mane, a boy:
  You hardly could suspect —   20
(So tight he kept his lips compressed,
  Scarce any blood came through)
You looked twice ere you saw his breast
  Was all but shot in two.

"Well," cried he, "Emperor, by God's grace   25
  We've got you Ratisbon!
The Marshal's in the market-place,
  And you'll be there anon
To see your flag-bird flap his vans
  Where I, to heart's desire,   30
Perched him!" The chief's eye flashed; his plans
  Soared up again like fire.

8. Note the rhyme-scheme: a b a b, c d c d.

The chief's eye flashed; but presently
    Softened itself, as sheathes
A film the mother-eagle's eye   35
    When her bruised eaglet breathes;
"You're wounded!"   "Nay," the soldier's pride
    Touched to the quick, he said:
."I'm killed, Sire!"   And his chief beside
    Smiling the boy fell dead.   40

HERVÉ RIEL

ROBERT BROWNING

I

On the sea and at the Hogue, sixteen hundred ninety-two,
  Did the English fight the French, — woe to France!
And, the thirty-first of May, helter-skelter through the blue,
Like a crowd of frightened porpoises a shoal of sharks
    pursue,
  Came crowding ship on ship to Saint-Malo on the
    Rance,   5
With. the English fleet in view.

II

'Twas the squadron that escaped, with the victor in full
    chase;
  First and foremost of the drove, in his great ship, Dam-
    freville;
    Close on him fled, great and small,
    Twenty-two good ships in all;   10

3. Name the line according to the number of accents and the kind of
foot. Is the metre rapid or slow?   4. Note that *which* is understood after
porpoises. 9-12. Is there any reason for short lines? Compare *The Re-
venge.*

And they signalled to the place
"Help the winners of a race!
    Get us guidance, give us harbor, take us quick — or,
        quicker still,
    Here's the English can and will!"

III

Then the pilots of the place put out brisk and leapt on
        board;   15
    "Why, what hope or chance have ships like these to
        pass?" laughed they:
"Rocks to starboard, rocks to port, all the passage scarred
        and scored, —
Shall the *Formidable* here, with her twelve and eighty guns,
    Think to make the river-mouth by the single narrow way,
Trust to enter — where 'tis ticklish for a craft of twenty
        tons,   20
    And with flow at full beside?
    Now, 'tis slackest ebb of tide.
    Reach the mooring?   Rather say,
While rock stands or water runs,
    Not a ship will leave the bay!"   25

IV

Then was called a council straight.
Brief and bitter the debate:
"Here's the English at our heels; would you have them
        take in tow
All that's left us of the fleet, linked together stern and bow,
For a prize to Plymouth Sound?   Better run the ships
        aground!"   30
    (Ended Damfreville his speech).

17. That is, scarred by rocks.

"Not a minute more to wait!
  Let the captains all and each
  Shove ashore, then blow up, burn the vessels on the
    beach!
France must undergo her fate.   35

V

"Give the word!" But no such word
Was ever spoke or heard;
For up stood, for out stepped, for in struck, amid all
    these —
A captain? A lieutenant? A mate — first, second, third?
  No such man of mark, and meet   40
  With his betters to compete,
  But a simple Breton sailor, pressed by Tourville for the
    fleet —
A poor coasting-pilot he, Hervé Riel the Croisickese.

VI

And, "What mockery or malice have we here?" cries Hervé
    Riel:
  "Are you mad, you Malouins? Are you cowards, fools,
    or rogues?   45
Talk to me of rocks and shoals, me who took the sound-
    ings, tell
On my fingers every bank, every shallow, every swell
  'Twixt the offing here and Grève, where the river dis-
    embogues!
Are you bought by English gold? Is it love the lying's for?
  Morn and eve, night and day   50
  Have I piloted your bay.

42. *Pressed* means *impressed* — forced into service. 43. *Croisickese*
means an inhabitant of Croisic, a little seashore town in the north of
France, where Browning spent many summers. See line 127. 48. *dis-
embogues*, a rare word for *empties; why did Browning use it?

Entered free and anchored fast at the foot of Solidor.
  Burn the fleet and ruin France? That were worse than
      fifty Hogues!
    Sirs, they know I speak the truth! Sirs, believe me
      there's a way!
Only let me lead the line,   55
  Have the biggest ship to steer,
  Get this *Formidable* clear,
Make the óthers follow mine,
And I lead them, most and least, by a passage I know well,
Right to Solidor, past Grève,   60
And there lay them safe and sound;
  And if one ship misbehave, —
    Keel so much as grate the ground,
Why, I've nothing but my life, — here's my head!" cries
  Hervé Riel.

VII

Not a minute more to wait.   65
"Steer us in, then, small and great!
  Take the helm, lead the line, save the squadron!" cried
    its chief.
Captains, give the sailor place!
  He is Admiral, in brief.
Still the north-wind, by God's grace!   70
See the noble fellow's face
As the big ship, with a bound,
Clears the entry like a hound,
Keeps the passage, as its inch of way were the wide sea's
    profound!
  See, safe thro' shoal and rock,   75
  How they follow in a flock,
Not a ship that misbehaves, not a keel that grates the
    ground,

Not a spar that comes to grief!
·The peril, see, is past.
All are harbored to the last,   80
And just as Hervé Riel hollas "Anchor!" sure as fate,
Up the English come, — too late!

VIII

So, the storm subsides to calm:
    They see the green trees wave
    On the heights o'erlooking Grève.   85
Hearts that bled are stanched with balm.
"Just our rapture to enhance,
    Let the English rake the bay,
Gnash their teeth and glare askance
    As they cannonade away!   90
'Neath rampired Solidor pleasant riding on the Rance!"
How hope succeeds despair on each captain's countenance!
Out burst all with one accord,
    "This is Paradise for Hell!
    Let France, let France's King   95
    Thank the man that did the thing!"
What a shout, and all one word,
    "Hervé Riel!"
As he stepped in front once more,
    Not a symptom of surprise   100
    In the frank blue Breton eyes —
Just the same man as before.

IX

Then said Damfreville, "My friend,
I must speak out at the end,
    Though I find the speaking hard.   105

90. Up to this point, which has received the most pleasure — the eye, the ear, or the muscular sense of motion?

Praise is deeper than the lips:
You have saved the King his ships,
   You must name your own reward.
'Faith, our sun was near eclipse!
Demand whate'er you will,   110
France remains your debtor still.
Ask to heart's content and have! or my name's not Dam-
    freville."

X

Then a beam of fun outbroke
On the bearded mouth that spoke,
As the honest heart laughed through   115
Those frank eyes of Breton blue:
"Since I needs must say my say,
   Since on board the duty's done —
   And from Malo Roads to Croisic Point, what is it but a
    run? —
Since 'tis ask and have, I may —   120
   Since the others go ashore —
Come! A good whole holiday!
   Leave to go and see my wife, whom I call the Belle
    Aurore!"
   That he asked and that he got — nothing more.

XI

Name and deed alike are lost: 125
Not a pillar nor a post
   In his Croisic keeps alive the feat as it befell;
Not a head in white and black
On a single fishing-smack,
In memory of the man but for whom had gone to wrack 130
   All that France saved from the fight whence England bore
    the bell.

131. "Bearing the bell" means being victorious. The allusion is to the
fact that little bells were once used as prizes in athletic contests.

Go to Paris: rank on rank

Search the heroes flung pell-mell

On the Louvre, face and flank!

You shall look long enough ere you come to Hervé Riel. 135

So, for better and for worse,

Hervé Riel, accept my verse!

In my verse, Hervé Riel, do thou once more

Save the squadron, honor France, love thy wife, the Belle

Aurore!

132–134. This merely means that there are thousands of portraits of French heroes in the gallery of the Louvre.

Has the poem unity? climax? clearness? force? Is its melody injured by any harsh sounds? Specify.

THE DESERTER FROM THE CAUSE

GERALD MASSEY

He is gone: better so. We should know who stand under

Our banner: let none but the trusty remain!

For there's stern work at hand, and the time comes shall

sunder

The shell from the pearl, and the chaff from the grain.

And the heart that through danger and death will be dutiful,

Soul that with Cranmer in fire would shake hands, 6

With a life like a palace-home built for the beautiful,

Freedom of all her belovèd demands.

He is gone from us! Yet shall we march on victorious,

Hearts burning like beacons — eyes fix'd on the goal! 10

And if we fall fighting, we fall like the glorious,

With face to the stars, and all heaven in the soul.

1. Name the line according to number of accents. Anapestic or dactyllic metre? What kind of ending? 2. What kind of ending? 6. Cranmer, burnt at the stake by Bloody Mary in 1556, thrust his right hand into the flames and let it burn first, because it had signed a cowardly recantation of his religious beliefs.

And aye for the brave stir of battle we'll barter
    The sword of life sheath'd in the peace of the grave;
And better the fieriest fate of the martyr,   15
    Than live like the coward, and die like the slave!

HEATHER ALE: A GALLOWAY LEGEND[1]

ROBERT LOUIS STEVENSON

From the bonny bells of heather
    They brewed a drink long-syne,
Was sweeter far than honey,
    Was stronger far than wine.
They brewed it and they drank it,   5
    And lay in a blessed swound
For days and days together
    In their dwellings underground.

There rose a king in Scotland,
    A fell man to his foes,   10
He smote the Picts in battle,
    He hunted them like roes.
Over miles of the red mountain
    He hunted as they fled,
And strewed the dwarfish bodies   15
    Of the dying and the dead.

Summer came in the country,
    Red was the heather bell;
But the manner of the brewing
    Was none alive to tell.   20

[1] Reprinted from "Ballads," by permission of Charles Scribner's Sons.

1. The metre is normally iambic, as appears in line 2; but, as so often happens in English, we have many *substitutions* of two short syllables for one long, thus: Frŏm thĕ bónnў bélls ŏf heáthĕr. 8. Might this stanza be written as four lines? Would it be as pleasant so written?

In graves that were like children's
   On many a mountain head,
The Brewsters of the Heather
   Lay numbered with the dead.

The king in the red moorland
   Rode on a summer's day;
And the bees hummed, and the curlews
   Cried beside the way.
The king rode, and was angry;
   Black was his brow and pale, ·
To rule in a land of heather
   And lack the Heather Ale.

It fortuned that his vassals,
   Riding free on the heath,
Came on a stone that was fallen
   And vermin hid beneath.
Rudely plucked from their hiding,
   Never a word they spoke:
A son and his aged father —
   Last of the dwarfish folk.

The king sat high on his charger,
   He looked on the little men;
And the dwarfish and swarthy couple
   Looked at the king again.
Down by the shore he had them;
   And there on the giddy brink —
"I will give you life, ye vermin,
   For the secret of the drink."

There stood the son and father
   And they looked high and low;
The heather was red around them,
   The sea rumbled below.

And up and spoke the father,
    Shrill was his voice to hear:
"I have a word in private,   55
    A word for the royal ear.

"Life is dear to the aged,
    And honor a little thing;
I would gladly sell the secret,"
    Quoth the Pict to the king.   60
His voice was small as a sparrow's,
    And shrill and wonderful clear:
"I would gladly sell my secret,
    Only my son I fear.

"For life is a little matter,   65
    And death is naught to the young;
And I dare not sell my honor
    Under the eye of my son.
Take *him*, O king, and bind him,
    And cast him far in the deep;   70
And it's I will tell the secret
    That I have sworn to keep."

They took the son and bound him,
    Neck and heels in a thong,
And a lad took him and swung him,   75
    And flung him far and strong,
And the sea swallowed his body,
    Like that of a child of ten;—
And there on the cliff stood the father,
    Last of the dwarfish men.   80

"True was the word I told you:
    Only my son I feared;
For I doubt the sapling courage
    That goes without the beard.

But now in vain is the torture,　　　　　　85
　　Fire shall never avail:
Here dies in my bosom
　　The secret of Heather Ale."

What colors are suggested in the ballad ? Why does not Stevenson linger on the pictures ?

ADAM OF GORDON

FOLK BALLAD　　　　　.

It fell about the Martinmas,
　　When the wind blew shrill and cold,
Said Adam of Gordon to his men,
　　"We maun draw to a hold.

"And whatna hold shall we draw to,　　　5
　　My merry men and me?
We will go to the house of Rodes,
　　To see that fair ladye."

The lady stood on her castle wall;
　　Beheld both dale and down;　　　　　10
There she was aware of a host of men
　　Came riding towards the town.

"O see ye not, my merry men all,
　　O see ye not what I see?
Methinks I see a host of men:　　　　　15
　　I marvel who they be."

4. *maun draw to a hold*, must proceed to a stronghold. 8. Iambic or trochaic ? Do accents fall on the syllables accented in ordinary speech ? Does not the folk ballad (see p. 1) seem to differ, in this matter of the accent, from artificial, written poetry ? Can you see any reasons why this should be so ? 12. *town*, the castle.

She had no sooner buskit herself,
   And putten on her gown,
Till Adam of Gordon and his men
   Were round about the town.   20

The lady ran to her tower-head,
   As fast as she could hie,
To see if by her fair speeches
   She could with him agree.

"Give o'er your house, ye lady fair,   25
   Give o'er your house to me!
Or I shall burn yourself therein,
   But and your babies three."

"I winna give o'er, ye false Gordon,
   To no sic traitor as thee;   .   30
And if ye burn my ain dear babes,
   My lord shall mak' ye dree.

—"Woe worth, woe worth ye, Jock, my man;
   I paid ye well your fee;
Why pull ye out the grund-wa' stone,   35
   Lets in the reek to me?

"And e'en woe worth ye, Jock, my man!
   I paid ye well your hire;
Why pull ye out the grund-wa' stone,
   To me lets in the fire?"   40

—"Ye paid me well my hire, ladye,
   Ye paid me well my fee;
But now I'm Adam of Gordon's man,—
   Must either do or dee."

17. *buskit*, clad.   22. In the Northern pronunciation, *hie* rhymes with *agree;* cf. line 44.   28. *but and*, and besides.   32. *dree*, rue.   36. *reek*, smoke.

O then bespake her little son,　　　45
　　Sat on the nurse's knee;
Says, "O mither dear, give o'er this house!
　　For the reek it smothers me."

— "I winna give up my house, my dear,
　　To no sic traitor as he:　　　50
Come weel, come woe, my jewel fair,
　　Ye maun take share with me."

O then bespake her daughter dear,—
　　She was both jimp and small:
"O row me in a pair of sheets,　　　55
　　And tow me o'er the wall!"

They row'd her in a pair of sheets,
　　And tow'd her o'er the wall;
But on the point of Gordon's spear
　　She gat a deadly fall.　　　60

O bonnie, bonnie was her mouth,
　　And cherry were her cheeks,
And clear, clear was her yellow hair,
　　Whereon the red blood dreeps!

Then with his spear he turn'd her o'er;　　　65
　　O gin her face was wan!
He said, "Ye are the first that e'er
　　I wish'd alive again.

"Busk and boun, my merry men all,
　　For ill dooms I do guess;—　　　70
I cannot look on that bonnie face
　　As it lies on the grass."

54. *jimp*, graceful. 55. *row*, roll. 66. *gin*, if. 69. *busk and boun*, make ready.

But when the ladye saw the fire
   Come flaming o'er her head,
She wept, and kiss'd her children twain,   75
   Says, "Bairns, we be but dead."

— O this way look'd her own dear lord,
   As he came o'er the lea;
He saw his castle all in a lowe,
   So far as he could see.   80

"Put on, put on, my mighty men,
   As fast as ye can dri'e!
For he that's hindmost of the thrang
   Shall ne'er get good of me!"

Then some they rade, and some they ran,   85
   Out-o'er the grass and bent;
But ere the foremost could win up,
   Both lady and babes were brent.

And after the Gordon he is gane,
   Sae fast as he might dri'e;   90
And soon i' the Gordon's foul heart's blood
   He's wroken his fair ladye.

79. *lowe*, flame. 82. *dri'e*, drive. 92. *wroken*, avenged.
Is the ballad simple? affecting? Select what seems to you the most
powerful stanza. Is there throughout the ballad a vivid appeal to the eye?

A PLANTATION HEROINE

George Cary Eggleston

It was nearing the end.

Every resource of the Southern states had been taxed
to the point of exhaustion.

The people had given up everything they had for "the cause." 5

Under the law of a "tax in kind," they had surrendered all they could spare of food products of every character. Under an untamable impulse of patriotism they had surrendered much more than they could spare in order to feed the army. 10

It was at such a time that I went to my home county on a little military business. I stopped for dinner at a house, the lavish hospitality of which had been a byword in the old days.

It found before me at dinner the remnants of a cold 15 boiled ham, some boiled mustard greens, which we Virginians called "salad," a pitcher of buttermilk, some corn pones, and — nothing else.

I carved the ham, and offered to serve it to the three women of the household. But they all declined. They 20 made their dinner on salad, buttermilk, and corn bread, the latter eaten very sparingly, as I observed. The ham went only to myself and to the three convalescent wounded soldiers, who were guests in the house.

Wounded men were at that time guests in every house 25 in Virginia.

I lay awake that night and thought over the circumstance. The next morning I took occasion to have a talk on the old familiar terms with the young woman of the family, with whom I had been on a basis of friend- 30 ship in the old days that even permitted me to kiss her upon due and proper occasion.

"Why didn't you take some ham last night?" I asked urgently.

"Oh, I didn't want it," she replied. 35

14. Might the first five paragraphs better be combined in one? 24. Might the sixth and seventh?

H

"Now, you know you're fibbing," I said. "Tell me the truth, won't you?"

She blushed, and hesitated. Presently she broke down and answered frankly: "Honestly, I did want the ham. I have hungered for meat for months. But I 40 mustn't eat it, and I won't. You see the army needs all the food there is, and more. We women can't fight, though I don't see at all why they shouldn't let us, and so we are trying to feed the fighting men — and there aren't any others. We've made up our minds not to eat 45 anything that can be sent to the front as rations."

"You are starving yourselves," I exclaimed.

"Oh, no," she said. "And if we were, what would it matter? Haven't Lee's soldiers starved many a day? But we aren't starving. You see we had plenty of salad 50 and buttermilk last night. And we even ate some of the corn bread. I must stop that, by the way, for corn meal is a good ration for the soldiers."

A month or so later this frail but heroic young girl was laid away in the Grub Hill churchyard. 55

Don't talk to me about the "heroism" that braves a fire of hell under enthusiastic impulse. That young girl did a higher act of self-sacrifice than any soldier who fought on either side during the war ever dreamed of doing. 60

THE ANGELS OF BUENA VISTA

JOHN GREENLEAF WHITTIER

Speak and tell us, our Ximena, looking northward far away,
O'er the camp of the invaders, o'er the Mexican array,
Who is losing? who is winning? are they far or come
    they near?

   1. Ximena (*zimdynya*). Is the metre iambic or trochaic?

Look abroad, and tell us, sister, whither rolls the storm we
    hear.
"Down the hills of Angostura still the storm of battle rolls;
Blood is flowing, men are dying; God have mercy on their
    souls!"   6
Who is losing? who is winning? — "Over hill and over
    · plain,
I see but smoke of cannon clouding through the mountain
    rain."

Holy Mother!· keep our brothers! Look, Ximena, look
    once more :
"Still I see the fearful whirlwind rolling darkly as
    before,   10
Bearing on, in strange confusion, friend and foeman, foot
    and horse,   ·
Like some wild and troubled torrent sweeping down its
    mountain course."

Look forth once more, Ximena! "Ah! the smoke has
    rolled away;
And I see the Northern rifles gleaming down the ranks of
    gray.
Hark! that sudden blast of bugles! there the troop of
    Minon wheels;   15
There the Northern horses thunder, with the cannon at
    their heels.

"Jesu, pity! how it thickens! now retreat and now advance!
Right against the blazing cannon shivers Puebla's charging
    lance!
Down they go, the brave young riders; horse and foot
    together fall;
Like a ploughshare in the fallow, through them plough
    the Northern ball."   20

Nearer came the storm and nearer, rolling fast and fright-
ful on:
Speak, Ximena, speak and tell us, who has lost, and who
has won?
"Alas! alas! I know not; friend and foe together fall,
O'er the dying rush the living: pray, my sisters, for them
all!"

"Lo! the wind the smoke is lifting: Blessed Mother, save
my brain!   25
I can see the wounded crawling slowly out from heaps of
slain.
Now they stagger, blind and bleeding; now they fall, and
strive to rise;
Hasten, sisters, haste and save them, lest they die before
our eyes!"

"Oh my heart's love! oh my dear one! lay thy poor head
on my knee;
Dost thou know the lips that kiss thee? Canst thou hear
me? canst thou see?   30
Oh, my husband, brave and gentle! oh, my Bernal, look
once more
On the blessed cross before thee! mercy! mercy! all is
o'er!"

Dry thy tears, my poor Ximena; lay thy dear one down to
rest;
Let his hands be meekly folded, lay the cross upon his
breast;
Let his dirge be sung hereafter, and his funeral masses
said;   35
To-day, thou poor bereaved one, the living ask thy aid.

29. Here Ximena speaks. There are two speakers in this poem besides
the poet; is there a dialogue, or are there two monologues?

Close beside her, faintly moaning, fair and young, a
    soldier lay,
Torn with shot and pierced with lances, bleeding slow his
    life away;
But, as tenderly before him, the lorn Ximena knelt,
She saw the Northern eagle shining on his pistol belt.   40

With a stifled cry of horror straight she turned away her
    head;
With a sad and bitter feeling looked she back upon her
    dead;
But she heard the youth's low moaning, and his struggling
    breath of pain,
And she raised the cooling water to his parching lips again.

Whispered low the dying soldier, pressed her hand and
    faintly smiled: 45
Was that pitying face his mother's? did she watch beside
    her child?
All his stranger words with meaning her woman's heart
    supplied;
With her kiss upon his forehead, "Mother!" murmured
    he, and died!

"A bitter curse upon them, poor boy, who led thee
    forth,
From some gentle, sad-eyed mother, weeping, lonely, in
    the North!"   50
Spake the mournful Mexic woman, as she laid him with
    her dead,
And turned to soothe the living, and bind the wounds
    which bled.

Look forth once more, Ximena! "Like a cloud before the
     wind
Rolls the battle down the mountains, leaving blood and
     death behind;
Ah! they plead in vain for mercy; in the dust the wounded
     strive;   55
Hide your faces, holy angels! oh, thou Christ of God,
     forgive!"

Sink, oh Night, among thy Mountains! let the cool, gray
     shadows fall;
Dying brothers, fighting demons, drop thy curtain over
     all!
Through the thickening winter twilight, wide apart the
     battle rolled,
In its sheath the sabre rested, and the cannon's lips grew
     cold.   60

But the noble Mexic women still their holy task pur-
     sued,
Through that long, dark night of sorrow, worn and faint
     and lacking food;
Over weak and suffering brothers, with a tender care they
     hung,
And the dying foeman blessed them in a strange and
     Northern tongue.

Not wholly lost, oh Father! is this evil world of ours;   65
Upward, through its blood and ashes, spring afresh the
     Eden flowers;
From its smoking hell of battle, Love and Pity send their
     prayer,
And still thy white-winged angels hover dimly in our air!

DECORATION [1]

Manibus date lilia plenis

THOMAS WENTWORTH HIGGINSON

'Mid the flower-wreathed tombs I stand,
Bearing lilies in my hand.
Comrades! in what soldier-grave
Sleeps the bravest of the brave?

Is it he who sank to rest   5
With his colors round his breast?
Friendship makes his tomb a shrine,
Garlands veil it; ask not mine.

One low grave, yon trees beneath,
Bears no roses, wears no wreath;   10
Yet no heart more high and warm
Ever dared the battle-storm.

Never gleamed a prouder eye .
In the front of victory;
Never foot had firmer tread   15
On the field where hope lay dead,

Than are hid within this tomb,
Where the untended grasses bloom;
And no stone with feigned distress,
Mocks the sacred loneliness.   20

[1] Reprinted from *The Afternoon Landscape*, by permission of Longmans, Green, & Co.

The Latin motto means "Strew handfuls of lilies." It is from Vergil, and refers to the death of the young Roman prince, Marcellus, son of Augustus Cæsar. The whole poem may be compared with Bryant's *The Conqueror's Grave*.

4. Do the simple, regular metre and simple rhyme-scheme (couplets) fit the theme?

Youth and beauty, dauntless will,
Dreams that life could ne'er fulfil
Here lie buried, — here in peace
Wrongs and woes have found release.

Turning from my comrades' eyes,   25
Kneeling where a woman lies,
I strew lilies on the grave
Of the bravest of the brave.

THE BURIAL OF SIR JOHN MOORE

CHARLES WOLFE

Not a drum was heard, not a funeral note,
    As his corse to the rampart we hurried;
Not a soldier discharged.his farewell shot
    O'er the grave where our hero we buried.

We buried him darkly at dead of night,   5
    The sods with our bayonets turning;
By the struggling moonbeam's misty light,
    And the lantern dimly burning.

No useless coffin enclosed his breast,
    Not in sheet nor in shroud we wound him;   10
But he lay like a warrior taking his rest
    With his martial cloak around him.

Few and short were the prayers we said,
    And we spoke not a word of sorrow;
But we steadfastly gazed on the face that was dead, 15
    And we bitterly thought of the morrow.

1. Name the line according to the accents and predominant foot. What
ending? 2. What ending? Does it hasten the movement?

We thought, as we hollowed his narrow bed,
  And smoothed down his lonely pillow,
That the foe and the stranger would tread o'er his head,
  And we far away on the billow!   20

Lightly they'll talk of the spirit that's gone,
  And o'er his cold ashes upbraid him, —
But little he'll reck, if they let him sleep on
  In the grave where a Briton has laid him.

But half of our heavy task was done,   25
  When the clock struck the hour for retiring;
And we heard the distant and random gun
  That the foe was sullenly firing.

Slowly and sadly we laid him down,
  From the field of his fame fresh and gory;   30
We carved not a line, and we raised not a stone —
  But we left him alone with his glory!

Which stanza presents the most striking picture? Which appeals the
most to the ear? Which seems the most genuine in its sadness?

ON THE AMERICAN REVOLUTION

WILLIAM PITT, EARL OF CHATHAM

I cannot, my lords, I *will not*, join in congratulation
on misfortune and disgrace. This, my lords, is a peril-
ous and tremendous moment: it is not a time for adula-
tion: the smoothness of flattery cannot save us in this
rugged and awful crisis. It is now necessary to instruct   5
the throne, in the language of TRUTH. We must, if pos-
sible, dispel the delusion and darkness which envelop
it; and display, in its full danger and genuine colors,
the ruin which is brought to our doors. Can ministers
still presume to expect support in their infatuation? 10

Can Parliament be so dead to its dignity and duty as to give their support to measures thus obtruded and forced upon them — measures, my lords, which have reduced this late flourishing empire to scorn and contempt. But yesterday, "and England might have stood against the world — NOW, none so poor to do her reverence." The people we at first despised as rebels, but whom we now acknowledge as enemies, are abetted against you, supplied with every military store, their interests consulted, and their ambassadors entertained by your inveterate enemy; and our ministers do not, and dare not, interpose with dignity or effect. The desperate state of our army abroad is in part known. No man more highly esteems and honors the English troops than I do: I know their virtue and their valor: I know they can achieve anything except impossibilities; and I know that the conquest of English America is an impossibility. You cannot, my lords, you CANNOT conquer America. What is your present situation there? We do not know the worst, but we know that in three campaigns we have done nothing, and suffered much. You may swell every expense, and strain every effort, accumulate every assistance, and extend your traffic to the shambles of every German despot; your attempts forever will be vain and impotent; doubly so indeed from this mercenary aid on which you rely; for it irritates to an incurable resentment the minds of your adversaries to overrun them with the mercenary sons of rapine and plunder, devoting them and their possessions to the rapacity of hireling cruelty. If I were an American, as I am an Englishman, while a foreign troop was landed in my country, I never would lay down my arms — NEVER! NEVER! NEVER!

Is the language of this passage colloquial or elevated? Is it high-flown, or was it warranted by the occasion?

CONCORD HYMN

SUNG AT THE COMPLETION OF THE BATTLE MONUMENT,
APRIL 19, 1836

RALPH WALDO EMERSON

By the rude bridge that arched the flood,
   Their flag to April's breeze unfurled,
Here once the embattled farmers stood,
   And fired the shot heard round the world.

The foe long since in silence slept;   5
   Alike the conqueror silent sleeps;
And Time the ruined bridge has swept
   Down the dark stream which seaward creeps.

On this green bank, by this soft stream,
   We set to-day a votive stone;   10
That memory may their deed redeem, .
   When, like our sires, our sons are gone.

Spirit, that made those heroes dare
   To die, and leave their children free,
Bid Time and Nature gently spare   15
   The shaft we raise to them and thee.

2. Name the line according to accents and feet. 3. *embattled* is a word of Emerson's coinage; is it good? 9. Why *soft?*

This poem was sung as a hymn. Which of the following things are particularly desirable in a hymn: elaborate phrases; words easily understood; complex, skilfully varied metre (like that of *The Revenge*); even, regular metre; tripping movement; stately movement; simple thought; complex thought; overwhelming emotion; sincere but controlled emotion?

Plan of Summary. — Reviewing the chapter, (1) enumerate the kinds of metre, designating them by the number of accents and the predominant foot. Then (2) say which poem is most noticeable for melody; (3) which for beauty of suggested sights; (4) which for pleasure of suggested sounds; (5) which for pleasure of suggested activity; (6) which for pleasure of suggested odors or tastes; (7) which is most easily understood; (8) which moves the reader most deeply; (9) which shows most skill in character drawing; (10) which has the best unity; (11) which, your critical judgment tells you, is the best piece of work; (12) which you like the best, — without regard to its deserved rank, or its fame.

CHAPTER III

THE HEROISM OF PEACE

THOUGH wars have sometimes been a moral necessity, as Hannah the Quakeress, p. 117. Miss Clarke implies in her stirring ballad of our American Revolution, and though, in Douglas Jerrold's words, "There is a peace more destructive of the manhood of living man than war is destructive to his material body," yet honorable peace is man's noblest achievement. When blood is up and thirst for revenge is hot, it is easy to go on fighting to the death. There are nations that live in eternal war with each other. Even in civilized lands, there are families between which exist feuds of centuries' standing. It is distinctly heroic, therefore, to be quickly reconciled with Reconciliation, p. 120. an enemy. Walt Whitman, as he pictures a soldier gazing upon the dead face of his foe, declares Reconciliation to be the most beautiful word in the world.

It is hard for the victor to refrain from unheroic exultation over his enemy, and harder for the vanquished to take up his broken life and make the most of it. Consider the The Confederate Soldier after the War, p.121. case of the Southern soldier, whom Mr. Grady, in a brilliant speech, sketched as returning to his ruined home. Northern youth of to-day cannot appreciate what it has cost the Southerners to reconstruct the South.

It is a great thing to save a state by force of arms. It is a greater thing to save it afterward from dishonesty and corruption. The soldiers who fought the battles of the Civil War found another fight to wage when they got home. Military heroes, both Northern and Southern, had now to protect the nation from greedy office-seeking and traitorous office-using. The poet Bayard Taylor told the Union veterans, as long ago as 1877, that their hardest work was yet to do. He declared that to the soldier of peace each true man is a friend, each false man a foe. Longfellow hated

The Arsenal at Springfield, p. 123.

war almost as much as he hated slavery. In one of his strongest short poems he declared that half the money spent on camps and forts could be so spent as to remove all need of camps and forts.

> Peace hath her victories,
> No less renowned than war,

sings Milton. Yet few of the individuals who win the victories of peace can be renowned. Homer says of a particular hour's fight that it were hard for him, though he were a god, to tell of all the deeds. Many a gallant fellow dies in battle without hope of the poet's praise, but more suffer a similar fate in time of peace. It is the unsung courage of nameless men that keeps the world moving. The fisherman on the winter ocean, the patrolman on the coast, the miner in the fire-damp, the engineer at the throttle, the fireman in the burning house, the nurse and the doctor in the plague,—all these are splendidly intrepid. Of a thousand

The Three Fishers, p. 125.
A Sea Story, p. 126.

such heroes but few have passed into literature. The duty of all fishermen stands out sternly in Kingsley's song of the three who lay dead on the shining sands. A young sailor relaxing his hold on the tiny raft, to save his friend who has a family, is the theme of Miss Hickey's *A Sea Story*.

Patroling Barnegat, p. 127.

In Whitman's *Patroling Barnegat*, the life-saver struggles steadily through the blinding night on his humane mission. The self-sacrifice of a rough miner is honored in one of Bret Harte's poems (*In the Tunnel*), and in another (*Guild's Signal*) that of the engineer who disdains to jump from his engine. The fidelity of Conductor Bradley did

not escape the notice of Whittier. The nurse in the plague
has never been written of more affectingly than by Mrs.
Phelps Ward in her story of the murderer Zerviah Hope,
who washed out his crime by giving his life for others.
The doctor appears in Whittier's *The Hero* as achieving
the impossible. This particular hero was Dr. Howe, who,
with infinite patience and skill, taught Laura Bridgman.
He found a way of enriching life for those born without
sight, hearing, and speech. Dr. Holmes has also praised
the physician, in his poem of *The Two Armies*. The duty
of one army is to slay; that of the other, the far nobler
band, is to save. A great fire reveals heroism not merely
in the ordinary fireman, like him of Mrs. Mulock Craik's
A True Hero, but in other people. Lowell tells — *An
Incident of the Fire at Hamburgh* — how, when the flames
were beating down his church, the old sexton stood by his
bells, and chimed, "All good souls praise the Lord," until
the tower came crashing down.

An Incident of the Fire at Hamburgh, p. 128.

Recognized or unrecognized in literature, great deeds
are not lacking in common life. Mr. Kipling is said to
have declared that there will be no dearth of subjects for
literature so long as the daily paper exists. Certainly that
is true of themes for heroic ballads. To-day it is the
account of a gamin unconcernedly losing an arm in saving
his chum amid the maze of tracks; to-morrow, that of a
painter dashing before a car and yielding his life for a
stranger's child, — I refer to Hovenden, whose picture,
"Breaking Home Ties," was at the Fair of 1893. It may
be a report of fine humanity from a quarter where it was
least expected. Dr. Conan Doyle has versified such a report
of a sporting man. He was a quiet fellow, riding to the
hounds with a party of friends. It is the custom of fox-
hunters to call out "'Ware Holes," when they see a rabbit-
burrow that may trip those behind. The "gent from

'Ware Holes, p. 130.

London" ran at full speed upon a deep, hidden quarry. He went down easily to his death, calmly singing out, "'Ware Holes," — and saved all three who were just behind him.[1]

The severest tests of heroism come when the hero has no immediate pattern to work by. Most persons have imagined themselves saving another's life, — though, indeed, that is not the same thing as performing the feat. But the actual demands for heroism are often of an unexpected sort. A new species of courage must be shown. A "loftier way," as Emerson said, must be found. For example, if physical courage is demanded, it is apt to be some absurd thing like controlling an irritable nerve. New forms of bravery are constantly being exhibited. Even in children the highest courage in enduring pain, both physical and mental, is often seen. The mere pains of fear felt by children are inconceivable to grown persons, — fear of the dark, fear of animals, fear of the bully, fear of ridicule, fear of death. To overcome any of these is a great achievement for a child. The following anecdote by Dr. Clay Trumbull, of Philadelphia, would be incredible to any but those who have studied children: —

"There was a tender-hearted, loving child in a New England home, to whom life was all gladness and joy. He loved as he was loved, and he was worthy of all the love which was given to him. One day, as he was starting out for a ride with his parents, he asked them where they were going; and they told him that they were going to take him up to the new cemetery, a beautiful city of the dead by the river's bank, beyond the town. His bright face grew

---

[1] On the day that these lines were sent to the printer, the newspapers were reporting the heroic death of a sporting man in New York. Mr. James McDonald threw his runaway horse to save a collision with approaching carriages. In so doing he was obliged to sacrifice his own life and that of his horse.

shadowed, and his little lips quivered, so that his father asked him, 'Why, Willy, don't you want to go there?' Quietly the trustful answer came back, 'Yes, if you think it best, papa.' And they rode on silently, in through the broad gateway; on, along the lovely tree-shaded and turf-bordered avenues.

"That bright boy seemed strangely quiet, clinging in love to his mother's side, and looking up from time to time with a face that seemed never so beautiful in its restful confidence. As they finally passed out again from the gateway they had entered, the dear child drew a breath of relief, and, looking up in new surprise, asked, 'Why, am I going *back* with you again?' 'Of course you are. Why should you doubt it?' 'Why, I thought that when they took little children to the cemetery, they left them there,' said that hero-child.

"And then it was found that with a child's imperfect knowledge that dear boy had supposed he was being taken, at the call of God, and by the parents whom he loved and trusted, to be buried in the place which he had heard of only as a place of burial. And all by himself he had had the struggle with himself, and had proved the victor."[1]

Children know so little of life that they can hardly be expected to have courage; they have few grounds for courage. Imagine an orphan girl in the hospital, a little creature like that in Mr. Henley's *Enter Patient*. Imagine this child overhearing a surgeon say that she must undergo an operation from which she can hardly hope to recover. Some idea of what an operation means can be had from Mr. Henley's poem on that subject. There is no parent to assure her that it will "not hurt much"; that "father will hold her hand all the while." Now we get the situation in Tennyson's poem on little Emmie. Her childish

Enter Patient, p. 132.

Operation, p. 133.

In the Children's Hospital, p. 134.

---

[1] "Character-shaping and Character-showing."

I

heart is shaken with fear, but she asks advice of Annie, who lies in the next cot. Annie advises an appeal to the Lord Jesus — on the wall there is a print of Him among the children. But Emmie is sceptical; how will He know who is who, among so many cots in the ward. "Tell Him it is the little girl with her arms lying out on the counterpane." This device serves, and Emmie falls asleep with courageous heart. In that repose of faith she is permitted to slip away into the world of light.

As life grows more complex, the occasions for unobserved courage become more numerous. San Lorenzo's mother, in Mrs. Meynell's lovely poem, had given her son to the cloister, and had not seen him since he reached his manhood. When one day a member of his order came, she thought she recognized her boy, and her heart sprang to meet him. But she had given him absolutely to the holy cause, and she would neither come between him and it, nor allow him to hide from her the Son that cannot change. Perhaps she was mistaken in her duty, but could any action be braver?

San Lorenzo Giustiniani's Mother, p. 139.

The poet Whittier celebrated many instances of moral courage. It was he who wrote of the Scotch Quaker Barclay, prefixing to his poem these words: "Among the earliest converts to the doctrine of Friends, in Scotland, was Barclay of Ury, an old and distinguished soldier, who had fought under Gustavus Adolphus, in Germany. As a Quaker, he became the object of persecution and abuse at the hands of the magistrates and the populace. None bore the indignities of the mob with greater patience and nobleness of soul than this once proud gentleman and soldier. One of his friends, on an occasion of uncommon rudeness, lamented that he should be treated so harshly in his old age, who had been so honored before. 'I find more satisfaction,' said Barclay, 'as well as honor in being thus

Barclay of Ury, p. 140.

insulted for my religious principles, than when, a few years ago, it was usual for the magistrates, as I passed the city of Aberdeen, to meet me on the road and conduct me to public entertainment in their hall, and then escort me out again, to gain my favor.' "

The same poet's hero, Davenport, was a man of superb self-control. About ten on the morning of 19th May, 1780, a strange darkness fell upon New England. To this day astronomers are not sure what caused it. In the Connecticut State House the legislators, fearful of the Judgment Day, were on the point of breaking up, when Abraham Davenport addressed the assembly and brought it to its senses. He admitted that this might be the Judgment Day, but

> Let God do his work, we will see to ours.
> Bring in the candles. And they brought them in.

That old New England blood was not watery. The Pilgrims were fanatics, perhaps, but much may be pardoned a fanatic if he is also a hero; and heroes they were. To cross, for conscience' sake, an unknown sea to a land of savages, where one is almost certain to perish, is an adequate test of moral courage. Of the poems that have been written about the Pilgrims, that by Mrs. Hemans is the most stirring, though Bryant's is finished and dignified. *Landing of the Pilgrim Fathers in New England,* p. 145.

A recent writer, Mrs. Stetson, has pointed out very emphatically the lack of the heroic in the business life. With what splendid scorn she repeats the common phrase "A man must live!" Imagine, she says, a soldier with that for a battle-cry! Mr. Heman White Chaplin has a story called *Eli*,[1] in which he pictures the high courage which faces loss of money, friends, and social position. A certain fisherman is summoned for jury service in a trial for bank *The Twenty-second of December,* p. 146. "A Man must Live," p. 147.

[1] In the admirable volume, "Five Hundred Dollars, and Other Stories." Boston: Little, Brown, & Co.

robbery. He believes the accused man innocent, though all the evidence is against him. Eli stands out against the persuasion of the other jurors. They give him to understand what such determination to defeat justice will mean.

"Lively times some folks'll hev', when they go home," said a spare tin-peddler, stroking his long yellow goatee. "Go into the store: nobody speak to you; go to cattle-show: everybody follow you 'round; go to the wharf: nobody weigh your fish; go to buy seed-cakes to the cart: baker won't give no tick." The butcher asks the foreman how much it costs "for a man 't's obliged to leave town, to move a family out West." A friend says to Eli, "They can kill your wife and break down your children. Women and children can't stand it." But Eli holds out, nor is he mistaken in his man.

The Hero, p. 148.

According to Robert Nicoll, the hero is not the soldier. "Go, mock at conquerors and kings." They are the inferiors of the poor man who works hard and makes no man, woman, or child unhappy. On the whole, young Nicoll was probably right. So was Whittier, when he said, in the poem on Dr. Howe, —

> Dream not helm and harness
> The sign of valor true;
> Peace hath higher tests of manhood
> Than battle ever knew.

HANNAH THE QUAKERESS

AN INCIDENT OF THE REVOLUTION

EDNAH PROCTOR CLARKE

Hannah the Quakeress sat
  And knit, by the parlor door;
And she heard within the Brethren's feet
  Pacing her sanded floor;

For to-day — in the hour of fear,   5
  Of defeat by land and sea,
When despair had clutched the hearts that fought
  Or prayed for Liberty,

When lives and gold seemed flung
  In a useless, hopeless fight   10
Waged by a handful of ragged boys
  Against great England's might,

They had met at Friend Isaac's house
  To vote for a shameful peace.
(Better their gold with a tyrant's bond   15
  Than Freedom's beggared lease!)

And Hannah, who curtsied them in
  By two and three and four,
With their brooding lips and their troubled eyes,
  Thought, as she scanned them o'er: 20

"They're wanting no woman's word;
  My counsel they'd scorn and mock;
But I'll set my chair by the parlor door,
  And turn the heel of my sock."

She was the gentlest dame,   25
  The most dutiful wife, in town;
Never a glint of her heart's fire slipped
  'Neath the veil of her lashes brown.

But swifter her needles clicked
  As the wavering footsteps went   30
To and fro till for "Peace!" for "Peace!"
  The clamorous voices blent.

"Peace!" — and her knitting stopped
  As the dastard votes were cast —
As the Elder read them one by one —   35
  And Isaac's name was the last!

Ah! — in through the wide-flung door
  Burst Hannah the Quakeress then,
And with heaving bosom and storming brow
  She faced the astounded men.   40

The blue yarn sock in her hand
  Shook with its bristling steel
As she snatched the votes from the Elder's grasp
  And ground them beneath her heel.

"Shame on you — traitors — cowards —   45
  Who fail at your Country's need!
Who would sell your birthright, sell your souls
  In your paltry selfish greed!

"We want not your Tory gold!
    The Lord God shields our right!   50
Yea, as He guided Israel's host,
    A pillar of fire by night,

"He will lead our Armies on!
    And when our land is free " —
The blue sock waved like a flag of war —   55
    "Traitors! where will you be?"

Speechless the Council stood,
    Dumb 'neath that storm of shame,
Till Isaac gasped: "She is distraught!
    Out! — to thy knitting, dame!"   60

Then how she flamed and turned!
    "Distraught with shame of thee!
Yea, Isaac Arnett, hold thy tongue —
    Thou'lt take this word from me!

"Now, as the Lord doth hear,   65
    Choose thou 'twixt peace and strife.
I married thee for an honest man;
    I'll be no traitor's wife!

"Thou canst keep thy house and thy King.
    I know my Country's worth!   70
I'd rather starve in her frozen fields
    Than feed at a traitor's hearth!"

Flushed Isaac's cold cheek then;
    The Brethren hung their heads;
And the Elder lifted the trampled votes   75
    And tore them into shreds.

"Thank God in this nest of fear
    There beats one loyal heart!
Hannah Arnett, to us this day
    A Flame of the Lord thou art!   80

"Friends, when a woman leads,
    No man is laggard found!
Here, to my Country's need and War
    I pledge an hundred pound."

Then the Elder lifted his pen   85
    And wrote his gift and name.
While with ten and twenty and fifty more
    The Brethren crowding came;

And stirred as the great deep stirs
    When a tempest smites the sea,   90
They pledged their honor, wealth, and lives
    Again to Liberty!

And what of Hannah the dame,
    With her heart of fire and steel?
Oh! she smoothed her kerchief, and set her cap,   95
    And finished her stocking heel.

RECONCILIATION[1]

WALT WHITMAN

Word over all, beautiful as the sky,
Beautiful that war and all its deeds of carnage must in time
        be utterly lost,
That the hands of the sisters Death and Night incessantly
        softly wash again, and ever again, this soil'd world;

[1] Reprinted by permission of Small, Maynard, & Co.

For my enemy is dead, a man divine as myself is dead,
I look where he lies white-faced and still in the coffin — I
    draw near,   5
Bend down and touch lightly with my lips the white face in
    the coffin.

. Having read the poem through silently several times, say whether it has
a definite metre; if not, whether it is rhythmical at all.
    Is any sense except the eye definitely appealed to? Which picture in
the poem is the most vivid? Which is the most imaginative?

THE CONFEDERATE SOLDIER AFTER THE WAR [1]

HENRY WOODFEN GRADY

You of the North have had drawn for you with a
master's hand the picture of your returning armies. You
have heard how, in the pomp and circumstance of war,
they came back to you, marching with proud and vic-
torious tread, reading their glory in a nation's eyes! 5
Will you bear with me while I tell you of another army
that sought its home at the close of the late war — an
army that marched home in defeat and not in victory,
in pathos and not in splendor, but in glory that equalled
yours, and to hearts as loving as ever welcomed heroes 10
home? Let me picture to you the footsore Confederate
soldier, as, buttoning up in his faded gray jacket the
parole which was to bear testimony to his children of

[1] Reprinted from "The New South," by permission of Robert Bonner's
Sons, publishers of the *New York Ledger*.
    5. The last seven words are a quotation from Gray's famous *Elegy
written in a Country Churchyard*. Mr. Grady does not use quotation
marks here, for he assumes that his audience will recognize the quotation.
The words thus treated may be called an *embedded* quotation. 11-54. Note
that the skilful orator understands the power of images.

his fidelity and faith, he turned his face southward from Appomattox in April, 1865. Think of him as 15 ragged, half-starved, heavy-hearted, enfeebled by want and wounds; having fought to exhaustion, he surrenders his gun, wrings the hands of his comrades in silence, and lifting his tear-stained and pallid face for the last time to the graves that dot the old Virginia hills, pulls 20 his gray cap over his brow and begins the slow and painful journey. What does he find — let me ask you, who went to your homes eager to find in the welcome you had justly earned, full payment for four years' sacrifice — what does he find when, having followed the 25 battle-stained cross against overwhelming odds, dreading death not half so much as surrender, he reaches the home he left so prosperous and beautiful? He finds his house in ruins, his farm devastated, his slaves free, his stock killed, his barns empty, his trade destroyed, 30 his money worthless; his social system, feudal in its magnificence, swept away; his people without law or legal status, his comrades slain, and the burdens of others heavy on his shoulders. Crushed by defeat, his very traditions are gone; without money, credit, em- 35 ployment, material, or training; and besides all this, confronted with the gravest problem that ever met human intelligence — the establishing of a status for the vast body of his liberated slaves.

What does he do — this hero in gray with a heart of 40 gold? Does he sit down in sullenness and despair? Not for a day. Surely God, who had stripped him of his prosperity, inspired him in his adversity. As ruin was never before so overwhelming, never was restoration swifter. The soldier stepped from the trenches into the 45 furrow; horses that had charged Federal guns marched before the plough, and fields that ran red with blood in

April were green with the harvest in June.   Never was
nobler duty confided to human hands than the uplifting
and building of the prostrate and bleeding South, mis- 50
guided, perhaps, but beautiful in her suffering; and
honest, brave, and generous always.   In the record of
her social, industrial, and political evolution we await
with confidence the verdict of the world.

THE ARSENAL AT SPRINGFIELD

HENRY WADSWORTH LONGFELLOW

This is the Arsenal.   From floor to ceiling,
    Like a huge organ, rise the burnished arms;
But from their silent pipes no anthem pealing
    Startles the villages with strange alarms.

Ah! what a sound will rise, how wild and dreary,   5
    When the death-angel touches those swift keys!
What loud lament and dismal Miserere
    Will mingle with their awful symphonies!

I hear even now the infinite fierce chorus,
    The cries of agony, the endless groan,   10
Which, through the ages that have gone before us,
    In long reverberations reach our own.

On helm and harness rings the Saxon hammer,
    Through Cimbric forest roars the Norseman's song,
And loud, amid the universal clamor,   15
    O'er distant deserts sounds the Tartar gong.

I hear the Florentine, who from his palace
    Wheels out his battle-bell with dreadful din,
And Aztec priests upon their teocallis
    Beat the wild war-drums made of serpent's skin;   20

The tumult of each sacked and burning village;
　The shout that every prayer for mercy drowns;
The soldiers' revels in the midst of pillage;　　　.
　The wail of famine in beleaguered towns;

The bursting shell, the gateway wrenched asunder,　　25
　The rattling musketry, the clashing blade;
And ever and anon, in tones of thunder,
　The diapason of the cannonade.

Is it, O man, with such discordant noises,
　With such accursed instruments as these,　　　30
Thou drownest Nature's sweet and kindly voices,
　And jarrest the celestial harmonies?

Were half the power, that fills the world with terror,
　Were half the wealth, bestowed on camps and courts,
Given to redeem the human mind from error,　　35
　There were no need of arsenals nor forts:

The warrior's name would be a name abhorred!
　And every nation, that should lift again
Its hand against a brother, on its forehead
　Would wear for evermore the curse of Cain!　　40

Down the dark future, through long generations,
　The echoing sounds grow fainter and then cease;
And like a bell, with solemn, sweet vibrations,
　I hear once more the voice of Christ say, "Peace!"

Peace! and no longer from its brazen portals　　45
　The blast of War's great organ shakes the skies!
But beautiful as songs of the immortals,
　The holy melodies of love arise.

Does Longfellow succeed in carrying the image of the organ through the poem?
　Does the poet make his appeal chiefly to the eye or to the ear?　Why?
　What emotions does the poem arouse?

THE THREE FISHERS

CHARLES KINGSLEY

Three fishers went sailing out into the West,
    Out into the West as the sun went down;
Each thought on the woman who lov'd him the best;
    And the children stood watching them out of the town;
For men must work, and women must weep,   5
And there's little to earn, and many to keep,
    Though the harbor bar be moaning.

Three wives sat up in the light-house tower,
    And they trimm'd the lamps as the sun went down;
They look'd at the squall, and they look'd at the shower, 10
    And the night rack came rolling up ragged and brown!
But men must work, and women must weep,
Though storms be sudden, and waters deep,
    And the harbor bar be moaning.

Three corpses lay out on the shining sands   15
    In the morning gleam as the tide went down,
And the women are weeping and wringing their hands
    For those who will never come back to the town;
For men must work, and women must weep,
And the sooner it's over, the sooner to sleep —   20
    And good-by to the bar and its moaning.

    This poem has often been set to music — a pretty sure sign that it is melodious. Is the refrain impressive?
    Is the story told continuously, or by scenes? Which is the better way for a narrative song? Why?

A SEA STORY

Emily H. Hickey

Silence.   Awhile ago
Shrieks went up piercingly;
But now is the ship gone down;
Good ship, well manned, was she.
There's a raft that's a chance of life for one,
    This day upon the sea.

A chance for one of two;
Young, strong, are he and he,
Just in the manhood prime,
The comelier, verily,
For the wrestle with wind and weather and wave
    In the life upon the sea.

One of them has a wife
And little children three;
Two that can toddle and lisp,
And a suckling on the knee;
Naked they'll go and hunger sore,
    If he be lost at sea.

One has a dream of home,
A dream that well may be;
He never has breathed it yet;
She never has known it, she.
But some one will be sick at heart,
    If he be lost at sea.

"Wife and kids at home! —   25
Wife, kids, nor home has he! —
Give us a chance, Bill!"   Then,
"All right, Jem!"   Quietly
A man gives up his life for a man,
     This day upon the sea.   30

Is this poem as musical as *The Three Fishers?* Which of the stanzas would sing best? Is the refrain impressive? Would the narrative in the last stanza be more or less impressive if it were less condensed and abrupt?

PATROLING BARNEGAT [1]

WALT WHITMAN

Wild, wild the storm, and the sea high running,
Steady the roar of the gale, with incessant undertone mut-
     tering,
Shouts of demoniac laughter fitfully piercing and pealing,
Waves, air, midnight, their savagest trinity lashing,
Out in the shadows there milk-white combs careering,   5
On beachy slush and sand spirts of snow fierce slanting,
Where through the murk the easterly death-wind breasting,
Through cutting swirl and spray watchful and firm ad-
          vancing,
(That in the distance! is that a wreck? is the red signal
     flaring?)
Slush and sand of the beach tireless till daylight wending, 10

[1] Reprinted by permission of Small, Maynard, & Co.

4. This vague line apparently means that waves, air, and midnight are lashing themselves together in the savagest possible trinity. Possibly it means that the midnight air is lashing the waves into spray; but it doesn't succeed in saying so.

Steadily, slowly, through hoarse roar never remitting,
Along the midnight edge by those milk-white combs careering,
A group of dim, weird forms, struggling, the night confronting,
That savage trinity warily watching.

Is the poem metrical or only rhythmical? Read it through line by line
for the images, which are startlingly vivid. Few poems appeal so strongly
and wholesomely to the senses of touch and muscular exertion. Note how
the fierce sounds come first, then a splash of white, then muscular exertion,
then sharp sensations on the face, then a splash of red, then more muscular
exertion, then more white, and finally a dim picture.

AN INCIDENT OF THE FIRE AT HAMBURGH

James Russell Lowell

The tower of old Saint Nicholas soared upward to the skies,
Like some huge piece of Nature's make, the growth of cen-
    turies;
You could not deem its crowding spires a work of human art,
They seemed to struggle lightward so from a sturdy living
    heart.

Not Nature's self more freely speaks in crystal or in oak   5
Than, through the pious builder's hand, in that gray pile she
    spoke;
And as from acorn springs the oak, so, freely and alone,
Sprang from his heart this hymn to God, sung in obedient
    stone.

It seemed a wondrous freak of chance, so perfect, yet so
    rough,
A whim of Nature crystallized slowly in granite tough;   10
The thick spires yearned toward the sky in quaint harmo-
    nious lines,
And in broad sunlight basked and slept, like a grove of
    blasted pines.

Never did rock or stream or tree lay claim with better right
To all the adorning sympathies of shadow and of light ;
And, in that forest petrified, as forester there dwells   15
Stout Herman, the old sacristan, sole lord of all its bells.

Surge leaping after surge, the fire roared onward, red as
    blood,
Till half of Hamburgh lay engulfed beneath the eddying
    flood ;
For miles away, the fiery spray poured down its deadly rain,
And back and forth the billows drew, and paused, and broke
    again.   20

From square to square, with tiger leaps, still on and on it
    came ;
The air to leeward trembled with the pantings of the flame,
And church and palace, which even now stood whelmed but
    to the knee,
Lift their black roofs like breakers lone amid the rushing sea.

Up in his tower old Herman sat and watched with quiet
    look ;   25
His soul had trusted God too long to be at last forsook :
He could not fear, for surely God a pathway would unfold
Through this red sea, for faithful hearts, as once he did of old.

But scarcely can he cross himself, or on his good saint call,
Before the sacrilegious flood o'erleaped the churchyard
    wall,   30
And, ere a *pater* half was said, 'mid smoke and crackling
    glare,
His island tower scarce juts its head above the wide despair.

---

31. *pater* (the *a* like *a* in *day*), the Lord's Prayer in Latin.

K

Upon the peril's desperate peak his heart stood up
    sublime ;
His first thought was for God above, his next was for his
    chime ;
" Sing now, and make your voices heard in hymns of praise,"
    cried he,   35
" As did the Israelites of old, safe-walking through the sea !

" Through this red sea our God hath made our pathway safe
    to shore ;
Our promised land stands full in sight ; shout now as ne'er
    before."
And, as the tower came crashing down, the bells, in clear
    accord,
Pealed forth the grand old German hymn — " All good souls
    praise the Lord ! "   40

'WARE HOLES [1]

A. CONAN DOYLE

['Ware Holes ! is the expression used in the hunting-field to warn those
behind against rabbit-burrows or other such dangers.]

    A sportin' death !   My word it was !
        An' taken in a sportin' way.
    Mind you, I wasn't there to see ;
        I only tell you what they say.

    They found that day at Shillinglee,   5
        An' ran 'im down to Chillinghurst ;
    The fox was goin' straight an' free
        For ninety minutes at a burst.

1 From " Songs of Action," Copyright, 1898, by Doubleday & McClure Co.

They 'ad a check at Ebernoe
  An' made a cast across the Down,   10
Until they got a view 'ollo
  An' chased 'im up to Kirdford town.

From Kirdford 'e run Bramber way,
  An' took 'em over 'arf the Weald.
If you 'ave tried the Sussex clay,   15
  You'll guess it weeded out the field.

Until at last I don't suppose
  As 'arf a dozen, at the most,
Came safe to where the grassland goes
  Switchbackin' southwards to the coast.   20

Young Captain 'Eadley, 'e was there,
  And Jim the whip an' Percy Day;
The Purcells an' Sir Charles Adair,
  An' this 'ere gent from London way.

For 'e 'ad gone amazin' fine,   25
  Two 'undred pounds between 'is knees;
Eight stone he was, an' rode at nine,
  As light an' limber as you please.

'E was a stranger to the 'Unt,
  There weren't a person as 'e knew there;   30
But 'e could ride, that London gent—
  'E sat 'is mare as if 'e grew there.

They seed the 'ounds upon the scent,
  But found a fence across their track,
And 'ad to fly it; else it meant   35
  A turnin' and a 'arkin' back.

'E was the foremost at the fence,
 And as 'is mare just cleared the rail
He turned to them that rode be'ind,
 For three was at 'is very tail.   40

" 'Ware 'oles !" says 'e, an' with the word,
 Still sittin' easy on his mare,
Down, down 'e went, an' down an' down,
 Into the quarry yawnin' there.

Some say it was two 'undred foot ;   45
 The bottom lay as black as ink.
I guess they 'ad some ugly dreams,
 Who reined their 'orses on the brink.

'E'd only time for that one cry ;
 " 'Ware 'oles !" says 'e, an' saves all three. 50
There may be better deaths to die,
 But that one's good enough for me.

For mind you, 'twas a sportin' end,
 Upon a right good sportin' day ;
They think a deal of 'im down 'ere,   55
 That gent what came from London way.

Sketch the character of the groom who is telling the story. Give your warrant for every statement.

ENTER PATIENT [1]

William Ernest Henley

The morning mists still haunt the stony street ;
The northern summer air is shrill and cold ;
And lo, the Hospital, gray, quiet, old,
Where Life and Death like friendly chafferers meet.

[1] Reprinted from " Poems," by permission of Charles Scribner's Sons.

4. Here is a striking simile. How can Life and Death be said to chaffer together ?

Thro' the loud spaciousness and draughty gloom 5
A small strange child — so agèd yet so young ! —
Her little arm besplintered and beslung,
Precedes me gravely to the waiting-room.
I limp behind, my confidence all gone,
The gray-haired soldier porter waves me on, 10
And on I crawl, and still my spirits fail :
A tragic meanness seems so to environ
These corridors and stairs of stone and iron,
Cold, naked, clean — half-workhouse and half-jail.

5. Why does not Mr. Henley say something like *loud, spacious room*, and *draughty, gloomy place?* Is it merely a desire to save words ? Did the child probably think of the *room?* 13. *environ* usually means *to surround.* Here is merely meant that the air of tragic meanness is associated with the corridors and stairs.

OPERATION [1]

WILLIAM ERNEST HENLEY

You are carried in a basket,
Like a carcase from the shambles,
To the theatre, a cockpit,
Where they stretch you on a table.

Then they bid you close your eyelids, 5
And they mask you with a napkin,
And the anæsthetic reaches
Hot and subtle through your being.

And you gasp and reel and shudder
In a rushing, swaying rapture, 10
While the voices at your elbow
Fade — receding — fainter — farther.

[1] Reprinted from "Poems," by permission of Charles Scribner's Sons.

2. *shambles*, slaughter-house. 7. *anæsthetic*, a numbing drug, like chloroform or ether.

Lights about you shower and tumble,
And your blood seems crystallizing —
Edged and vibrant, yet within you   15
Racked and hurried back and forward.

Then the lights grow fast and furious,
And you hear a noise of waters,
And you wrestle, blind and dizzy,
In an agony of effort,   20

Till a sudden lull accepts you,
And you sound an utter darkness . . .
And awaken . . . with a struggle . . .
On a hushed, attentive audience.

15. *vibrant*, that is, pulsing, blood is clear enough; *edged* is harder to understand, but it probably meant something to the patient.

The curious thing about this powerful poem is that it deals with physical sensations that seem *within* the nerves, not produced by outside sights and sounds. Why do we not miss the *rhyme* very much?

IN THE CHILDREN'S HOSPITAL

Alfred, Lord Tennyson

EMMIE

I

Our doctor had call'd in another, I never had seen him
    before,
But he sent a chill to my heart when I saw him come in at
    the door,
Fresh from the surgery-schools of France and of other
    lands —
Harsh red hair, big voice, big chest, big merciless hands!
Wonderful cures he had done, O yes, but they said too of
    him   5

He was happier using the knife than in trying to save the
    limb,
And that I can well believe, for he look'd so coarse and so
    red,
I could think he was one of those who would break their
    jests on the dead,
And mangle the living dog that had loved him and fawn'd
    at his knee —
Drench'd with the hellish oorali — that ever such things
    should be!   10

II

Here was a boy — I am sure that some of our children
    would die
But for the voice of Love, and the smile, and the com-
    forting eye —
Here was a boy in the ward, every bone seem'd out of its
    place —
Caught in a mill and crush'd — it was all but a hopeless
    case:
And he handled him gently enough; but his voice and his
    face were not kind,   15
And it was but a hopeless case, he had seen it and made up
    his mind,
And he said to me roughly, "The lad will need little more
    of your care."
"All the more need," I told him, "to seek the Lord Jesus
    in prayer;
They are all his children here, and I pray for them all as
    my own:"
But he turn'd to me, "Ay, good woman, can prayer set a
    broken bone?"   20

---

10. *oorali,* an anæsthetic drug.

Then he mutter'd half to himself, but I know that I heard
    him say,
"All very well — but the good Lord Jesus has had his day."

III

Had? has it come?   It has only dawn'd.   It will come by
    and by.
O how could I serve in the wards if the hope of the world
    were a lie?
How could I bear with the sights and the loathsome smells
    of disease   25
But that He said, "Ye do it to me, when ye do it to these"?

IV

So he went.   And we past to this ward where the younger
    children are laid:
Here is the cot of our orphan, our darling, our meek little
    maid;
Empty you see just now!   We have lost her who loved her
    so much —
Patient of pain tho' as quick as a sensitive plant to the
    touch;   30
Hers was the prettiest prattle, it often moved me to tears,
Hers was the gratefullest heart I have found in a child of
    her years —
Nay you remember our Emmie; you used to send her the
    flowers;
How she would smile at 'em, play with 'em, talk to 'em
    hours after hours!
They that can wander at will where the works of the Lord
    are reveal'd   35
Little guess what joy can be got from a cowslip out of the
    field;

Flowers to these "spirits in prison" are all they can know
 of the spring,
They freshen and sweeten the wards like the waft of an
 Angel's wing;
And she lay with a flower in one hand and her thin hands
 crost on her breast —
Wan, but as pretty as heart can desire, and we thought her
 at rest,   40
Quietly sleeping — so quiet, our doctor said, "Poor little
 dear,
Nurse, I must do it to-morrow; she'll never live thro' it, I
 fear."

v

I walk'd with our kindly old doctor as far as the head of
 the stair,
Then I return'd to the ward; the child didn't see I was
 there.

VI

Never since I was nurse, had I been so grieved and so
 vext!   45
Emmie had heard him. Softly she call'd from her cot to
 the next,
"He says I shall never live thro' it, O Annie, what shall I
 do?"
Annie consider'd. "If I," said the wise little Annie, "was
 you,
I should cry to the dear Lord Jesus to help me, for, Emmie,
 you see,
It's all in the picture there: 'Little children should come
 to me.'"   50

(Meaning the print that you gave us, I find that it always
    can please
Our children, the dear Lord Jesus with children about his
    knees.)
"Yes, and I will," said Emmie, "but then if I call to the
    Lord,
How should he know that it's me? such a lot of beds in
    the ward!"   .   54
That was a puzzle for Annie.   Again she consider'd and said,
"Emmie, you put out your arms, and you leave 'em out-
    side on the bed —
The Lord has so *much* to see to! but, Emmie, you tell it
    him plain,
It's the little girl with her arms lying out on the coun-
    terpane."

VII

I had sat three nights by the child — I could not watch her
    for four —   59
My brain had begun to reel — I felt I could do it no more.
That was my sleeping-night, but I thought that it never
    would pass.
There was a thunderclap once, and a clatter of hail on the
    glass,
And there was a phantom cry that I heard as I tost about,
The motherless bleat of a lamb in the storm and the dark-
    ness without;
My sleep was broken besides with dreams of the dreadful
    knife   65
And fears for our delicate Emmie who scarce would escape
    with her life;
Then in the gray of the morning it seem'd she stood by
    me and smiled,
And the doctor came at his hour, and we went to see to the
    child.

VIII

He had brought his ghastly tools: we believed her asleep
    again —
Her dear, long, lean, little arms lying out on the counter-
    pane;   70
Say that His day is done! Ah; why should we care what
    they say?
The Lord of the children had heard her, and Emmie had
    past away.

The stanzas are of unequal length; does each represent a real step?
Has the poem plot, *i.e.* does it arouse suspense? If so, at what line is
the suspense finally relieved? Is the poem simple or complex in thought?
Is it pathetic? Is it gloomy or serene in spirit?

SAN LORENZO GIUSTINIANI'S MOTHER [1]

ALICE MEYNELL

I had not seen my son's dear face
(He chose the cloister by God's grace)
    Since it had come to full flower-time
    I hardly guessed at its perfect prime,
That folded flower of his dear face.   5

Mine eyes were veiled by mists of tears
When on a day in many years
    One of his Order came. I thrilled,
    Facing, I thought, that face fulfilled.
I doubted, for my mists of tears.   10

[1] Reprinted by permission of Mr. John Lane. The author's name is
pronounced Mennell.

5. The *folded flower* perhaps means that the son's face was quiet in its
beauty, like a flower folded at night. 8. *Order*, religious order of monks;
thus, the Order of St. Francis, or Franciscan order.

His blessing be with me forever!
My hope and doubt were hard to sever.
— That altered face, those holy weeds.
I filled his wallet and kissed his beads,
And lost his echoing feet forever.   15

If to my son my alms were given
I know not, and I wait for Heaven.
He did not plead for child of mine,
But for another Child divine,
And unto Him it was surely given.   20

There is One alone who cannot change;
Dreams are we, shadows, visions strange;
And all I give is given to One.
I might mistake my dearest son,
But never the Son who cannot change.   25

13. *weeds*, garments of sombre hue. The Order of St. Francis wore
rough sack-cloth, girt with a rope instead of a girdle. 14. *wallet*. The
travelling friars depended on charity for their food. 22. Perhaps it would
be well to write a paragraph for the instructor, explaining your idea of what
Mrs. Meynell means by this line.

BARCLAY OF URY

JOHN GREENLEAF WHITTIER

Up the streets of Aberdeen,
By the kirk and college green,
Rode the Laird of Ury;
Close behind him, close beside,
Foul of mouth and evil-eyed,   5
Pressed the mob in fury.

Flouted him the drunken churl,
Jeered at him the serving girl,
    Prompt to please her master;
And the begging carlin, late   10
Fed and clothed at Ury's gate,
    Cursed him as he passed her.

Yet, with calm and stately mien,
Up the streets of Aberdeen
    Came he slowly riding;   15
And, to all he saw and heard
Answering not with bitter word,
    Turning not for chiding.

Came a troop with broadswords swinging,
Bits and bridles sharply ringing,   20
    Loose and free and forward;
Quoth the foremost, "Ride him down!
Push him! prick him! through the town
    Drive the Quaker coward!"

But from out the thickening crowd   25
Cried a sudden voice and loud:
    "Barclay! Ho! a Barclay!"
And the old man at his side
Saw a comrade, battle tried,
    Scarred and sunburned darkly;   30

Who with ready weapon bare,
Fronting to the troopers there,
    Cried aloud: "God save us!
Call ye coward him who stood
Ankle deep in Lutzen's blood,   35
    With the brave Gustavus?"

10. *carlin*, a contemptuous term for a woman.

"Nay, I do not need thy sword,
Comrade mine," said Ury's lord;
 "Put it up I pray thee:
Passive to His holy will,   40
Trust I in my Master still,
 Even though He slay me."

"Pledges of thy love and faith,
Proved on many a field of death,
 Not by me are needed."   45
Marvelled much that henchman bold,
That his laird, so stout of old,
 Now so meekly pleaded.

"Woe's the day," he sadly said,
With a slowly shaking head,   50
 And a look of pity;
"Ury's honest lord reviled,
Mock of knave and sport of child,
 In his own good city!

"Speak the word, and, master mine, 55
As we charged on Tilly's line,
 And his Walloon lancers,
Smiting through their midst we'll teach
Civil look and decent speech
 To these boyish prancers!"   60

"Marvel not, mine ancient friend,
Like beginning, like the end:"
 Quoth the Laird of Ury,
"Is the sinful servant more
Than his gracious Lord who bore   65
 Bonds and stripes in Jewry?

"Give me joy that in His name
I can bear, with patient frame,
    All these vain ones offer;
While for them He suffereth long,   70
Shall I answer wrong with wrong,
    Scoffing with the scoffer?

"Happier I, with loss of all,
Hunted, outlawed, held in thrall,
    With few friends to greet me,   75
Than when reeve and squire were seen,
Riding out from Aberdeen,
    With bared heads, to meet me.

"When each good wife, o'er and o'er,
Blessed me as I passed her door;   80
    And the snooded daughter,
Through her casement glancing down,
Smiled on him who bore renown
    From red fields of slaughter.

"Hard to feel the stranger's scoff,   85
Hard the old friend's falling off,
    Hard to learn forgiving:
But the Lord His own rewards,
And His love with theirs accords,
    Warm and fresh and living.   90

"Through this dark and stormy night
Faith beholds a feeble light
    Up the blackness streaking;
Knowing God's own time is best,
In a patient hope I rest   95
    For the full day-breaking!"

76. *reeve*, an officer of justice.   81. *snood*, a head-band worn by Scottish maidens.

So the Laird of Ury said,
Turning slow his horse's head
    Toward the Tolbooth prison,
Where, through iron gates, he heard   100
Poor disciples of the Word
    Preach of Christ arisen!

Not in vain, Confessor old,
Unto us the tale is told
    Of thy day of trial;   105
Every age on him, who strays
From its broad and beaten ways,
    Pours its sevenfold vial.

Happy he whose inward ear
Angels comfortings can hear,   110
    O'er the rabble's laughter;
And, while Hatred's fagots burn,
Glimpses through the smoke discern
    Of the good hereafter.

Knowing this, that never yet   115
Share of Truth was vainly set
    In the world's wide fallow;
After hands shall sow the seed,
After hands from hill and mead
    Reap the harvests yellow.   120

Thus, with somewhat of the Seer,
Must the moral pioneer
    From the Future borrow;
Clothe the waste with dreams of grain,
And, on midnight's sky of rain,   125
    Paint the golden morrow!

LANDING OF THE PILGRIM FATHERS IN NEW ENGLAND

FELICIA BROWNE HEMANS

Look now abroad! Another race has fill'd
 Those populous borders — wide the wood recedes,
And towns shoot up, and fertile realms are till'd;
 The land is full of harvests and green meads. — *Bryant.*

The breaking waves dash'd high
 On a stern and rock-bound coast,
And the woods against a stormy sky
 Their giant branches toss'd;

And the heavy night hung dark   5
 The hills and waters o'er,
When a band of exiles moor'd their bark
 On the wild New England shore.

Not as the conqueror comes,
 They, the true-hearted, came;   10
Not with the roll of the stirring drums,
 And the trumpet that sings of fame;

Not as the flying come,
 In silence and in fear; —
They shook the depths of the desert gloom   15
 With their hymns of lofty cheer.

Amidst the storm they sang,
 And the stars heard and the sea;
And the sounding aisles of the dim woods rang
 To the anthem of the free!   20

L

The ocean eagle soared
   From his nest by the white wave's foam;
And the rocking pines of the forest roared,—
   This was their welcome home!

There were men with hoary hair,   25
   Amidst that pilgrim band;—
Why had they come to wither there,
   Away from their childhood's land?

There was woman's fearless eye,
   Lit by her deep love's truth;   30
There was manhood's brow serenely high,
   And the fiery heart of youth.

What sought they thus afar?
   Bright jewels of the mine?.
The wealth of seas, the spoils of war?   35
   They sought a faith's pure shrine!

Ay, call it holy ground,
   The soil where first they trod!
They left unstained what there they found,—
   Freedom to worship God!   40

THE TWENTY-SECOND OF DECEMBER

William Cullen Bryant

Wild was the day; the wintry sea
   Moaned sadly on New England's strand,
When first, the thoughtful and the free,
   Our fathers, trod the desert land.

They little thought how pure a light,   5
    With years, should gather round that day;
How love should keep their memories bright,
    How wide a realm their sons should sway.

Green are their bays; but greener still
    Shall round their spreading fame be wreathed,   10
And regions, now untrod, shall thrill
    With reverence, when their names are breathed.

Till when the sun, with softer fires,
    Looks on the vast Pacific's sleep,
The children of the pilgrim sires   15
    This hallowed day like us shall keep.

"A MAN MUST LIVE"[1]

CHARLOTTE PERKINS STETSON

A man must live.   We justify
Low shift and trick to treason high,
    A little vote for a little gold
    To a whole senate bought and sold,
By that self-evident reply.   5

But is it so?   Pray tell me why
Life at such cost you have to buy?
    In what religion were you told
        A man must live?

---

[1] Reprinted by permission of Small, Maynard, & Co.

There are times when a man must die. 10
Imagine, for a battle-cry,
   From soldiers, with a sword to hold,—
   From soldiers, with the flag unrolled,—
This coward's whine, this liar's lie,—
   A man must live! 15

THE HERO

ROBERT NICOLL

My hero is na deck'd wi' gowd,
   He has nae glittering state;
Renown upon a field o' blood
   In war he hasna met.
He has nae siller in his pouch, 5
   Nae menials at his ca';
The proud o' earth frae him would turn,
   And bid him stand awa'.

His coat is hame-spun hodden-gray,
   His shoon are clouted sair, 10
His garments, maist unhero-like,
   Are a' the waur o' wear:
His limbs are strong — his shoulders broad,
   His hands were made to plough;
He's rough without, but sound within; 15
   His heart is bauldly true.

He toils at e'en, he toils at morn,
   His wark is never through;
A coming life o' weary toil
   Is ever in his view. 20

1. *gowd*, gold. 9. *hodden-gray*, natural color of the wool. 10. *clouted*, patched.

But on he trudges, keeping aye
    A stout heart to the brae,
And proud to be an honest man
    Until his dying day.

His hame a hame o' happiness   25
    And kindly love may be;
And monie a nameless dwelling-place
    Like his we still may see.
His happy altar-hearth so bright
    Is ever bleezing there;   30
And cheerfu' faces rcund it set   .
    Are an unending prayer.

The poor man in his humble hame,
    Like God, who dwells aboon,
Makes happy hearts around him there,   35
    Sae joyfu' late and soon.
His toil is sair, his toil is lang;
    But weary nights and days,
Hame — happiness akin to his —
    A hunder-fauld repays.   40

Go, mock at conquerors and kings!
    What happiness give they?
Go, tell the painted butterflies
    To kneel them down and pray!
Go, stand erect in manhood's pride,   45
    Be what a man should be,
Then come, and to my hero bend
    Upon the grass your knee!

22. *brae*, hillside, precipice. 43-44. Is the metaphor mixed?

Plan of Summary. — Reviewing the chapter, (1) enumerate the kinds of metre, designating them by the number of accents and by the predominant foot. Then (2) say which poem is most noticeable for melody; (3) which for beauty of suggested sights; (4) which for pleasure of suggested sounds; (5) which for pleasure of suggested activity; (6) which for pleasure of suggested odors or tastes; (7) which is most easily understood; (8) which moves the reader most deeply; (9) which shows most skill in character drawing; (10) which has the best unity; (11) which, your critical judgment tells you, is the best piece of work; (12) which you like the best, without regard to its deserved rank or its fame.

CHAPTER IV

THE ATHLETE

ART admires the beauty and strength of the human body more than anything else in the physical creation. Greek sculpture, the world's one perfect art, was devoted entirely to this subject. To use the metaphor of a famous scholar, the Greek was a Narcissus, gazing enraptured at the picture of his own beauty that he had just discovered in the pool. The Greek artists did not, it is true, represent men exactly as they are, though the Greek race was just then at its physical perfection. They made the human figure less animal than it usually is, refining it in various ways. Their statues are not so true to nature as Michael Angelo's, but they are physically more beautiful. The so-called Venus of Melos is taller than most women; but it is the loveliest and noblest of female figures.

The worship of beauty was a part of the Greek's religion. The object of his athletics was not prize-money, inter-collegiate renown, or the exploitation of muscular prodigies; it was the development of grace and strength, on the ground that these were qualities of the gods. Accordingly any particular physical gift was revered and cherished. Just as Homer calls attention to the especial beauty of each character, — the silver-footed Thetis, the snowy-armed Juno, the fair-cheeked Briseis, the bright-eyed Pallas, the graceful Paris, the yellow-haired Menelaus, — so the Grecian master of the games looked among his candidates for one whose strength of arm or neck or thigh might make him victor in one special strife. Greece was rich in pan-athletes, — "all-round" men, — but one secret of Greek athletics lay in recognizing that neither beauty nor strength is often symmetrically developed. Homer's men reveal the principles of Greek strength and beauty. Homer has an Achilles, unique in his union of many powers; but he has many heroes famous for one especial strength. Of the two Ajaces the first is a giant, frequently likened to a tower, while the second is famed for fleetness of foot. Even when a Homeric character is ugly or weak in one respect, he is beautiful or strong in another. Dolon is distorted in face, but he is the man on whose nimbleness Hector depends for the safety of the Trojans. This reminds us of the handsome Lord Byron, who, in spite of his deformed foot, was an expert swimmer — as, indeed, one might guess from his lines on that subject.

Christians saw that the Greeks had cultivated the body to the detriment of the soul. In the Middle Ages, therefore, the body was not honored as in pagan days. A pale complexion was supposed to mean that the owner had spent the night in fasting, and it was accordingly considered beautiful. In our own time people have learned that, as Browning puts it, body helps spirit as much as spirit body. Nowadays the ideal is a sound mind in a sound body. We think no human body perfectly beautiful unless a gleam of kindly intelligence is in the beautiful eye, and no human soul wholly admirable unless it has developed whatever body heaven may have given it for its servant.

The scientist Huxley, sketching the liberally educated man, does not forget to say that his ideal scholar "has been so trained in youth that his body is the ready servant of his will, and does with ease and pleasure all the work that, as a mechanism, it is capable of." Richard Jefferies draws a picture of the wood-cutter who has enormous dead strength, but no physical training; the man in whose muscles is no mind. Quickness of response by muscle to will is one of the chief aims in athletics; no game can be successful without it. It is illustrated in the runner — who is photographed by Walt Whitman just when the will has every muscle under control. It is better illustrated in the football player, because this game demands weight and fleetness, and an electric quickness of thought. Football requires a very difficult thing, — the perfect control of a large frame. A sonnet by the late Edward Lefroy dwells on these merits of the individual player. He is heavy, but open-eyed, quick, aggressive. A second sonnet by the same author suggests the importance of the very same qualities in a team. It is team-work that wins. It is characteristic of childish play to be hilarious and unorganized. That will not do in football; the men must take direction and keep their mouths shut. The beauty and effectiveness of organized, perfectly consonant exertion is shown in the late Judge Hughes's pictures of football and boat-racing in "Tom Brown." The working of such a mechanism as a well-trained team engaged in either of these sports is a keen satisfaction to the eye.

The Runner, p. 159.

A Football Player, p. 159. Childhood and Youth, p. 160.

Different individual mechanisms are capable of different things. The giant John Ridd, who is the hero of the terrible Devonshire winter in Dr. Blackmore's novel of "Lorna Doone," had muscles which enabled him to tear gnarled branches from oak trees. The poet Bryant, on the other hand, was a frail lad whom his father, a physician, used to dip head first into a cold spring every morning to prevent his dying of too big a brain. Such a poet's muscular power would never be very large; yet Bryant, by regular exercise for an hour before breakfast and a two-mile walk after breakfast, preserved himself in perfect physical condition till eighty. Professor Blackie, the famous Greek scholar, was a little man, but our astronomer Newcomb

The Great Winter, p. 161.

Driven beyond Endurance, p. 166.

described him as "the liveliest little man of sixty he ever saw." Some suggestion of how Blackie kept himself lively may be had from his poem *My Bath*. A man who would habitually plash about and dash about in the foaming, bubbling linn, vying with the glancing trout in that cloud-fed fountain, would very likely remain agile.

When we are in perfect health, the health that "snuffs the morning air," we are almost unconscious of our bodies. All we feel is the "prime vigor" that Browning celebrates in Saul. We simply know that the machine does what we want it to do, and all we ask for is exercise. Browning has chosen the moment in Saul's life when the king is grievously ill, and has sent for David to sing to him with the help of the harp. The whole poem is a guess at what David would sing under these circumstances. The youth tries every kind of song he knows, — that of the shepherd to his sheep, those which appeal to the quail, the crickets, the jerboa; that of the reapers, that of the funeral, that of the marriage, that of the priests, and, finally, that of "our manhood's prime vigor." With every muscle playing free, the strong man springs from rock up to rock, and plunges into the pool of living water; he hunts without fear; he eats with zest, and sleeps, on the ground, the sleep of the just.

Whenever the poets have stopped to think about the ways in which all this glorious life goes on, they are filled with wonder. One sacred writer speaks in curious Oriental imagery of the nerve as the silver cord, and the skull as the golden bowl. Another calls the body the temple of God. The physician-poet Holmes takes this last image for the title of his poem on the human body, *The Living Temple*. He sings the strange mystery of the breath and the unresting heart; the living marble we call limbs; the exquisite adjustments of sight and hearing; the unsolved secret of brain and nerve. Tennyson has a poem in which

he speaks of the dead body as a house deserted by its care-
less tenants. Edgar Poe's *The Haunted Palace* is a still
more imaginative conception. It shadows forth what hap-
pens to the body when reason fails. There was once a stately
palace tenanted by good angels. "Banners yellow, golden,
glorious on its roof did float and flow." Through two lumi-
nous windows were seen the ruler of the realm, and spirits that
moved to music. But now all is changed. The windows are
red-litten, and through the pale door rush hideous things that
can laugh, — as the insane laugh, — but cannot smile.

The
Haunted
Palace,
p. 179.

Physical breakdown of any organ is due to under-
exercise, or over-exercise, or lack of proper nutrition, or
poisoning of some sort. One of these facts was never
learned by a poet-naturalist of our own time, Richard
Jefferies, who is certainly the most enthusiastic writer of
our century concerning the beauty of the human body and
the possibilities of its improvement. His marvellous ad-
miration of physical strength, shown everywhere in his
autobiography, led him into dangerous excess of exercise.
But Jefferies did not poison himself. In this respect he
was wiser than Franklin, who exercised so little that he got
that particular form of blood-poisoning called the gout.
He was wiser, too, than Robert Louis Stevenson, dear to
all boys. The latter, like Jefferies, fought a heroic battle
with disease, keeping himself alive for years after the
doctors had told him he must soon yield to phthisis; but
he handicapped his vital powers desperately by surcharging
his system with nicotine.

The Lyra
Prayer,
p. 188.

Dialogue
between
Franklin
and the
Gout,
p. 181.

The last hero in this chapter is Tennyson's Sir Galahad,[1]
who sums up the athletic ideal of cleanness, strength, and

Sir Gala-
had, p. 191.

---

[1] Galahad was one of the knights who cherished the ideal of searching
until they found the holy cup, the grail, from which Christ drank at the last
supper. Tennyson regarded such a search, even in fable, as a fanatic and
useless one. He made his perfect king, Arthur, refuse to join in the quest.
Arthur stayed at home and attended to the business of his kingdom.

courage, with the added grace of a fine idealism. Tennyson, himself a manly figure, broad-shouldered and lean-waisted, liked to write of the athletic ideal. His best friend, Hallam, he somewhere calls a Galahad, and again praises for being clean, but no ascetic.

> High nature amorous of the good,
>> But touched with no ascetic gloom.
>> And passion pure in snowy bloom
> Through all the years of April blood.

SWIMMING

GEORGE GORDON NOËL, LORD BYRON

How many a time have I
Cloven, with arm still lustier, breast more daring,
The wave all roughened; with a swimmer's stroke
Flinging the billows back from my drenched hair,
And laughing from my lip the audacious brine,   5
Which kissed it like a wine-cup, rising o'er
The waves as they arose, and prouder still
The loftier they uplifted me; and oft,
In wantonness of spirit, plunging down
Into their green and glassy gulfs, and making   10
My way to shells and seaweed, all unseen
By those above, till they waxed fearful; then
Returning with my grasp full of such tokens
As showed that I had searched the deep; exulting,
With a far-dashing stroke, and drawing deep   15
The long-suspended breath, again I spurned
The foam which broke around me, and pursued
My track like a sea-bird. — I was a boy then.

The metre is iambic pentameter, or blank verse. Shakspere's plays are mostly in blank verse, and Milton's epic poem of Paradise Lost is in the same metre.

THE PHYSIQUE OF A WOOD-CUTTER[1]

RICHARD JEFFERIES

He was standing in the ditch leaning heavily upon the long handle of his axe. It was a straight stick of ash, roughly shaved down to some sort of semblance of smoothness, such as would have worked up an unpractised hand into a mass of blisters in ten minutes' usage, 5 but which glided easily through those horny palms, leaving no mark of friction. The continuous outdoor labor, the beating of innumerable storms, and the hard, coarse fare, had dried up all the original moisture of the hand, till it was rough, firm, and cracked or chapped 10 like a piece of wood exposed to the sun and weather. The natural oil of the skin, which gives to the hand its beautiful suppleness and delicate sense of touch, was gone like the sap in the tree he was felling, for it was early in the winter. However the brow might perspire, 15 there was no dampness on the hand, and the helve of the axe was scarcely harder and drier. In order, therefore, that the grasp might be firm, it was necessary to artificially wet the palms, and hence that custom which so often disgusts lookers-on, of spitting on the hands before 20 commencing work. This apparently gratuitous piece of dirtiness is in reality absolutely necessary. Men with hands in this state have hardly any feeling in them; they find it difficult to pick up anything small, as a pin — the fingers fumble over it; and as for a pen, they hold it 25 like a hammer. His chest was open to the north wind, which whistled through the bare branches of the tall elm

---

[1] Reprinted from "The Toilers of the Fields," by permission of Longmans, Green, & Co.

overhead as if they were the cordage of a ship, and came
in sudden blasts through the gaps in the hedge, blowing
his shirt back, and exposing the immense breadth of 30
bone and rough dark skin tanned to a brown-red by the
summer sun while mowing.   The neck rose from it short
and thick like that of a bull, and the head was round,
and covered with a crop of short grizzled hair not yet
quite gray, but fast losing its original chestnut color. 35
The features were fairly regular, but coarse, and the nose
flattened.   An almost worn-out old hat thrown back on
the head showed a low, broad, wrinkled forehead.   The
eyes were small and bleared, set deep under shaggy eye-
brows.   The corduroy trousers, yellow with clay and 40
sand, were shortened below the knee by leather straps
like garters, so as to exhibit the whole of the clumsy
boots, with soles like planks, and shod with iron at heel
and tip.   These boots weigh seven pounds the pair;
and in wet weather, with clay and dirt clinging to them, 45
must reach nearly double that.

In spite of all the magnificent muscular development
which this man possessed, there was nothing of the Her-
cules about him.   The grace of strength was wanting,
the curved lines were lacking; all was gaunt, angular, 50
and square.   The chest was broad enough, but flat, a
framework of bones hidden by a rough hairy skin; the
breasts did not swell up like the rounded prominences
of the antique statue.   The neck, strong enough as it
was to bear the weight of a sack of corn with ease, was 55
too short, and too much a part, as it were, of the shoulders.
It did not rise up like a tower, distinct in itself; and the
muscles on it, as they moved, produced hollow cavities
distressing to the eye.   It was strength without beauty;
a mechanical kind of power, like that of an engine, 60
working through straight lines and sharp angles.   There

was too much of the machine, and too little of the ani-
mal; the lithe, easy motion of the lion or the tiger was
not there. The impression conveyed was, that such
strength had been gained through a course of incessant 65
exertion of the rudest kind, unassisted by generous food
and checked by unnatural exposure.

THE RUNNER [1]

WALT WHITMAN

On a flat road runs the well-train'd runner,
He is lean and sinewy with muscular legs,
He is thinly clothed, he leans forward as he runs,
With lightly closed fists and arms partially rais'd.

THE FOOTBALL PLAYER [2]

EDWARD CRACROFT LEFROY

If I could paint you, friend, as you stand there,
Guard of the goal, defensive, open-eyed,
Watching the tortured bladder slide and glide
Under the twinkling feet; arms bare, head bare,
The breeze a-tremble through crow-tufts of hair;   5
Red-brown in face, and ruddier having spied
A wily foeman breaking from the side,

[1] Reprinted by permission of Small, Maynard, & Co.
[2] Reprinted by permission of Mr. John Lane.

Aware of him, — of all else unaware:
If I could limn you, as you leap and fling
Your weight against his passage, like a wall;   10
Clutch him, and collar him, and rudely cling,
For one brief moment till he falls — you fall:
My sketch would have what Art can never give —
Sinew and breath and body; it would live.

What form of poem? Give the rhyme-scheme. Does it differ from
that of a preceding poem of the same number of lines? Does Mr. Lefroy
divide his poem into two thought divisions, as did Mr. Watts-Dunton?

CHILDHOOD AND YOUTH [1]

A CONTRAST

EDWARD CRACROFT LEFROY

I love to watch a rout of merry boys
Released from school for play, and nothing loth
To make amends for late incurious sloth
By wild activity and strident noise;
But more to mark the lads of larger growth   5
Move fieldward with such perfect equipoise,
As if constricted by an inward oath
To scorn the younger age and clamorous joys;
Prepared no less for pastime all their own,
A silent strenuous game of hand and knee,   10
Where no man speaks, but a round ball is thrown
And kicked and run upon with solemn glee,
And every struggle takes an earnest tone,
And rudest sport a sober dignity.

[1] Reprinted by permission of Mr. John Lane.

CHAPTERS FROM " LORNA DOONE "[1]

R. D. BLACKMORE

THE GREAT WINTER

It must have snowed most wonderfully to have made that depth of covering in about eight hours. For one of Master Stickles' men, who had been out all the night, said that no snow began to fall until nearly midnight. And there it was, blocking up the doors, stopping the 5 ways and the watercourses, and making it very much worse to walk than in a saw-pit newly used. However, we trudged along in a line; I first, and the other men after me; trying to keep my track, but finding legs and strength not up to it. Most of all, John Fry was groan- 10 ing; certain that his time was come, and sending messages to his wife, and blessings to his children. For all this time it was snowing harder than it ever had snowed before, so far as a man might guess at it; and the leaden depth of the sky came down, like a mine turned upside 15 down on us. Not that the flakes were so very large; for I have seen much larger flakes in a shower of March, while sowing peas; but that there was no room between them, neither any relaxing, nor any change of direction.

Watch, like a good and faithful dog, followed us very 20 cheerfully, leaping out of the depth, which took him over his back and ears already, even in the level places; while in the drifts he might have sunk to any distance out of sight, and never found his way up again. However, we helped him now and then, especially through 25 the gaps and gateways; and so, after a deal of flounder-ing, some laughter, and a little swearing, we came all

[1] The style is in imitation of the seventeenth century. The gigantic young hero, John Ridd, tells the story.

M

safe to the lower meadow, where most of our flock was huddled.

But behold, there was no flock at all! None, I mean, 30 to be seen anywhere; only at one corner of the field, by the eastern end, where the snow drove in, a great white billow, as high as a barn and as broad as a house. This great drift was rolling and curling beneath the violent blast, tufting and combing with rustling swirls, and 35 carved (as in patterns of cornice) where the grooving chisel of the wind swept round. Ever and again the tempest snatched little whiffs from the channeled edges, twirled them round and made them dance over the chine of the monster pile, then let them lie like herring-bones, 40 or the seams of sand where the tide has been. And all the while from the smothering sky, more and more fiercely at every blast, came the pelting, pitiless arrows, winged with murky white, and pointed with the barbs of frost.

But although, for people who had no sheep, the sight 45 was a very fine one (so far at least as the weather permitted any sight at all), yet for us, with our flock beneath it, this great mount had but little charm. Watch began to scratch at once, and to howl along the sides of it; he knew that his charge was buried there, and his 50 business taken from him. But we four men set to in earnest, digging with all our might and main, shovelling away at the great white pile, and pitching it into the meadow. Each man made for himself a cave, scooping at the soft cold flux, which slid upon him at every stroke, 55 and throwing it out behind him, in piles of castled fancy. At last we drove our tunnels in (for we worked indeed for the lives of us), and all converging toward the middle, held our tools and listened.

The other men heard nothing at all; or declared that 60

39. *chine* means spine.

they heard nothing, being anxious now to abandon the matter, because of the chill in their feet and knees. But I said, "Go, if you choose, all of you. I will work it out by myself, you pie-crusts!" and upon that they gripped their shovels, being more or less of English- 65 men; and the least drop of English blood is worth the best of any other when it comes to lasting out.

But before we began again, I laid my head well into the chamber; and there I heard a faint "ma-a-ah," coming through some ells of snow, like a plaintive buried 70 hope, or a last appeal. I shouted aloud to cheer him up, for I knew what sheep it was — to wit, the most valiant of all the wethers, who had met me when I came home from London, and been so glad to see me. (And then we all fell to again, and very soon we hauled him 75 out.) Watch took charge of him at once, with an air of the noblest patronage, lying on his frozen fleece, and licking all his face and feet, to restore his warmth to him. Then fighting Tom jumped up at once, and made a little butt at Watch, as if nothing had ever ailed him, 80 and then set off to a shallow place, and looked for something to nibble at.

Further in, and close under the bank, where they had huddled themselves for warmth, we found all the rest of the poor sheep, packed as closely as if they were in a 85 great pie. It was strange to observe how their vapor, and breath, and the moisture exuding from their wool, had scooped, as it were, a covered room for them, lined with a ribbing of deep yellow snow. Also the churned snow beneath their feet was as yellow as gamboge. Two 90 or three of the weaklier hoggets were dead from want of air, and from pressure; but more than three-score were as lively as ever, though cramped and stiff for a little while.

92. *hoggets*, two-year-old sheep.

"However shall us get 'em home?" John Fry asked, in great dismay, when we had cleared about a dozen of 95 them; which we were forced to do very carefully, so as not to fetch the roof down. "No manner of maning to draive 'un, drough all they girt driftnesses."

"You see to this place, John," I replied, as we leaned on our shovels a moment, and the sheep came rubbing 100 round us. "Let no more of them out for the present; they are better where they be. Watch! here, boy, keep them."

Watch came, with his little scut of a tail cocked as sharp as duty; and I set him at the narrow mouth of the great snow antre. All the sheep sidled away, and got 105 closer, that the other sheep might be bitten first, as the foolish things imagine; whereas no good sheep-dog even so much as lips a sheep to turn it.

Then of the outer sheep (all now snowed and frizzled like a lawyer's wig) I took the two finest and heaviest, 110 and with one beneath my right arm, and the other beneath my left, I went straight home to the upper sheppey, and set them inside, and fastened them. Sixty-and-six I took home in that way, two at a time on each journey; and the work grew harder and harder each 115 time, as the drifts of the snow were deepening. No other man should meddle with them: I was resolved to try my strength against the strength of the elements; and try it I did, ay, and proved it. A certain fierce delight burned in me, as the struggle grew harder; but rather 120 would I die than yield; and at last I finished it. People talk of it to this day: but none can tell what the labor was, who had not felt that snow and wind.

---

97. *No manner of maning* is about equivalent to "I don't by any means intend." 98. *'un*, them. *girt*, a provincial expression for big, powerful. John Fry applies it to snowdrifts; but John Ridd himself was known as "Girt Jan Ridd." 105. *antre* is an old word for cave.

Of the sheep upon the mountain, and the sheep upon
the western farm, and the cattle on the upper barrows, 125
scarcely one in ten was saved, do what we would for
them. And this was not through any neglect (now that
our wits were sharpened), but from the pure impossi-
bility of finding them at all. That great snow never
ceased a moment for three days and nights; and then 130
when all the earth was filled, and the topmost hedges
were unseen, and the trees broke down with weight
(wherever the wind had not lightened them), a brilliant
sun broke forth and showed the loss of all our customs.

All our house was quite snowed up, except where we 135
had purged a way by dint of constant shovellings. The
kitchen was as dark, and darker, than the cider-cellar,
and long lines of furrowed scollops ran even up to the
chimney-stacks. Several windows fell right inward,
through the weight of the snow against them; and the 140
few that stood bulged in, and bent like an old bruised
lantern. We were obliged to cook by candle-light; we
were forced to read by candle-light; as for baking we
could not do it, because the oven was too chill; and a load
of fagots only brought a little wet down the sides of it. 145

For when the sun burst forth at last upon the world of
white, what he brought was neither warmth, nor cheer,
nor hope of softening; only a clearer shaft of cold,
from the violent depths of sky. Long-drawn alleys of
white haze seemed to lead toward him, yet such as 150
he could not come down, with any warmth remaining.
Broad white curtains of the frost-fog looped around the
lower sky, on the verge of hill and valley, and above the
laden trees. Only round the sun himself, and the spot
of heaven he claimed, clustered a bright purple-blue, 155
clear, and calm, and deep.

134. *customs* here means profits.

That night such a frost ensued as we had never dreamed of, neither read in ancient books, nor histories of Frobisher. The kettle by the fire froze, and the crock upon the hearth-cheeks; many men were killed, and cattle rigid in their head-ropes. Then I heard that 160 fearful sound which never I had heard before, neither since have heard (except during that same winter), the sharp yet solemn sound of trees burst open by the frost-blow. Our great walnut lost three branches, and has been dying ever since; though growing meanwhile, as 165 the soul does. And the ancient oak at the cross was rent, and many score of ash trees. But why should I tell all this? The people who have not seen it (as I have) will only make faces, and disbelieve, till such another frost comes, which perhaps may never be. . . . 170

DRIVEN BEYOND ENDURANCE

Everything was settled smoothly, and without any fear or fuss that Lorna might find end of troubles, and myself of eager waiting, with the help of Parson Bowden, and the good wishes of two counties. I could scarce believe my fortune when I looked upon her beauty, gentleness, 5 and sweetness, mingled with enough of humor, and warm woman's feeling, never to be dull or tiring; never themselves to be weary.

For she might be called a woman now, although a very young one, and as full of playful ways, or perhaps I 10 may say ten times as full, as if she had known no trouble: to wit, the spirit of bright childhood, having been so curbed and straightened ere its time was over, now broke forth, enriched and varied with the garb of conscious maidenhood. And the sense of steadfast love, and eager 15 love enfolding her, colored with so many tinges all her looks, and words, and thoughts, that to me it was the noblest vision even to think about her.

But this was far too bright to last, without bitter break, and the plunging of happiness in horror, and of passion- 20 ate joy in agony. My darling, in her softest moments, when she was alone with me, when the spark of defiant eyes was veiled beneath dark lashes, and the challenge of gay beauty passed into sweetest invitation; at such times of her purest love and warmest faith in me, a deep 25 abiding fear would flutter in her bounding heart, as of deadly fate's approach. She would cling to me, and nestle to me, being scared of coyishness, and lay one arm around my neck, and ask if I could do without her.

Hence, as all emotions haply, of those who are more 30 to us than ourselves, find within us stronger echo, and more perfect answer, so I could not be regardless of some hidden evil, and my dark misgivings deepened as the time drew nearer. I kept a steadfast watch on Lorna, neglecting a field of beans entirely, as well as a litter 35 of young pigs, and a cow somewhat given to jaundice. And I let Jem Slocome go to sleep in the tallat all one afternoon and Bill Dadds draw off a bucket of cider, without so much as a "by your leave." For these men knew that my knighthood, and my coat of arms, and 40 (most of all) my love, were greatly against good farming: the sense of our country being — and perhaps it may be sensible — that a man who sticks up to be anything must allow himself to be cheated.

But I never did stick up, nor would, though all the 45 parish bade me; and I whistled the same tunes to my horses, and held my plough-tree just the same as if no King nor Queen had ever come to spoil my tune or hand. For this thing nearly all the men around our parts up-

37. *tallat*, hayloft.

braided me, but the women praised me; and for the most 50
part these are right, when themselves are not concerned.

However humble I might be, no one knowing any-
thing of our part of the country would for a moment
doubt that now here was a great to-do and talk of John
Ridd and his wedding. The fierce fight with the 55
Doones so lately, and my leading of the combat (though
I fought not more than need be), and the vanishing of Sir
Counsellor, and the galloping madness of Carver, and
the religious fear of the women that this last was gone
to hell — for he himself had declared that his aim, while 60
he cut through the yeomanry — also their remorse that
he should have been made to go thither, with all his
children left behind — these things, I say (if ever I can
again contrive to say anything), had led to the broadest
excitement about my wedding of Lorna. We heard that 65
people meant to come from more than thirty miles
around, upon excuse of seeing my stature and Lorna's
beauty; but in good truth, out of sheer curiosity and
the love of meddling.

Our clerk had given notice that not a man should 70
come inside the door of his church without shilling-fee,
and women (as sure to see twice as much) must every
one pay two shillings. I thought this wrong; and, as
church-warden, begged that the money might be paid
into mine own hands when taken. · But the clerk said 75
that was against all law; and he had orders from the
parson to pay it to him without any delay. So, as I
always obey the parson when I care not much about a
thing, I let them have it their own way, though feeling
inclined to believe sometimes that I ought to have some 80
of the money.

Dear mother arranged all the ins and outs of the way
in which it was to be done; and Annie and Lizzie, and

all the' Snowes, and even Ruth Huckaback (who was there, after great persuasion), made such a sweeping of 85 dresses that I scarcely knew where to place my feet, and longed for a staff to put by their gowns. Then Lorna came out of a pew halfway, in a manner which quite astonished me, and took my left hand in her right, and I prayed God that it were done with. 90

My darling looked so glorious that I was afraid of glancing at her, yet took in all her beauty. She was in a fright, no doubt, but nobody should see it; whereas I said (to myself, at least), "I will go through it like a grave-digger." 95

Lorna's dress was of pure white, clouded with faint lavender (for the sake of the old Earl Brandir), and as simple as need be, except for perfect loveliness. I was afraid to look at her, as I said before, except when each of us said, "I will"; and then each dwelt upon the other. 100

It is impossible for any who have not loved as I have to conceive my joy and pride when, after ring and all was done, and the parson had blessed us, Lorna turned to look at me with her glances of subtle fun subdued by this great act. 105

Her eyes, which none on earth may ever equal or compare with, told me such a depth of comfort, yet awaiting further commune, that I was almost amazed, thoroughly as I knew them. Darling eyes, the sweetest eyes, the loveliest, the most loving eyes — the sound of 110 a shot rang through the church, and those eyes were filled with death.

Lorna fell across my knees when I was going to kiss her, as the bridegroom is allowed to do, and encouraged, if he needs it; a flood of blood came out upon the 115 yellow wood of the altar steps; and at my feet lay Lorna, trying to tell me some last message out of her faithful eyes. I lifted her up, and petted her, and coaxed her, but it was no good; the only sign of life remaining was a spirit of bright red blood.   120

Some men know what things befall them in the supreme time of their life — far above the time of death — but to me comes back as a hazy dream, without any knowledge in it, what I did, or felt, or thought, with my wife's arms flagging, flagging, around my neck, as I 125 raised her up, and softly put them there. She sighed a long sigh on my breast, for her last farewell to life, and then she grew so cold, and cold, that I asked the time of year.

It was now Whit-Tuesday, and the lilacs all in blos- 130 som; and why I thought of the time of year, with the young death in my arms, God or His angels may decide, having so strangely given us. Enough that so I did, and looked; and our white lilacs were beautiful. Then I laid my wife in my mother's arms, and begging that 135 no one would make any noise, went forth for my revenge.

Of course I knew who had done it. There was but one man in the world, or, at any rate, in our part of it, who could have done such a thing — such a thing. I use no harsher word about it, while I leaped upon our 140 best horse, with bridle but no saddle, and set the head of Kickums toward the course now pointed out to me. Who showed me the course, I cannot tell. I only knew that I took it. And the men fell back before me.   .

Weapon of no sort had I. Unarmed, and wondering 145 at my strange attire (with a bridal vest wrought by our Annie, and red with the blood of the bride), I went forth just to find out this — whether in this world there be or be not God of justice.

With my vicious horse at a furious speed, I came upon 150

120. *spirit*, spirt.

Black Barrow Down, directed by some shout of men, which seemed to me but a whisper. And there about a furlong before me, rode a man on a great black horse, and I knew that the man was Carver Doone.

"Your life, or mine," I said to myself; "as the will 155 of God may be. But we two live not upon this earth one more hour together."

I knew the strength of this great man; and I knew that he was armed with a gun — if he had time to load again, after shooting my Lorna — or at any rate with 160 pistols, and a horseman's sword as well. Nevertheless, I had no more doubt of killing the man before me than a cook has of spitting a headless fowl.

Sometimes seeing no ground beneath me, and sometimes heeding every leaf, and the crossing of the grass- 165 blades, I followed over the long moor, reckless whether seen or not. But only once the other man turned round and looked back again, and then I was beside a rock, with a reedy swamp behind me.

Although he was so far before me, and riding as hard 170 as ride he might, I saw that he had something on the horse in front of him; something which needed care, and stopped him from looking backward. In the whirling of my wits, I fancied first that this was Lorna; until the scene I had been through fell across hot brain and 175 heart, like the drop at the close of a tragedy. Rushing there through crag and quag at utmost speed of a maddened horse, I saw, as of another's fate, calmly (as on canvas laid), the brutal deed, the piteous anguish, and the cold despair. 180

The man turned up the gully leading from the moor to Cloven Rocks, through which John Fry had tracked Uncle Ben, as of old related. But as Carver entered it, he turned round, and beheld me not a hundred yards

behind; and I saw that he was bearing his child, little 185
Ensie, before him.   Ensie also descried me, and
stretched his hands and cried to me; for the face of
his father frightened him.

Carver Doone, with a vile oath, thrust spurs into his
flagging horse, and laid one hand on a pistol-stock, 190
whence I knew that his slung carbine had received no
bullet since the one that had pierced Lorna.   And a cry
of triumph rose from the black depths of my heart.
What cared I for pistols?   I had no spurs, neither was
my horse one to need the rowel; I rather held him in 195.
than urged him, for he was fresh as ever; and I knew that
the black steed in front, if he breasted the steep ascent,
where the track divided, must be in our reach at once.

His rider knew this, and, having no room in the
rocky channel to turn and fire, drew rein at the cross- 200
ways sharply, and plunged into the black ravine leading
to the Wizard's Slough.   "Is it so?" I said to myself,
with brain and head cold as iron: "though the foul fiend
come from the slough to save thee, thou shalt carve it,
Carver."   205

I followed my enemy carefully, steadily, even lei-
surely; for I had him as in a pitfall, where no escape
might be.   He thought that I feared to approach him,
for he knew not where he was: and his low disdainful
laugh came back.   "Laugh he who wins," thought I.   210

A gnarled and half-starved oak, as stubborn as my
own resolve, and smitten by some storm of old, hung
from the crag above me.   Rising from my horse's back,
although I had no stirrups, I caught a limb, and tore it
(like a mere wheat-awn) from the socket.   Men show 215
the rent even now with wonder; none with more wonder
than myself.

Carver Doone turned the corner suddenly on the black

and bottomless bog; with a start of fear he reigned back
his horse, and I thought he would have turned upon me. 220
But instead of that, he again rode on, hoping to find a
way round the side.

Now there is a way between cliff and slough for those
who know the ground thoroughly, or have time enough
to search it; but for him there was no road, and he lost 225
some time in seeking it. Upon this he made up his
mind; and wheeling, fired, and then rode at me.

His bullet struck me somewhere, but I took no heed
of that. Fearing only his escape, I laid my horse
across the way, and with the limb of the oak struck full 230
on the forehead his charging steed. Ere the slash of
the sword came nigh me, man and horse rolled over,
and well-nigh bore my own horse down with the power
of their onset.

Carver Doone was somewhat stunned, and could not 235
arise for a moment. Meanwhile I leaped on the ground
and awaited, smoothing my hair back, and baring my
arms, as though in the ring for wrestling. Then the
little boy ran to me, clasped my leg, and looked up at
me; and the terror in his eyes made me almost fear 240
myself.

"Ensie, dear," I said quite gently, grieving that he
should see his wicked father killed, "run up yonder
round the corner, and try to find a pretty bunch of blue-
bells for the lady." The child obeyed me, hanging 245
back, and looking back, and then laughing, while I pre-
pared for business. There and then I might have killed
mine enemy with a single blow while he lay unconscious,
but it would have been foul play.

With a sullen and black scowl, the Carver gathered 250
his mighty limbs and arose, and looked round for his
weapons; but I had put them well away. Then he

came to me and gazed, being wont to frighten thus
young men.

"I would not harm you, lad," he said, with a lofty 255
style of sneering. "I have punished you enough, for
most of your impertinence. For the rest I forgive you,
because you have been good and gracious to my little
son. Go and be contented."

For answer I smote him on the cheek, lightly, and 260
not to hurt him, but to make his blood leap up. I
would not sully my tongue by speaking to a man like
this.

There was a level space of sward between us and the
slough. With the courtesy derived from London, and 265
the processions I had seen, to this place I led him.
And that he might breathe himself, and have every fibre
cool, and every muscle ready, my hold upon his coat I
loosed, and left him to begin with me whenever he
thought proper. 270

I think he felt that his time was come. I think that
he knew from my knitted muscles, and the firm arch of
my breast, and the way in which I stood, but most of
all from my stern blue eyes, that he had found his mas-
ter. At any rate a paleness came, an ashy paleness on 275
his cheeks, and the vast calves of his legs bowed in as
if he was out of training.

Seeing this, villain as he was, I offered him first
chance. I stretched forth my left hand, as I do to a
weaker antagonist, and I let him have the hug of me. 280
But in this I was too generous; having forgotten my
pistol-wound, and the cracking of one of my short lower
ribs. Carver Doone caught me round the waist with such
a grip as never yet had been laid upon me.

I heard my rib go; I grasped his arm, and tore the 285
muscle out of it (as the string comes out of an orange);

then I took him by the throat, which is not allowed in wrestling, but he had snatched at mine; and now was no time of dalliance. In vain he tugged, and strained, and writhed, dashed his bleeding fist into my face, and 290 flung himself on me with gnashing jaws. Beneath the iron of my strength — for God that day was with me — I had him helpless in two minutes, and his fiery eyes lolled out.

"I will not harm thee any more," I cried, so far as I 295 could for panting, the work being very furious. "Carver Doone, thou art beaten; own it, and thank God for it; and go thy way, and repent thyself."

It was all too late. Even if he had yielded in his ravening frenzy — for his beard was like a mad dog's 300 jowl — even if he would have owned that, for the first time in his life, he had found his master; it was all too late.

The black bog had him by the feet; the sucking of the ground drew on him, like the thirsty lips of death. 305 In our fury, we had heeded neither wet nor dry; nor thought of earth beneath us. I myself might scarcely leap, with the last spring of o'erlabored legs, from the ingulfing grave of slime. He fell back, with his swarthy breast (from which my gripe had tore all clothing), like 310 a hummock of bog-oak, standing out the quagmire; and then he tossed his arms to heaven, and they were black to the elbow, and the glare of his eyes was ghastly. I could only gaze and pant; for my strength was no more than an infant's, from the fury and the horror. Scarcely 315 could I turn away, while, joint by joint, he sunk from sight.

MY BATH

JOHN STUART BLACKIE

(*Scene:* Kinnaird Burn, near Pitlochrie)

Come here, good people great and small, that wander far
    abroad,
To drink of drumly German wells, and make a weary road
To Baden and to Wiesbaden, and how they all are nam'd,
To Carlsbad and to Kissingen, for healing virtue fam'd;
Come stay at home, and keep your feet from dusty travel
    free,   5
And I will show you what rare bath a good God gave to
    me;
'Tis hid among the Highland hills beneath the purple brae,
With cooling freshness free to all, nor doctor's fee to pay.

No craft of mason made it here, nor carpenter, I wot;
Nor tinkering fool with hammering tool to shape the
    charmed spot;   10
But down the rocky-breasted glen the foamy torrent falls
Into the amber caldron deep, fenced round with granite
    walls.

Nor gilded beam, nor pictur'd dome, nor curtain, roofs it in,
But the blue sky rests, and white clouds float, above the
    bubbling linn,
Where God's own hand hath scoop'd it out in Nature's
    Titan hall,   15
And from her cloud-fed fountains drew its waters free to all.

2. *drumly*, Scotch for *muddy*. 3. *and how they all are nam'd* is a German idiom equivalent to "all of them, however named." 14. *linn*, a pool. The "colony by the pool" is the sense of *Linn-colonia*, shortened into *Lincoln*.

Oh come and see my Highland bath, and prove its freshen-
    ing flood,
And spare to taint your skin with swathes of drumly Ger-
    man mud :
Come plunge with me into the wave like liquid topaz fair,
And to the waters give your back that spout down bravely
    there ;   20
Then float upon the swirling flood, and, like a glancing
    trout,
Plash about, and dash about, and make a lively rout,
And to the gracious sun display the glory of your skin,
As you dash about and splash about in the foamy-bubbling
    linn.

Oh come and prove my bonnie bath ; in sooth 'tis furnish'd
    well   25
With trees, and shrubs, and spreading ferns, all in the rocky
    dell,
And roses hanging from the cliff in grace of white and red,
And little tiny birches nodding lightly overhead,
And spiry larch with purple cones, and tips of virgin green,
And leafy shade of hazel copse with sunny glints between :
Oh might the Roman wight be here who praised Bandusia's
    well,   31
He'd find a bath to Nymphs more dear in my sweet High-
    land dell.

Some folks will pile proud palaces, and some will wander
    far
To scan the blinding of a sun, or the blinking of a star ;
Some sweat through Afric's burning sands ; and some will
    vex their soul   35
To find heaven knows what frosty prize beneath the Arctic
    pole.
    N

God bless them all; and may they find what thing delights
    them well
In east or west, or north or south, — but I at home will dwell
Where fragrant ferns their fronds uncurl, and healthful
    breezes play,   39
And clear brown waters grandly swirl beneath the purple brae.

Oh come and prove my Highland bath, the burn, and all
    the glen,
Hard-toiling wights in dingy nooks, and scribes with inky pen,
Strange thoughtful men with curious quests that vex your
    fretful brains,
And scheming sons of trade who fear to count your slippery
    gains;
Come wander up the burn with me, and thread the winding
    glen,   45
And breathe the healthful power that flows down from the
    breezy Ben,
And plunge you in the deep brown pool; and from beneath
    the spray
You'll come forth like a flower that blooms 'neath freshen-
    ing showers in May!

41. *burn*, a brook.   42. *wights*, mortals.   46. *Ben* is a Celtic word for mountain.

Name the metre according to the number of accents. Is it trochaic or iambic? Is the movement solemn or cheerful? What is the rhyme-scheme? What colors are attributed to the pool of mountain water?

OH, OUR MANHOOD'S PRIME VIGOR

ROBERT BROWNING

Oh, our manhood's prime vigor! No spirit feels waste,
Not a muscle is stopped in its playing nor sinew unbraced.
Oh, the wild joys of living! the leaping from rock up to rock.

The strong rending of boughs from the fir tree, the cool
    silver shock
Of the plunge in a pool's living water, the hunt of the
    bear,   5
And the sultriness showing the lion is couched in his lair.
And the meal, the rich dates yellowed over with gold dust
    divine,
And the locust-flesh steeped in the pitcher, the full draught
    of wine,
And the sleep in the dried river-channel where bulrushes
    tell
That the water was wont to go warbling so softly and well. 10
How good is man's life, the mere living ! how fit to employ
All the heart and the soul and the senses forever in joy !

THE HAUNTED PALACE

EDGAR ALLAN POE

In the greenest of our valleys,
    By good angels tenanted,
Once a fair and stately palace
    (Radiant palace) reared its head.
In the monarch Thought's dominion   5
    It stood there !
Never seraph spread a pinion
    Over fabric half so fair.

Banners yellow, glorious, golden,
    On its roof did float and flow   10
(This, all this, was in the olden
    Time long ago) ;

And every gentle air that dallied
In that sweet day,
Along the ramparts plumed and pallid,   15
A wingèd odor went away.   ,

Wanderers in that happy valley
Through two luminous windows saw
Spirits moving musically,
To a lute's well-tunèd law,   20
Round about a throne, where, sitting
(Porphyrogene !)
In state his glory well befitting,
The ruler of the realm was seen.

And all with pearl and ruby glowing   25
Was the fair palace door,
Through which came flowing, flowing, flowing,
And sparkling evermore,
A troop of Echoes, whose sweet duty
Was but to sing,   30
In voices of surpassing beauty,
The wit and wisdom of their king.

But evil things, in robes of sorrow,
Assailed the monarch's high estate
(Ah ! let us mourn, for never morrow   35
Shall dawn upon him desolate);
And round about his home the glory
That blushed and bloomed
Is but a dim-remembered story
Of the old time entombed.   40
And travellers now within that valley
Through the red-litten windows see

22. *Porphyrogene* means born to the purple, *i.e.* to royalty.

Vast forms that move fantastically
To a discordant melody,
While, like a ghastly, rapid river,   45
Through the pale door
A hideous throng rush out forever,
And laugh — but smile no more.

What two lines of the poem are the most melodious ?
Explain the allegory stanza by stanza, but do not be surprised if every detail (*e.g.* the lute) is not clear; Poe perhaps intended a little beautiful vagueness now and then.

DIALOGUE BETWEEN FRANKLIN AND THE GOUT

BENJAMIN FRANKLIN

MIDNIGHT, October 22, 1780.

Franklin. Eh ! oh ! eh ! What have I done to merit these cruel sufferings?

Gout. Many things : you have ate and drank too freely, and too much indulged those legs of yours in their indolence.   5

Franklin. Who is it that accuses me?

Gout. It is I, even I, the Gout.

Franklin. What ! my enemy in person?

Gout. No, not your enemy.

Franklin. I repeat it : my enemy ; for you would not 10 only torment my body to death, but ruin my good name ; you reproach me as a glutton and a tippler ; now all the world, that knows me, will allow that I am neither the one nor the other.

Gout. The world may think as it pleases ; it is always 15 very complaisant to itself, and sometimes to its friends ;

but I very well know that the quantity of meat and drink proper for a man who takes a reasonable degree of exercise, would be too much for another who never takes any.

Franklin.   I take — eh! oh! — as much exercise — 20 eh! — as I can, Madam Gout.   You know my sedentary state, and on that account, it would seem, Madam Gout, as if you might spare me a little, seeing it is not altogether my own fault.

Gout.   Not a jot; your rhetoric and your politeness 25 are thrown away; your apology avails nothing.   If your situation in life is a sedentary one, your amusements, your recreations, at least, should be active.   You ought to walk or ride, or if the weather prevents that, play at billiards.   But let us examine your course of life.   While 30 the mornings are long, and you have leisure to go abroad, what do you do?   Why, instead of gaining an appetite for breakfast by salutary exercise, you amuse yourself with books, pamphlets, or newspapers, which commonly are not worth the reading.   Yet you eat an inordinate breakfast, 35 — four dishes of tea, with cream, and one or two buttered toasts, with slices of hung beef, which, I fancy, are not things the most easily digested.   Immediately afterward you sit down to write at your desk, or converse with persons who apply to you on business.   Thus the time passes 40 till one, without any kind of bodily exercise.   But all this I could pardon, in regard, as you say, to your sedentary condition.   But what is your practice after dinner? Walking in the beautiful gardens of those friends with whom you have dined, would be the choice of a man of 45 sense; yours is to be fixed down to chess, where you are found engaged for two or three hours!   This is your perpetual recreation, which is the least eligible of any for a

25. Here *rhetoric* is used partly in the old sense — the art of persuasion — and partly in the sense of fine, high-sounding language.

sedentary man, because, instead of accelerating the motion
of the fluids, the rigid attention it requires helps to retard 50
the circulation and obstruct internal secretions. Wrapt
in the speculations of this wretched game, you destroy
your constitution. What can be expected from such a
course of living, but a body replete with stagnant humors,
ready to fall a prey to all kinds of dangerous maladies, if I, 55
the Gout, did not occasionally bring you relief by agitating
those humors, and so purifying or dissipating them? If it
was in some nook or alley in Paris, deprived of walks, that
you played awhile at chess after dinner, this might be
excusable; but the same taste prevails with you in Passy, 60
Auteuil, Montmartre, or Savoy, — places where there are
the finest gardens and walks, a pure air, beautiful women,
and most agreeable and instructive conversation; all of
which you might enjoy by frequenting the walks. But
these are rejected for this abominable game of chess. 65
Fie, then, Mr. Franklin! But, amidst my instructions, I
had almost forgot to administer my wholesome correc-
tions; so take that twinge, — and that!

Franklin. Oh! eh! oh! ohhh! As much instruction
as you please, Madam Gout, and as many reproaches; 70
but pray, madam, a truce with your corrections!

Gout. No, sir, no: I will not abate a particle of what
is so much for your good, — therefore —

Franklin. Oh! ehhh! — It is not fair to say I take
no exercise, when I do very often, going out to dine, and 75
returning in my carriage.

Gout. That, of all imaginable exercises, is the most
slight and insignificant, if you allude to the motion of a
carriage suspended on springs. By observing the degree
of heat obtained by different kinds of motion, we may 80
form an estimate of the quantity of exercise given by
each. Thus for example, if you turn out to walk in

winter with cold feet, in an hour's time you will be in a glow all over; ride on horseback, the same effect will scarcely be perceived by four hours' round trotting; but if you loll in a carriage, such as you have mentioned, you may travel all day, and gladly enter the last inn to warm your feet by the fire.   Flatter yourself then no longer, that half an hour's airing in your carriage deserves the name of exercise.   Providence has appointed few to roll in carriages, while he has given to all a pair of legs, which are machines infinitely more commodious and service-able.   Be grateful, then, and make a proper use of yours. Would you know how they forward the circulation of your fluids, in the very action of transporting you from place to place : observe, when you walk, that all your weight is alternately thrown from one leg to the other; this occasions a great pressure on the vessels of the foot, and repels their contents; when relieved, by the weight of being thrown on the other foot, the vessels of the first are allowed to replenish, and, by a return of this weight, this repulsion again succeeds; thus accelerating the cir-culation of the blood.   The heat produced in any given time depends on the degree of this acceleration; the fluids are shaken, the humors alternated, the secretions facilitated, and all goes well; the cheeks are ruddy, and health is established.   Behold your fair friend at Auteuil; a lady who received from bounteous nature more really useful science than half a dozen such pretenders to philosophy as you have been able to extract from all your books.   When she honors you with a visit, it is on foot.   She walks all hours of the day, and leaves indolence and its concomitant maladies to be endured by her horses.   In this see at once the preservative of her health and personal charms.   But when you go to Auteuil, you must have your carriage, though it is no

further from Passy to Auteuil than from Auteuil to
Passy.

Franklin. Your reasonings grow very tiresome.

Gout. I stand corrected. I will be silent and con- 120
tinue my office; take that, and that.

Franklin. Oh! ohh! Talk on, I pray you!

Gout. No, no; I have a good number of twinges
for you to-night, and you may be sure of some more
to-morrow.   125

Franklin. What, with such a fever! I shall go dis-
tracted. Oh! eh! Can no one bear it for me?

Gout. Ask that of your horses; they have served you
faithfully.

Franklin. How can you so cruelly sport with my 130
torments?

Gout. Sport! I am very serious. I have here a list
of offences against your own health distinctly written,
and can justify every stroke inflicted on you.

Franklin. Read it, then.   135

Gout. It is too long a detail; but I will briefly men-
tion some particulars.

Franklin. Proceed. I am all attention.

Gout. Do you remember how often you have prom-
ised yourself, the following morning a walk in the grove 140
of Bologne, in the Garden de la Muette, or in your own
garden, and have violated your promise, alleging at one
time it was too cold, at another too warm, too windy, too
moist, or what else you pleased; when in truth it was too
nothing but your inseparable love of ease?   145

Franklin. That, I confess, may have happened oc-
casionally; probably ten times in a year.

Gout. Your confession is very far short of the truth;
the gross amount is one hundred and ninety-nine times.

Franklin. Is it possible?   150

Gout. So possible that it is fact; you may rely on the accuracy of my statement. You know M. Brillon's gardens, and what fine walks they contain; you know the handsome flight of an hundred steps, which lead from the terrace above to the lawn below. You have 155 been in the practice of visiting this amiable family twice a week after dinner, and it is a maxim of your own, that "a man may take as much exercise in walking a mile, up and down stairs, as in ten on level ground." What an opportunity was here for you to have had exercise in 160 both these ways! Did you embrace it, and how often?

Franklin. I cannot immediately answer that question.

Gout. I will do it for you. Not once.

Franklin. Not once?

Gout. Even so. During the summer you went there 165 at six o'clock. You found the charming lady with her lovely children and friends, eager to walk with you and entertain you with their agreeable conversation; and what has been your choice? Why, to sit on the terrace, satisfy yourself with the fine prospect, and passing your 170 eye over the beauties of the garden below, without taking one step to descend and walk about in them. On the contrary, you call for tea and the chessboard; and lo! you are occupied in your seat till nine o'clock, and that besides two hours' play after dinner; and then, instead 175 of walking home, which would have bestirred you a little, you step into your carriage. How absurd to suppose that all this carelessness can be reconcilable with health, without my interposition!

Franklin. I am convinced now of the justness of 180 Poor Richard's remark, that "Our debts and our sins are always greater than we think for."

Gout. So it is. You philosophers are sages in your maxims, and fools in your conduct.

Franklin. But do you charge among my crimes that 185
I return in a carriage from M. Brillon's?

Gout. Certainly; for, having been seated all the
while, you cannot object the fatigue of the day, and can-
not want, therefore, the relief of a carriage.

Franklin. What, then, would you have me do with 190
my carriage?

Gout. Burn it if you choose : you would at least get
heat out of it once in this way; or, if you dislike that
proposal, here's another for you : observe the poor
peasants, who work in the vineyards and grounds about 195
the villages of Passy, Auteuil, Chaillot, etc., you may find
every day among these deserving creatures, four or five
old men and women, bent and perhaps crippled by weight
of years and too long and too great labor. After a most
fatiguing day, these people have to trudge a mile or two 200
to their smoky huts. Order your coachman to set them
down. This is an act that will be good for your soul;
and at the same time after your visit to the Brillons, if
you return on foot that will be good for your body.

Franklin. Ah ! how tiresome you are !   205

Gout. Well, then, to my office ; it should not be for-
gotten that I am your physician. There !

Franklin. Oh-h-h ! What a devil of a physician !

Gout. How ungrateful you are to say so ! Is it not
I who, in the character of your physician, have saved you 210
from the palsy, dropsy, and apoplexy ? one or other of
which would have done for you long ago, but for me.

Franklin. I submit, and thank you for the past, but
entreat the discontinuance of your visits for the future ;
for, in my mind, one had better die than be cured so 215
dolefully. Permit me just to hint, that I have also not
been unfriendly to you. I never feed physician or quack
of any kind, to enter the list against you ; if then you

do not leave me to my repose, it may be said you are
ungrateful too.   220

Gout. I can scarcely acknowledge that as an objec-
tion. As to quacks, I despise them; they may kill you
indeed, but cannot injure me. And, as to regular physi-
cians, they are at last convinced that the gout, in such
a subject as you are, is no disease, but a remedy; and 225
wherefore cure a remedy? — But to our business; there !

Franklin. Oh ! oh ! — for Heaven's sake leave me,
and I promise faithfully never more to play at chess, but
to take exercise daily and live temperately.

Gout. I know you too well. You promise fair; but 230
after a few months of good health you will return to your
old habits; your fine promises will be forgotten like the
forms of the last year's clouds. Let us then finish the
account, and I will go. But I leave you with an assur-
ance of visiting you again at a proper time and place; 235
for my object is your good, and you are sensible now that
I am your *real friend.*

THE LYRA PRAYER

RICHARD JEFFERIES

One evening, when the bright white star in Lyra was
shining almost at the zenith over me, and the deep con-
cave was the more profound in the dusk, I formulated it
[his soul's-desire] into three divisions. First, I desired
that I might do or find something to exalt the soul, some-   5
thing to enable it to live its own life, a more powerful
existence now. Secondly, I desired to be able to do
something for the flesh, to make a discovery or perfect

---

[1] Reprinted from "The Story of my Heart," by permission of Long-
mans, Green, & Co.

a method by which the fleshly body might enjoy more
pleasure, longer life, and suffer less pain. Thirdly, to 10
construct a more flexible engine with which to carry into
execution the design of the will. I called this the Lyra
prayer, to distinguish it from the far deeper emotion in
which the soul was alone concerned.

Of the three divisions, the last was of so little impor- 15
tance that it scarcely deserved to be named in conjunc-
tion with the others. Mechanism increases convenience
—in no degree does it confer physical or moral perfec-
tion. The rudimentary engines employed thousands of
years ago in raising buildings were in that respect equal 20
to the complicated machines of the present day. Con-
trol of iron and steel has not altered or improved the
bodily man. I even debated some time whether such
a third division should be included at all. Our bodies
are now conveyed all round the world with ease, but 25
obtain no advantage. As they start, so they return. The
most perfect human families of ancient times were almost
stationary, as those of Greece. Perfection of form was
found in Sparta; how small a spot compared to those
continents over which we are now taken so quickly! 30
Such perfection of form might perhaps again dwell, con-
tented and complete in itself, on such a strip of land as
I could see between me and the sand of the sea. Again,
a watch keeping correct time is no guarantee that the
bearer shall not suffer pain. The owner of the watch 35
may be soulless, without mind-fire, a mere creature. No
benefit to the heart or to the body accrues from the
most accurate mechanism. Hence I debated whether
the third division should be included. But I reflected
that time cannot be put back on the dial, we cannot 40
return to Sparta; there is an existent state of things, and
existent multitudes; and possibly a more powerful engine,

flexible to the will, might give them that freedom which
is the one, and the one only, political or social idea I
possess.   For liberty, therefore, let it be included.   45

For the flesh, this arm of mine, the limbs of others
gracefully moving, let me find something that will give
them greater perfection, that the bones may be firmer,
somewhat larger if that would be an advantage, certainly
stronger, that the cartilage and sinews may be more en- 50
during, and the muscles more powerful, something after
the manner of those ideal limbs and muscles sculptured
of old, these in the flesh and real.   That the organs of
the body may be stronger in their action, perfect, and
lasting.   That the exterior flesh may be yet more beauti- 55
ful; that the shape may be finer, and the motions grace-
ful.   These are the soberest words I can find, purposely
chosen; for I am so rapt in the beauty of the human
form, and so earnestly, so inexpressibly, prayerful to see
that form perfect, that my full thought is not to be 60
written.   Unable to express it fully, I have considered it
best to put it in the simplest manner of words.   I
believe in the human form; let me find something,
some method, by which that form may achieve the
utmost beauty.   Its beauty is like an arrow, which may 65
be shot any distance according to the strength of the
bow.   So the idea expressed in the human shape is
capable of indefinite expansion and elevation of beauty.

Of the mind, the inner consciousness, the soul, my
prayer desired that I might discover a mode of life for 70
it, so that it might not only conceive of such a life for it,
but actually enjoy it on the earth.   I wished to search
out a new and higher set of ideas on which the mind
should work.   The simile of a new book of the soul is
the nearest to convey the meaning — a book drawn from 75
the present and future, not the past.   Instead of a set of

ideas based on tradition, let me give the mind a new thought drawn straight from the wondrous present, direct this very hour. Next, to furnish the soul with the means of executing its will, of carrying thought into action. In 80 other words, for the soul to become a power. These three formed the Lyra prayer, of which the two first are immeasurably the more important. I believe in the human being, mind and flesh, form and soul.

SIR GALAHAD

ALFRED, LORD TENNYSON

My good blade carves the casques of men,
  My tough lance thrusteth sure,
My strength is as the strength of ten,
  Because my heart is pure.
The shattering trumpet shrilleth high,   5
  The hard brands shiver on the steel,
The splinter'd spear-shafts crack and fly,
  The horse and rider reel:
They reel, they roll in clanging lists,
  And when the tide of combat stands,   10
Perfume and flowers fall in showers,
  That lightly rain from ladies' hands.

How sweet are looks that ladies bend
  On whom their favors fall!
For them I battle till the end,   15
  To save from shame and thrall:
But all my heart is drawn above,
  My knees are bow'd in crypt and shrine:

I never felt the kiss of love,
  Nor maiden's hand in mine.   20
More bounteous aspects on me beam,
  Me mightier transports move and thrill;
So keep I fair thro' faith and prayer
  A virgin heart in work and will.

When down the stormy crescent goes,   25
  A light before me swims,
Between dark stems the forest glows,
  I hear a noise of hymns:
Then by some secret shrine I ride;
  I hear a voice but none are there;   30
The stalls are void, the doors are wide,
  The tapers burning fair.
Fair gleams the snowy altar-cloth,
  The silver vessels sparkle clean,
The shrill bell rings, the censer swings,   35
  And solemn chants resound between.

Sometimes on lonely mountain-meres
  I find a magic bark;
I leap on board: no helmsman steers:
  I float till all is dark.   40
A gentle sound, an awful light!
  Three angels bear the Holy Grail:
With folded feet, in stoles of white,
  On sleeping wings they sail.
Ah, blessed vision! blood of God!   45
  My spirit beats her mortal bars,
As down dark tides the glory slides,
  And star-like mingles with the stars.

37. *meres*, lakes.

When on my goodly charger borne
   Thro' dreaming towns I go,   50
The cock crows ere the Christmas morn,
   The streets are dumb with snow.
The tempest crackles on the leads,
   And, ringing, spins from brand and mail;
But o'er the dark a glory spreads,   55
   And gilds the driving hail.
I leave the plain, I climb the height;
   No branchy thicket shelter yields;
But blessed forms in whistling storms
   Fly o'er waste fens and windy fields.   60

A maiden knight — to me is given
   Such hope, I know not fear;
I yearn to breathe the airs of heaven
   That often meet me here.
I muse on joy that will not cease,   65
   Pure spaces cloth'd in living beams,
Pure lilies of eternal peace,
   Whose odors haunt my dreams;
And, stricken by an angel's hand,
   This mortal armor that I wear,   70
This weight and size, this heart and eyes,
   Are touch'd, are turn'd to finest air.

The clouds are broken in the sky,
   And thro' the mountain-walls
A rolling organ-harmony   75
   Swells up, and shakes and falls.
Then move the trees, the copses nod,
   Wings flutter, voices hover clear:

53. *leads*, the leaden plates of the roofs.

o

"O just and faithful knight of God !
Ride on ! the prize is near."   80
So pass I hostel, hall, and grange ;
By bridge and ford, by park and pale,
All-arm'd I ride, whate'er betide,
Until I find the Holy Grail.

The poem is a panorama, beginning with a picture of the actual jousts of knighthood, then proceeding with magic picture after magic picture of what happened to Galahad on his quest. These pictures are partly from the old Celtic legends of the miraculous sights that Galahad saw; but they are mostly the product of Tennyson's imagination. Try to tell from memory the successive pictures, entering into the mysterious feeling of the poem.

Plan of Summary. — Reviewing the chapter, (1) enumerate the kinds of metre, designating them by the number of accents, and by the predominant foot. Then (2) say which poem is most noticeable for melody; (3) which for beauty of suggested sights; (4) which for pleasure of suggested sounds; (5) which for pleasure of suggested activity; (6) which for pleasure of suggested odors or tastes; (7) which is most easily understood; (8) which moves the reader most deeply; (9) which shows most skill in character drawing; (10) which has the best unity; (11) which, your critical judgment tells you, is the best piece of work; (12) which you like the best, without regard to its deserved rank, or its fame.

CHAPTER V

THE ADVENTURER

Boys do not need to be urged to read the Leather-Stocking Tales, in which the actors have to depend on their native gifts of eye and ear and limb, like that embodiment of self-reliance, Natty Bumppo. It is a sign of old age not to like a good story of pioneer life, or of shipwreck on a desert island.

Some forms of adventure are best told in verse. Rhythm is necessary in order to suggest the sense of freedom felt by a roving cow-boy. Longfellow, who was fond of travelling by imagination, usually chose verse rather than prose to express the dreamy flight his fancy took to other lands. He watches the red sand in the hour-glass, and gradually he sees, in his mind's eye, the wastes of Arabia, the caravans, the sand-storms, and even the biblical scenes that we associate with the desert. Longfellow finds that the impulse to explore the sea and the mysterious lands beyond it is a poetic impulse. His poem reminds grown men of the days when they fancied that everything beyond the horizon was strange and new, and that the very soil of foreign lands was magically different from our own. But chiefly it reminds them that the secret of the sea always remains a secret except to those who brave its dangers. The Cow-Boy, p. 198. Sand of the Desert in an Hour-Glass, p. 200. The Secret of the Sea, p. 202.

Nor are the adventurers celebrated in song less brave than those of prose. Longfellow told in simple verse the story of the old Viking who discovered the North Cape. Such a man was surely as venturesome as Jim Hawkins in Treasure Island. The parrots and savages of Crusoe's acquaintance are inconsiderable when compared with the creatures of the haunted isles seen by the old Irish voyagers in Tennyson's *Maeldune*. And Pathfinder's excursions through the woods or the prairies were not more wonderful than the voyage of Ulysses beyond the sunset and the baths of all the western stars.

Tennyson's *Maeldune* is an old Irish legend of a hero who put to sea with his friends to find the slayer of his father. As they approached the murderer's island home, a wind blew them out and away into the boundless sea. They came to an island where all was silence ; even the waterfall made no sound ; then to one where all was shouting and uproar. They sailed on to an isle of flowers — nothing but flowers — then to one all fruits. Some of their number perished at the land of fire, and others at the magic isle under the sea. At the isle of bounty a magic hand fed all until they became slothful and quarrelsome. Then the isle of witches tried to coax their ship upon the rocks. After that they passed to the isle of the double towers, strange buildings that rocked against each other, one smooth, one sculptured. Here they insanely fell to fighting each other over the merits of the opposing towers, and half were slain. At last they came to the isle of a saint, who bade Maeldune remember that vengeance is the Lord's, and sent him back home, exhausted and awed.

Tennyson's *Ulysses* is in the spirit of the antique, but it represents that hero as doing something not told of in the Odyssey. Once restored to his native Ithaca after long wanderings, he cannot rest, but must adventure again. He calls to his friends to embark once more with him, and sitting well in order ·smite the sounding furrows. He will sail into the uttermost west. It may be that the gulfs will wash him down ; it may be he will reach the happy isles of the dead. At all events, he is determined to strive, to seek, to find, and not to yield. The brave Norse explorer who built and ventured in the *Fram* has given a new force to these last words by quoting them as the expression of his own ambition.

To speak of discoverers is to recall the famous finding of Livingstone. It used to be said that a redskin would make an appointment, months ahead, to be at a certain tree in a far-distant region at precisely such an hour, and would keep the appointment to the minute. But the Indian, achieving such a feat in a temperate climate, among tribes closely related to him in nature and speech, is less remarkable than young Stanley, fighting his way for months through unmapped tropical forests, amid the gravest dangers from heat, miasma, serpents, wild beasts, and wilder savages, yet reaching the hut he sought. Stanley himself has told the story with fine restraint. Every American is glad that their young countryman did not gush at the last moment, but merely said, " Dr. Livingstone, I presume."

A Meeting in the Heart of Africa, p. 214.

In one of his poems Mr. Kipling speaks of the "out-trail," — the path of the adventurer. The " out-trail " calls to the blood of every youth, and in one form or another it must be obeyed. It may call neither to Africa, nor China, nor the plains. It may call the country lad to that worst of wildernesses, the city. It often summons the ambitious son of poverty to school, whither he thought he never could afford to go. To start out, with no visible means of support, to get an education, is as adventurous as piracy. But, whithersoever the out-trail may call, the youth ought to leave home with a pang. A youth who is unqualifiedly glad to get away from home promises ill. Robert Louis Stevenson's ballad of a *Christmas at Sea* puts this matter in just the right light. A young sailor is telling of the trouble his ship had in putting to sea on a given Christmas Day. The winds seemed determined to drive the craft on the rocks.

It so happened that all this occurred very close to the spot
where the young sailor's father lived.   The boy could see
the homestead easily, and imagine his parents by the fireside.

> " And well I knew the talk they had, the talk that was of me,
> Of the shadow on the household and the son that went to sea ;
> And, oh, the wicked fool I seemed, in every kind of way,
> To be here and hauling frozen ropes on blessed Christmas Day.

> " And they heaved a mighty breath, every soul on board but me,
> As they saw her nose again pointing handsome out to sea ;
> But all that I could think of in the darkness and the cold,
> Was just that I was leaving home, and my folks were growing old."

THE COW-BOY

JOHN ANTROBUS

> " What care I, what cares he,
> What cares the world of the life we know !
> Little they reck of the shadowless plains,
> The shelterless mesa, the sun and the rains,
> The wild, free life, as the winds that blow."   5
>   With his broad sombrero,
>   His worn chapparejos,
>   And clinking spurs,
>   Like a Centaur he speeds,
>   Where the wild bull feeds ;   10
> And he laughs ha, ha ! who cares, who cares !

> Ruddy and brown — careless and free —
> A king in the saddle — he rides at will
> O'er the measureless range where rarely change,
> The swart gray plains so weird and strange,   15
> Treeless, and streamless, and wondrous still !

4. *mesa*, table-land. 7. *chapparejos* (chapparayhos), leather breeches.

With his slouch sombrero,
His torn chapparejos,
And clinking spurs,
Like a Centaur he speeds   20
Where the wild bull feeds;
And he laughs ha, ha ! who cares, who cares !

He of the towns, he of the East,
Has only a vague dull thought of him;
In his far-off dreams the cow-boy seems   25
A mythical thing, a thing he deems
A Hun or a Goth, as swart and grim !
    With his stained sombrero,
    His rough chapparejos,
    And clinking spurs,   30
    Like a Centaur he speeds
    Where the wild bull feeds ;
And he laughs ha, ha ! who cares, who cares !

Swift and strong, and ever alert,
Yet sometimes he rests on the dreary vast ;   35
And his thoughts, like the thoughts of other men,
Go back to his childhood's days again,
And to many a loved one in the past.
    With his gay sombrero,
    His rude chapparejos,   40
    And clinking spurs,
    He rests awhile,
    With a tear and a smile,
Then he laughs ha, ha ! who cares, who cares !

'Tis over late at the ranchman's gate —   45
He and his fellows, perhaps a score,
Halt in a quarrel o'er night begun,
With a ready blow and a random gun —
There's a comrade dead, dead ! nothing more.

With his slouched sombrero,   50
   His dark chapparejos,
   And clinking spurs,
   He dashes past
   With face o'ercast
And growls in his throat — who cares, who cares ! 55

The author of this poem was also a painter, and had a picture on the same subject. Note that the refrain has four unrhymed lines. Does this irregular refrain commend itself after several readings ? If so, why ? Are there any gains in the changes in the refrain from stanza to stanza ?

SAND OF THE DESERT IN AN HOUR–GLASS

HENRY WADSWORTH LONGFELLOW

A handful of red sand, from the hot clime
   Of Arab deserts brought,
Within this glass becomes the spy of Time,
   The minister of Thought.

How many weary centuries has it been   5
   About those deserts blown !
How many strange vicissitudes has seen,
   How many histories known !

Perhaps the camels of the Ishmaelite
   Trampled and passed it o'er,   10
When into Egypt from the patriarch's sight
   His favorite son they bore.

Perhaps the feet of Moses, burnt and bare,
   Crushed it beneath their tread ;
Or Pharaoh's flashing wheels into the air   15
   Scattered it as they sped ;

Or Mary, with the Christ of Nazareth
    Held close in her caress,
Whose pilgrimage of hope and love and faith
    Illumed the wilderness ;   20

Or anchorites beneath Engaddi's palms
    Pacing the Dead Sea beach,
And singing slow their old Armenian psalms
    In half-articulate speech ;

Or caravans, that from Bassora's gate   25
    With westward steps depart ;
Or Mecca's pilgrims, confident of Fate,
    And resolute in heart !

These have passed over it, or may have passed !
    Now in this crystal tower   30
Imprisoned by some curious hand at last,
    It counts the passing hour.

And as I gaze, these narrow walls expand ; —
    Before my dreamy eye
Stretches the desert with its shifting sand,   35
    Its unimpeded sky.

And borne aloft by the sustaining blast,
    This little golden thread
Dilates into a column high and vast,
    A form of fear and dread.   40

And onward, and across the setting sun,
    Across the boundless plain,
The column and its broader shadow run,
    Till thought pursues in vain.

The vision vanishes ! These walls again 45
   Shut out the lurid sun,
Shut out the hot, immeasurable plain ;
   The half-hour's sand is run !

THE SECRET OF THE SEA

HENRY WADSWORTH LONGFELLOW

Ah ! what pleasant visions haunt me
   As I gaze upon the sea !
All the old romantic legends,
   All my dreams come back to me.

Sails of silk and ropes of sendal, 5
   Such as gleam in ancient lore ;
And the singing of the sailors,
   And the answer from the shore !

Most of all, the Spanish ballad
   Haunts me oft, and tarries long, 10
Of the noble Count Arnaldos
   And the sailor's mystic song.

Like the long waves on a sea-beach,
   Where the sand as silver shines,
With a soft, monotonous cadence, 15
   Flow its unrhymed lyric lines ; —

Telling how the Count Arnaldos,
   With his hawk upon his hand,
Saw a fair and stately galley,
   Steering onward to the land ; — 20

How he heard the ancient helmsman
   Chant a song so wild and clear,
That the sailing sea-bird slowly
   Poised upon the mast to hear,

Till his soul was full of longing,   25
   And he cried, with impulse strong, —
"Helmsman ! for the love of heaven,
   Teach me, too, that wondrous song !"

"Wouldst thou," — so the helmsman answered,
   "Learn the secret of the sea?   30
Only those who brave its dangers
   Comprehend its mystery !"

In each sail that skims the horizon,
   In each landward-blowing breeze,
I behold that stately galley,   35
   Hear those mournful melodies ;

Till my soul is full of longing
   For the secret of the sea,
And the heart of the great ocean
   Sends a thrilling pulse through me.   40

THE VOYAGE OF MAELDUNE

(FOUNDED ON AN IRISH LEGEND A.D. 700)

ALFRED, LORD TENNYSON

I

I was the chief of the race — he had stricken my father
   dead —
But I gather'd my fellows together, I swore I would strike
   off his head.
Each of them look'd like a king, and was noble in birth as
   in worth,
And each of them boasted he sprang from the oldest race
   upon earth.   4

---

1. What earlier poem in the book has the same metre ?

Each was as brave in the fight as the bravest hero of song,
And each of them liefer had died than have done one
    another a wrong.
He lived on an isle in the ocean — we sail'd on a Friday
    morn —
He that had slain my father the day before I was born.

II

And we came to the isle in the ocean, and there on the
    shore was he.
But a sudden blast blew us out and away thro' a boundless
    sea.   10

III

And we came to the Silent Isle that we never had touch'd
    at before,
Where a silent ocean always broke on a silent shore,
And the brooks glitter'd on in the light without sound, and
    the long waterfalls
Pour'd in a thunderless plunge to the base of the mountain
    walls,
And the poplar and cypress unshaken by storm flourish'd up
    beyond sight,   15
And the pine shot aloft from the crag to an unbelievable
    height,
And high in the heaven above it there flicker'd a songless
    lark,
And the cock couldn't crow, and the bull couldn't low, and
    the dog couldn't bark.
And round it we went, and thro' it, but never a murmur, a
    breath —
It was all of it fair as life, it was all of it quiet as death, 20

8–10. Why is this stanza so short?   18. Is this line longer than its
neighbors? Note the medial rhyme.

And we hated the beautiful Isle, for whenever we strove to
  speak
Our voices were thinner and fainter than any flittermouse-
  shriek ;
And the men that were mighty of tongue and could raise
  such a battle-cry
That a hundred who heard it would rush on a thousand
  lances and die —
O they to be dumb'd by the charm ! — so fluster'd with
  anger were they   25
They almost fell on each other ; but after we sail'd away.

IV

And we came to the Isle of Shouting, we landed, a score of
  wild birds
Cried from the topmost summit with human voices and
  words ;
Once in an hour they cried, and whenever their voices
  peal'd
The steer fell down at the plough and the harvest died
  from the field,   30
And the men dropt dead in the valleys and half of the cattle
  went lame,
And the roof sank in on the hearth, and the dwelling broke
  into flame ;
And the shouting of these wild birds ran into the hearts of
  my crew,
Till they shouted along with the shouting and seized one
  another and slew ;
But I drew them the one from the other ; I saw that we
  could not stay,   35
And we left the dead to the birds and we sail'd with our
  wounded away.

22. *flittermouse*, bat.

V

And we came to the Isle of Flowers: their breath met us
    out on the seas,
For the Spring and the middle Summer sat each on the lap
    of the breeze;
And the red passion-flower to the cliffs, and the dark-blue
    clematis clung,
And starr'd with a myriad blossom the long convolvulus
    hung;   40
And the topmost spire of the mountain was lilies in lieu of
    snow,
And the lilies like glaciers winded down, running out below
Thro' the fire of the tulip and poppy, the blaze of gorse, and
    the blush
Of millions of roses that sprang without leaf or a thorn from
    the bush;
And the whole isle-side flashing down from the peak without
    ever a tree   45
Swept like a torrent of gems from the sky to the blue of the
    sea;
And we roll'd upon capes of crocus and vaunted our kith
    and our kin,
And we wallow'd in beds of lilies, and chanted the triumph
    of Finn,
Till each like a golden image was pollen'd from head to feet
And each was as dry as a cricket, with thirst in the middle-
    day heat.   50
Blossom and blossom, and promise of blossom, but never a
    fruit!
And we hated the Flowering Isle, as we hated the isle that
    was mute,

38. Note the accent (the correct one always) of *clematis.* 47. The one
who boasts of his kin is like a promising blossom without fruit.

And we tore up the flowers by the million and flung them
    in bight and bay,
And we left but a naked rock, and in anger we sail'd away.

VI

And we came to the Isle of Fruits : all round from the cliffs
    and the capes,   55
Purple or amber, dangled a hundred fathom of grapes,
And the warm melon lay like a little sun on the tawny sand,
And the fig ran up from the beach and rioted over the land,
And the mountain arose like a jewell'd throne thro' the
    fragrant air,
Glowing with all-color'd plums and with golden masses of
    pear,   60
And the crimson and scarlet of berries that flamed upon
    bine and vine,
But in every berry and fruit was the poisonous pleasure of wine ;
And the peak of the mountain was apples, the hugest that
    ever were seen,
And they prest, as they grew, on each other, with hardly a
    leaflet between,
And all of them redder than rosiest health or than utterest
    shame,   65
And setting, when Even descended, the very sunset aflame ;
And we stay'd three days, and we gorged and we madden'd,
    till every one drew
His sword on his fellow to slay him, and ever they struck
    and they slew ;
And myself, I had eaten but sparely, and fought till I
    sunder'd the fray,
Then I bade them remember my father's death, and we
    sail'd away.   70

61. *bine*, slender stem of a plant.

VII

And we came to the Isle of Fire : we were lured by the
    light from afar,
For the peak sent up one league of fire to the Northern
    Star ;
Lured by the glare and the blare, but scarcely could stand
    upright,
For the whole isle shudder'd and shook like a man in a
    mortal affright ;
We were giddy besides with the fruits we had gorged, and
    so crazed that at last   75
There were some leap'd into the fire ; and away we sail'd,
    and we past
Over that undersea isle, where the water is clearer than air :
Down we look'd : what a garden !   O bliss, what a Paradise
    there !
Towers of a happier time, low down in a rainbow deep
Silent palaces, quiet fields of eternal sleep !   80
And three of the gentlest and best of my people, whate'er
    I could say,
Plunged head down in the sea, and the Paradise trembled
    away.

VIII

And we came to the Bounteous Isle, where the heavens lean
    low on the land,
And ever at dawn from the cloud glitter'd o'er us a sunbright
    hand,
Then it open'd and dropt at the side of each man, as he rose
    from his rest,   85
Bread enough for his need till the laborless day dipt under
    the West ;

77. Poe's City in the Sea and Southey's Curse of Kehama, § XVI, fur-
nish interesting comparisons.

And we wander'd about it and thro' it. O never was time
　　so good !
And we sang of the triumphs of Finn, and the boast of our
　　ancient blood,
And we gazed at the wandering wave as we sat by the gurgle
　　of springs,
And we chanted the songs of the Bards and the glories of
　　fairy kings ;　　　　　　　　　　　　　　　　　　90
But at length we began to be weary, to sigh, and to stretch
　　and yawn,
Till we hated the Bounteous Isle and the sunbright hand of
　　the dawn,
For there was not an enemy near, but the whole green Isle
　　was our own,
And we took to playing at ball, and we took to throwing the
　　stone,
And we took to playing at battle, but that was a perilous
　　play,　　　　　　　　　　　　　　　　　　　　95
For the passion of battle was in us, we slew and we sail'd
　　away.

IX

And we past to the Isle of Witches and heard their musical
　　cry —
" Come to us, O come, come " in the stormy red of a sky
Dashing the fires and the shadows of dawn on the beautiful
　　shapes,
For a wild witch naked as heaven stood on each of the
　　loftiest capes,　　　　　　　　　　　　　　　　100
And a hundred ranged on the rock like white sea-birds in
　　a row,
And a hundred gamboll'd and pranced on the wrecks in the
　　sand below,

---

94. Anglo-Saxon poets habitually called battle the " sword-play."

P

And a hundred splash'd from the ledges, and bosom'd the
    burst of the spray,
But I knew we should fall on each other, and hastily sail'd
    away.

x

And we came in an evil time to the Isle of the Double
    Towers,   105
One was of smooth-cut stone, one carved all over with
    flowers,
But an earthquake always moved in the hollows under the
    dells,
And they shock'd on each other and butted each other with
    clashing of bells,
And the daws flew out of the Towers and jangled and
    wrangled in vain,
And the clash and boom of the bells rang into the heart and
    the brain.   110
Till the passion of battle was on us, and all took sides with
    the Towers,
There were some for the clean-cut stone, there were more
    for the carven flowers,
And the wrathful thunder of God peal'd over us all the day,
For the one half slew the other, and after we sail'd away.

XI

And we came to the Isle of a Saint who had sail'd with
    St. Brendan of yore,   115
He had lived ever since on the Isle and his winters were
    fifteen score,
And his voice was low as from other worlds, and his eyes
    were sweet,
And his white hair sank to his heels and his white beard fell
    to his feet,

And he spake to me, "O Maeldune, let be this purpose of
    thine !
Remember the words of the Lord when he told us 'Ven-
    geance is mine !'   120
His fathers have slain thy fathers in war or in single strife,
Thy fathers have slain his fathers, each taken a life for a life,
Thy father had slain his father, how long shall the murder
    last?
Go back to the Isle of Finn and suffer the Past to be Past."
And we kiss'd the fringe of his beard and we pray'd as we
    heard him pray,   125
And the Holy man he assoil'd us, and sadly we sail'd away.

XII

And we came to the Isle we were blown from, and there on
    the shore was he,
The man that had slain my father. I saw him and let
    him be.
O weary was I of the travel, the trouble, the strife and
    the sin,
When I landed again, with a tithe of my men, on the Isle
    of Finn.   130

    Tennyson is remarkable among poets for the number of beautiful images
he can suggest in a line. Take the sixth stanza, for example, and read it
several times, trying to realize all it conveys. Could any painting represent
all that is suggested here?

ULYSSES

ALFRED, LORD TENNYSON

It little profits that an idle king,
By this still hearth, among these barren crags,
Match'd with an aged wife, I mete and dole
Unequal laws unto a savage race,

    1. What is the metre? What previous example of it have we seen?

That hoard, and sleep, and feed, and know not me.   5
I cannot rest from travel : I will drink
Life to the lees : all times I have enjoy'd
Greatly, have suffer'd greatly, both with those
That lov'd me, and alone ; on shore, and when
Thro' scudding drifts the rainy Hyades   10
Vex'd the dim sea.   I am become a name ;
For always roaming with a hungry heart
Much have I seen and known : cities of men
And manners, climates, councils, governments,
Myself not least, but honor'd of them all ;   15
And drunk delight of battle with my peers,
Far on the ringing plains of windy Troy.
I am a part of all that I have met ;
Yet all experience is an arch wherethro'
Gleams that untravell'd world, whose margin fades   20
For ever and for ever when I move.
How dull it is to pause, to make an end,
To rust unburnish'd, not to shine in use !   .
As tho' to breathe were life.   Life pil'd on life
Were all too little, and of one to me   25
Little remains : but every hour is sav'd
From that eternal silence, something more,
A bringer of new things ; and vile it were
For some three suns to store and hoard myself,
And this gray spirit yearning in desire   30
To follow knowledge like a sinking star,
Beyond the utmost bound of human thought.
    This is my son, mine own Telemachus,

10. The *Hyades* are a constellation of seven stars. When they rose with
the sun they were thought by the ancients to denote the approach of
rain. 11. *I am become a name*, that is, have become famous. 29. *suns*
here means yearly revolutions of the sun. 30. Note the compression of the
phrase *gray spirit,* — transfer of *gray* from gray head to spirit. An adjective
so applied is called a *transferred epithet*.

To whom I leave the sceptre and the isle —
Well-lov'd of me, discerning to fulfil   35
This labor, by slow prudence to make mild
A rugged people, and thro' soft degrees
Subdue them to the useful and the good.
Most blameless is he, centred in the sphere
Of common duties, decent not to fail   40
In offices of tenderness, and pay
Meet adoration to my household gods,
When I am gone.   He works his work, I mine.
    There lies the port ; the vessel puffs her sail :
There gloom the dark broad seas.   My mariners,   45
Souls that have toil'd, and wrought, and thought with me —
That ever with a frolic welcome took
The thunder and the sunshine, and oppos'd
Free hearts, free foreheads — you and I are old ;
Old age hath yet his honor and his toil ;   50
Death closes all ; but something ere the end,
Some work of noble note, may yet be done,
Not unbecoming men that strove with Gods.
The lights begin to twinkle from the rocks :
The long day wanes : the slow moon climbs : the deep   55
Moans round with many voices.   Come, my friends,
'Tis not too late to seek a newer world.
Push off, and sitting well in order smite
The sounding furrows ; for my purpose holds
To sail beyond the sunset, and the baths   60
Of all the western stars, until I die.
It may be that the gulfs will wash us down :
It may be we shall touch the Happy Isles,
And see the great Achilles, whom we knew.
Tho' much is taken, much abides ; and tho'   65

---

45. Note the compression of *gloom ;* a noun is made into a verb and
does the work of a long phrase.

We are not now that strength which in old days
Mov'd earth and heaven, that which we are, we are :
One equal temper of heroic hearts,
Made weak by time and fate, but strong in will
To strive, to seek, to find, and not to yield.   70

This stately and inspiriting poem is somewhat in the Greek spirit; it
sounds like Homer, though less simple than Homer. Lines 43–70 are emi-
nently worth learning by heart.

Is the poem lyrical, expressing a personal mood of the author, or narra-
tive? or is it a dramatic monologue?

A MEETING IN THE HEART OF AFRICA

HENRY MORTON STANLEY

We push on rapidly, lest the news of our coming might
reach the people of Bunder Ujiji before we come in sight
and are ready for them. We halt at a little brook, then
ascend the long slope of a naked ridge, the very last of
the myriads we have crossed. This alone prevents us 5
from seeing the lake in all its vastness. We arrive at the
summit, travel across and arrive at its western rim, and —
pause, reader — the port of Ujiji is below us, embowered
in the palms, only five hundred yards from us ! At this
grand moment we do not think of the five hundred miles 10
we have marched, of the hundreds of hills that we have
ascended and descended, of the many forests we have
traversed, of the jungles and thickets that annoyed us,
of the fervid salt plains that blistered our feet, of the hot
suns that scorched us, nor the dangers and difficulties, 15
now happily surmounted. At last the sublime hour has
arrived ! our dreams, our hopes and anticipations, are
about to be realized ! Our hearts and feelings are with
our eyes as we peer into the palms and try to make out in

which hut or house lives the white man with the gray 20 beard we heard about on the Malagarazi.

" Unfurl the flags, and load your guns ! "

" Ay Wallah, ay Wallah, bana ! " respond the men, eagerly.

.." One, two, three, fire ! "   25

A volley from nearly fifty guns roars like a salute from a battery of artillery ; we shall note its effect presently on the peaceful-looking village below.

" Now, kirangozi, hold the white man's flag up high, and let the Zanzibar flag bring up the rear. And you 30 men keep close together, and keep firing until we halt in the market-place, or before the white man's house. You have said to me often that you could smell the fish of the Tanganika. I can smell the fish of the Tanganika now. There are fish, and beer, and a long rest waiting for you. 35 March ! "

Before we had gone a hundred yards our repeated volleys had the effect desired. We had awakened Ujiji to the knowledge that a caravan was coming, and the people were witnessed rushing up in hundreds to meet 40 us. The mere sight of the flags informed every one immediately that we were a caravan, but the American flag, borne aloft by the gigantic Asmani, whose face was one vast smile on this day, rather staggered them at first. However, many of the people who now approached us 45 remembered the flag. They had seen it float above the American Consulate, and from the masthead of many a ship in the harbor of Zanzibar, and they were soon heard welcoming the beautiful flag with cries of " Bindera kisungu ! " — a white man's flag ! " Bindera Merikani ! " 50 — the American flag !

Then we were surrounded by them — by Wajiji, Wan- yamwezi, Wangwana, Warundi, Waguhha, Wamanyuema,   ◞

and Arabs — and were almost deafened with the shouts
of "Yambo, yambo, bana! Yambo, bana! Yambo, 55
bana!" To all and each of my men the welcome was
given.

We were now about three hundred yards from the
village of Ujiji, and the crowds are dense about me.
Suddenly I hear a voice on my right say : — 60

"Good morning, sir!"

Startled at hearing this greeting in the midst of such a
crowd of black people, I turn sharply around in search
of the man, and see him at my side, with the blackest of
faces, but animated and joyous — a man dressed in a long 65
white shirt, with a turban of American sheeting around
his woolly head, and I ask : —

"Who the mischief are you?"

"I am Susi, the servant of Dr. Livingstone," said he,
smiling, and showing a gleaming row of teeth. 70

"What! Is Dr. Livingstone here?"

"Yes, sir."

"In this village?"

"Yes, sir."

"Are you sure?" 75

"Sure, sure, sir. Why, I leave him just now."

"Good morning, sir," said another voice.

"Hallo," said I, "is this another one?"

"Yes, sir."

"Well, what is your name?" 80

"My name is Chumah, sir."

"What! are you Chumah, the friend of Wekotani?"

"Yes, sir."

"And is the Doctor well?"

"Not very well, sir." 85

"Where has he been so long?"

"In Manyuema."

" Now, you Susi, run, and tell the Doctor I am coming."

" Yes, sir," and off he darted like a madman.

By this time we were within two hundred yards of the 90
village, and the multitude was getting denser, and almost
preventing our march. Flags and streamers were out;
Arabs and Wangwana were pushing their way through the
natives in order to greet us, for, according to their
account, we belonged to them. But the great wonder of 95
all was, " How did you come from Unyanyembe?"

Soon Susi came running back, and asked me my name;
he had told the Doctor that I was coming, but the Doctor
was too surprised to believe him, and, when the Doctor
asked him my name, Susi was rather staggered. 100

But, during Susi's absence, the news had been con-
veyed to the Doctor that it was surely a white man that
was coming, whose guns were firing and whose flag could
be seen; and the great Arab magnates of Ujiji — Moham-
med bin Sali, Sayd bin Majid, Abid bin Suliman, Moham- 105
med bin Gharib, and others — had gathered together
before the Doctor's house, and the Doctor had come out
from his veranda to discuss the matter and await my
arrival.

In the meantime the head of the expedition had halted, 110
and the kirangozi was out of the ranks, holding his flag
aloft, and Selim said to me : " I see the Doctor, sir. Oh,
what an old man ! He has got a white beard." And I
— what would I not have given for a bit of friendly wil-
derness, where, unseen, I might vent my joy in some 115
mad freak, such as idiotically biting my hand, turning a
somersault, or slashing at trees, in order to allay those
exciting feelings that were well-nigh uncontrollable. My
heart beats fast, but I must not let my face betray my
emotions, lest it shall detract from the dignity of a white 120
man appearing under such extraordinary circumstances.

So I did that which I thought was most dignified. I
pushed back the crowds, and, passing from the rear,
walked down a living avenue of people, until I came in
front of the semicircle of Arabs, in the front of which 125
stood the white man with the gray beard. As I advanced
slowly toward him I noticed he was pale, looked wearied,
had a gray beard, wore a bluish cap with a faded gold
band round it, had on a red-sleeved waistcoat, and a pair
of gray tweed trousers. I would have run to him, only I 130
was a coward in the presence of such a mob ; would have
embraced him, only, he being an Englishman, I did not
know how he would receive me ; so I did what cowardice
and false pride suggested was the best thing; walked
deliberately to him, took off my hat, and said : —   135

" Dr. Livingstone, I presume ? "

"Yes," said he, with a kind smile, lifting his cap
slightly.

I replace my hat on my head, and he puts on his cap,
and we both grasp hands, and I then say aloud : —   140

" I thank God, Doctor, I have been permitted to see
you."

He answered : " I feel thankful that I am here to
welcome you."

I turn to the Arabs, take off my hat to them in response 145
to the saluting of " Yambos " I receive, and the Doctor
introduces them to me by name. Then, oblivious of
the crowds, oblivious of the men who shared with me my
dangers, we — Livingstone and I — turn our faces toward
his tembe. He points to the veranda, or, rather, mud 150
platform, under the broad overhanging eaves ; he points
to his own particular seat, which I see his age and expe-
rience in Africa have suggested, namely, a straw mat with
a goatskin over it, and another skin nailed against the
wall to protect his back from contact with the cold mud. 155

I protest against taking this seat, which so much more befits him than me, but the Doctor will not yield ; I must take it.

We are seated — the Doctor and I — with our backs to the wall. The Arabs take seats on our left. More than a 160 thousand natives are in our front, filling the whole square densely, indulging their curiosity, and discussing the fact of two white men meeting at Ujiji — one just come from Manyuema, in the west, the other from Unyanyembe, in the east. 165

Conversation began. What about? I declare I have forgotten. Oh ! we simultaneously asked questions of one another, such as " How did you come here ? " and " Where have you been all this long time ? The world has believed you to be dead." Yes, that was the way it 170 began ; but whatever the Doctor informed me, and that which I communicated to him, I cannot correctly report, for I found myself gazing at him, conning the wonderful man at whose side I now sat in Central Africa. Every hair of his head and beard, every wrinkle of his face, the 175 wanness of his features, and the slightly wearied look he wore, were all imparting intelligence to me ; the knowledge I craved for so much ever since I heard the words, " Take what you want, but find Livingstone." What I saw was deeply interesting intelligence to me, and unvar- 180 nished truth. I was listening and reading at the same time. What did these dumb witnesses relate to me ?

Oh, reader, had you been at my side on this day in Ujiji, how eloquently could be told the nature of this man's work ! Had you been there but to see and hear ! 185 His lips gave me the details ; lips that never lie. I cannot repeat what he said ; I was too much engrossed to take my note-book out and begin to stenograph his story. He had so much to say that he began at the end, seem-

ingly oblivious of the fact that five or six years had to be 190
accounted for. But his account was oozing out; it was
growing fast into grand proportions, into a most marvel-
lous history of deeds.

The Arabs rose up, with a delicacy I approved, as if
they intuitively knew that we ought to be left to our- 195
selves. I sent Bombay with them, to give them the news
they also wanted so much to know about the affairs at
Unyanyembe. Sayd bin Majid was the father of the
gallant young man whom I saw at Masange, and who
fought with me at Zimbizo, and who soon afterward was 200
killed by Mirambo's Ruga-Ruga in the forest of Wilyan-
kuru; and, knowing that I had been there, he earnestly
desired to hear the tale of the fight; but they had all
friends at Unyanyembe, and it was but natural that they
should be anxious to hear of what concerned them.　　205

After giving orders to Bombay and Asmani for the
provisioning of the men of the expedition, I called
" Kaif-Halek," or " How-do-ye-do," and introduced him
to Dr. Livingstone as one of the soldiers in charge of
certain goods left at Unyanyembe, whom I had com- 210
pelled to accompany me to Ujiji, that he might deliver in
person to his master the letter-bag he had been intrusted
with by Dr. Kirk. This was that famous letter-bag
marked " Nov. 1st, 1870," which was now delivered
into the Doctor's hands 365 days after it left Zanzi- 215
bar! How long, I wonder, had it remained at Unyan-
yembe had I not been despatched into Central Africa in
search of the great traveller!

The Doctor kept the letter-bag on his knee, then pres-
ently opened it, looked at the letters contained there, and 220
read one or two of his children's letters, his face, in the
meanwhile, lighting up.

He asked me to tell him the news. " No, Doctor,"

said I ; " read your letters first, which I am sure you must
be impatient to read." 225

" Ah," said he, " I have waited years for letters, and
I have been taught patience. I can surely afford to wait
a few hours longer. No, tell me the general news ; how
is the world getting along ? "

" You probably know much already. Do you know 230
that the Suez canal is a fact — is opened, and a regular
trade carried on between Europe and India through it ? "

" I did not hear about the opening of it. Well, that is
grand news ! What else ? "

Shortly I found myself enacting the part of an annual 235
periodical to him. There was no need of exaggeration —
of any penny-a-line news, or of any sensationalism. The
world had witnessed and experienced much the last few
years. The Pacific Railroad had been completed ; Grant
had been elected President of the United States ; Egypt 240
had been flooded with savans ; the Cretan rebellion had
terminated ; a Spanish revolution had driven Isabella from
the throne of Spain, and a regent had been appointed ;
General Prim was assassinated ; a Castelar had electrified
Europe with his advanced ideas upon the liberty of 245
worship ; Prussia had humbled Denmark and annexed
Schleswig-Holstein, and her armies were now around
Paris ; the " Man of Destiny " was a prisoner at Wil-
helmshöhe ; the Queen of Fashion and the Empress of
the French was a fugitive ; and the child born in the 250
purple had lost forever the imperial crown intended for
his head ; the Napoleon dynasty was extinguished by the
Prussians, Bismarck and Von Moltke ; and France, the
proud empire, was humbled to the dust.

What could a man have exaggerated of these facts ? 255
What a budget of news it was to one who had emerged
from the depths of the primeval forests of Manyuema !

The reflection of the dazzling light of civilization was cast on him while Livingstone was thus listening in wonder to one of the most exciting pages of history ever repeated. 260 How the puny deeds of barbarism paled before these ! Who could tell under what new phases of uneasy life Europe was laboring even then, while we, two of her lonely children, rehearsed the tale of her late woes and glories? More worthily, perhaps, had the tongue of a 265 lyric Demodocus recounted them ; but, in the absence of the poet, the newspaper correspondent performed his part as well and truthfully as he could.

Not long after the Arabs had departed, a dishful of hot hashed-meat cakes was sent to us by Sayd bin Majid, 270 and a curried chicken was received from Mohammed bin Sali, and Moeni Kheri sent a dishful of stewed goat-meat and rice ; and thus presents of food came in succession, and as fast as they were brought we set to. I had a healthy, stubborn digestion. The exercise I had taken 275 had put it in prime order ; but Livingstone — he had been complaining that he had no appetite, that his stomach refused everything but a cup of tea now and then — he ate also, ate like a vigorous, hungry man ; and, as he vied with me in demolishing the pancakes, he kept 280 repeating, "You have brought me new life ; you have brought me new life."

"Oh, by George !" I said ; "I have forgotten something. Hasten, Selim, and bring that bottle ; you know which. And bring me the silver goblets. I brought 285 this bottle on purpose for this event, which I hoped would come to pass, though often it seemed useless to expect it."

Selim knew where the bottle was, and he soon returned

266. *Demodocus,* a famous minstrel mentioned in Homer's Odyssey.

with it — a bottle of Sillery champagne; and, handing 290
the Doctor a silver goblet brimful of the exhilarating
wine, and pouring a small quantity into my own, I
said : —

"Dr. Livingstone, to your very good health, sir."

"And to yours," he responded. 295

And the champagne I had treasured for this happy
meeting was drunk with hearty good wishes to each other.

Plan of Summary. — Reviewing the chapter, (1) enumerate the
kinds of metre, designating them by the number of accents, and by the
predominant foot. Then (2) say which poem is most noticeable for mel-
ody; (3) which for beauty of suggested sights; (4) which for pleasure
of suggested sounds; (5) which for pleasure of suggested activity;
(6) which for pleasure of suggested odors or tastes; (7) which is
most easily understood; (8) which moves the reader most deeply;
(9) which shows most skill in character drawing; (10) which has the
best unity; (11) which, your critical judgment tells you, is the best
piece of work; (12) which you like the best, — without regard to its
deserved rank, or its fame.

CHAPTER VI

THE HEARTH

THE instinct to get away from apron-strings is very active in strong young natures. If it were not, there would never be any men, but only grown-up infants. The instinct spends itself in adventure, pioneering, making one's way in the world, and ends by producing a self-reliant head of a new household. The young man who learns to take care of himself is he who comes to care most for his old home. A really appreciative affection for one's parents is a sign of manhood, because only the grown man can appreciate his parents. Charles Kingsley seems to suggest this fact in *The* *"Old, Old Song."* At all events, when Kingsley prays that the wild lad, after creeping home spent and maimed, may find one face there he loved when all was young, what face would he so probably have in mind as that of the mother?

The " Old, Old Song." p. 229.

In war-time some parents are foolish enough to oppose a strong, healthy son in his wish to leave home and serve his country. Sons are sometimes inconsiderate enough to abandon parents who can ill spare them, and go to war for the sake of adventure and glory. If, in any case of running away to the war, the youth be killed, the satisfaction of having said good-bye is then denied the survivors. If he gets back home, in spite of false rumors that he is among the missing, the situation is somewhat better, as in Mrs. Osgood's poem.

Driving Home the Cows, p. 230.

But an honest good-bye and an honest return make the best case of all. The boy whose going causes honest tears and whose coming causes honest joy will not miss his welcome when he is the head of a house. His homecoming will be, to him and his, one of the few great pleasures that our checkered life has to give. Many a king never knows what such a poem as *There's Nae Luck about the House* means to the nation that produces it. There's Nae Luck, p. 232.

Few subjects have appealed to the poets more than the mother's love for the child. Some of the greatest lyrics in literature picture the tragic grief of the mother over her child. Tennyson's *Rizpah* is such a masterpiece, revealing the heart of an old woman who goes by night to collect, from the ground beneath a gibbet, the bones of her luckless son. Two poems in the present chapter exhibit this passionate motherly love for the dead child. One is by Barnes of Dorsetshire, — William Barnes, who wrote in the Dorsetshire dialect. The peasant woman, " Mëary-Ann," is alone with her babe, in her house with the trees overhead. There is a storm outside. In the evening she notices that the child is not well. He grows worse with the advancing night, and she clasps him to her bosom. His struggles grow weak, and his cries die away. By a gleam of the moon she sees that his face is white as ashes. The other poem, Sydney Dobell's *How's my Boy?* is a short dramatic dialogue, almost a monologue. The mother is asking for news of her sailor boy. The sailor stares at her, and in her vexation she declares that she might as well have asked some landsman. Finally he tells her that her boy's ship has gone down. " What cares she for the ship? How is her boy?" " Every man on the ship went down." Even then she will not listen to the awful news, but cries, " What care I for the men, sailor? How's my boy — my boy?" Mary-Ann's Child, p. 234. How's my Boy? p. 236.

In Matthew Arnold's beautiful little myth, *The Forsaken Merman*, there is a mother of most unmotherly heart. The poet imagines a merman, a sea king, who has won a mortal maiden for his bride. By some magic, Margaret is enabled The Forsaken Merman, p. 238.

Q

to live in the deep sea-caves. But by and by she grows anxious for her soul. It is Easter-time in the world, and she says she must go and pray in the little gray church on the shore. The merman lovingly bids her farewell for the time. Margaret departs, and does not return. Her husband and her little ones wait for her in vain. Then they steal up and gaze at her through the window of the church. He whispers to her, and the little ones call to her, but she gives them no look. They return with sad hearts to their pearly caves; but the father promises the children that they shall go again by night and gaze on the white, sleeping town.

In Arnold's *Merman* it is really the father's love that charms us. Poetry is full of that, too. From the terrible warrior Hector playing with his babe Astyanax, beautiful as a star, to the serene thinker Emerson, voicing in his *Threnody* his anguish for the star-eyed boy whom he lost, there is something about a father's love that ennobles its possessor. King David was never so kingly as in his grief over Absalom. Longfellow's *The Chamber over the Gate* is the modern version of that story, though nothing can match the pathos of the account in Samuel, translated into the short, simple words of our mother tongue.

avid and
bsalom,
235.

he Toys,
243.

Coventry Patmore wrote a poem in which a father grieves at his own harshness to his child. Mr. James Whitcomb Riley has a few heart-breaking lines on a similar subject. The parent cannot forget his cross rebuke of the baby, now dead, who came rowdying up to interrupt her busy father.

Dante tells of a Florentine, Ugolino, whose enemy starved him and his sons in a tower. When the poet met him in the lower world, Ugolino told the story of the boys' death in this hunger-tower. " I did not suffer; I grew as hard as stone. It was they who suffered." Ugolino's depth of grief and his hatred for his tormentor made him tearless. But

there may be tearless grief without hate. Symonds,[1] the
heroic man of letters who banished himself to the higher
Alps in order to live, just as Stevenson banished himself to
Samoa, has a poem of how a father's love may control a
father's grief. Again the story is of an Italian. The artist
Luca Signorelli belonged to the great painters that made
Italy in the fifteenth century a new Athens. Friends
brought home the painter's son dead, a youth of seventeen.
Luca did not weep. He would do the boy one last honor,
and make for himself and the world one sad but enduring
pleasure. He seized his brush, and began to paint the lad's
picture. All day long he worked, and at eve they found
him still painting with unerring handstroke. He was firm
and dry-eyed.

An Epi-
sode,
p. 244.

Neither in Ugolino's case nor in Luca's was there any
chance for self-sacrifice on the part of the parent. Ugolino
would have grasped eagerly any chance of starving to save
his children from this fate. That was what the father of
little Rhodopè did, with a willingness so quiet that his child
did not suspect. Landor tells this story in prose which has
never been surpassed for beauty.

The Selling
of Rho-
dopè,
p. 245.

Some such simplicity as Ugolino's, the simplicity which
arises when a mourner can utter but few words, and must
let these stand for all the unspoken anguish, appears in
Kingsley's *The Merry Lark*. Like the other two songs by
the same author (pp. 125, 229), this one is very sad, but it is
perhaps more beautiful than either. Some father or mother
is speaking of a great loss. The lark was merry, the hare
was feeding in the field, the bells were ringing to the laughter
of the child. Now the hare is killed, the lark has gone, the
bells are silent, the baby lies in its cradle in the churchyard
till the bells shall bring the parent there too.

The Merry
Lark,
p. 252.

Time cannot change the parent's love. Even the sin of`

---

[1] The *y* in *Symonds* is short, like *y* in *Lynn*.

Two Sons,
p. 253.
the child cannot destroy it. The old man in Mr. Robert Buchanan's poem has two sons, but these twain are one. There is the rough, cold soldier across the water; there is the sinless little child upon his mother's knee. The first is a hard reality; the second is a memory.

Though filial love is a rare theme in poetry, there are Sohrab and Rustum, p. 254. some glorious exceptions. Matthew Arnold's *Sohrab and Rustum*, one of the great poems of the century, is such an exception. It is based on an old Persian legend of the love between a child and a parent, made known to each too late. In its Persian form the story of Sohrab and Rustum was the work of the poet Firdusi, who lived in the tenth century, and wrote the national epic, *The Shah-Nameh*, "Book of Kings." As Arnold tells it, modifying the ancient version somewhat, the story is this. Rustum, the mightiest of Persian warriors, made a long visit, when a young man, to the king of the Koords. The king gave Rustum his daughter in marriage. Before Rustum became a father, the old desire of wandering seized him, and he departed. He gave his wife a seal, that she might prick it on the arm of the babe she bore. The princess gave birth to a son, whom she named Sohrab. He grew in stature and strength, and became a warrior of the greatest promise. Learning the name of his father, Sohrab longed to see him, and determined at last to seek him through the world. He joined the Tartars in their war on the Persians, chiefly in the hope of finding his father. When the two armies were encamped beside the Oxus, Sohrab proposed that the enemy be challenged to send a champion to meet him in single combat; for thus, he reasoned, he should come to the notice of the man he sought. The Persians persuaded Rustum himself to accept the challenge. Of course the latter did not know the identity of Sohrab. Likewise it happened that the mighty Rustum concealed his own name, being ashamed to have it said he had stooped to meet any one man on equal terms. The two champions stood forth. In a long fight Sohrab proved a match for his antagonist; but when the latter finally shouted "Rustum!" as a war-cry, the youth was unmanned, and before he could recover himself was struck down. Dying, he showed to Rustum the seal upon his arm. The love he had so long borne to this unseen parent he now poured out with his blood. He crawled upon the ground to where his heart-broken father lay, and kissed him, and called him back to life.

THE "OLD, OLD SONG"

CHARLES KINGSLEY

When all the world is young, lad,
   And all the trees are green;
And every goose a swan, lad,
   And every lass a queen, —
Then hey for boot and horse, lad,   5
   And round the world away;
Young blood must have its course, lad,
   And every dog his day.

When all the world is old, lad,
   And all the trees are brown;   10
And all the sport is stale, lad,
   And all the wheels run down, —
Creep home, and take your place there,
   The spent and maimed among:
God grant you find one face there   15
   You loved when all was young.

DRIVING HOME THE COWS

KATE PUTNAM OSGOOD

Out of the clover and blue-eyed grass
    He turned them into the river lane ;
One after another he let them pass,
    Then fastened the meadow bars again.

Under the willows, and over the hill,   5
    He patiently followed their sober pace ;
The merry whistle for once was still,
    And something shadowed the sunny face.

Only a boy ! and his father had said
    He never could let his youngest go :   10
Two already were lying dead
    Under the feet of the trampling foe.

But after the evening work was done,
    And the frogs were loud in the meadow-swamp,
Over his shoulder he slung his gun   15
    And stealthily followed the footpath damp.

Across the clover and through the wheat
    With resolute heart and purpose grim,
Though cold was the dew on his hurrying feet,
    And the blind bat's flitting startled him.   20

Thrice since then had the lanes been white,
    And the orchards sweet with apple-bloom ;
And now, when the cows come back at night,
    The feeble father drove them home.

For news had come to the lonely farm   25
    That three were lying where·two had lain ;
And the old man's tremulous, palsied arm
    Could never lean on a son's again.

The summer day grew cool and late :
    He went for the cows when the work was done ;   30
But down the lane, as he opened the gate,
    He saw them coming, one by one —

Brindle, Ebony, Speckle, and Bess,
    Shaking their horns in the evening wind ;
Cropping the buttercups out of the grass, —   35
    But who was it following close behind ?

Loosely swayed in the idle air
    The empty sleeve of army blue ;
And worn and pale, from the crisping hair,
    Looked out a face that the father knew.   40

For gloomy prisons will sometimes yawn,
    And yield their dead unto life again :
And the day that comes with a cloudy dawn
    In golden glory at last may wane.

The great tears sprang to their meeting eyes ;   45
    For the heart must speak when the lips are dumb :
And under the silent evening skies
    Together they followed the cattle home.

Name the metre according to the number of accents. Trochaic or iam-
bic ? Name the stanza and give the rhyme-scheme.

Supposing that Mrs. Osgood could have commanded such quantities of
picturesque detail as appear in *The Voyage of Maeldune*, would she have
done well to fill this poem with such detail ? Give your reasons.

THERE'S NAE LUCK ABOUT THE HOUSE

WILLIAM JULIUS MICKLE (?)

JEAN ADAMS (?)

And are ye sure the news is true !
  And are ye sure he's weel?
Is this a time to think of wark !
  Mak haste, lay by your wheel ;
Is this the time to spin a thread,   5
  When Colin's at the door !
Reach me my cloak, I'll to the quay,
  And see him come ashore.

    For there's nae luck about the house,
      There's nae luck at a' ;   10
    There's little pleasure in the house
      When our gudeman's awa.

And gie to me my bigonet,
  My bishop's satin gown ;
For I maun tell the baillie's wife   15
  That Colin's come to town.
My Turkey slippers maun gae on,
  My stockings pearly blue ;
It's a' to pleasure my gudeman,
  For he's baith leal and true.   20

Rise, lass, and mak a clean fireside,
  Put on the muckle pot,
Gie little Kate her button gown,
  And Jock his Sunday coat ;

13. *bigonet*, a woman's cap. 22. *muckle*, large.

And mak their shoon as black as slaes,   25
    Their hose as white as snaw,
It's a' to please my ain gudeman,
    For he's been long awa.

There's twa fat hens upo' the bank
    Been fed this month and mair,   30
Mak haste and thraw their necks about,
    That Colin weel may fare ;
And mak the table neat and clean,
    Gar ilka thing look braw,
For wha can tell how Colin far'd   35
    When he was far awa?

Sae true his heart, sae smooth his speech,
    His breath like caller air,
His very foot has music in't
    As he comes up the stair !   40
And will I see his face again,
    And will I hear him speak?
I'm downright dizzy wi' the thought,
    In troth I'm like to greet.

If Colin's weel, and weel content,   45
    I hae nae mair to crave :
And gin I live to keep him sae,
    I'm blest aboon the lave.
And will I see his face again,
    And will I hear him speak?   50
I'm downright dizzy wi' the thought,
    In troth I'm like to greet.

---

25. *slaes*, sloes. 34. Make everything look neat. 38. *caller*, sweet, fresh.
41. The Scotch, like the Americans, are weak in their knowledge of *shall*
and *will*. 44. *greet*, cry. 47. *gin*, if. 48. *aboon the lave*, above the rest.

For there's nae luck about the house,
    There's nae luck at a' ;
There's little pleasure in the house   55
    When our gudeman's awa.

Is this poem purely narrative or purely lyrical, or a mixture of both tones ? The familiar Scotch music to which it is set is excellent.

MARY–ANN'S CHILD

WILLIAM BARNES

Mary-Ann was alone with her baby in arms,
    In her house with the trees overhead,
For her husband was out in the night and the storms,
    In his business a-toiling for bread ;
And she, as the wind in the elm-heads did roar,   5
Did grieve to think he was all night out of door.

And her kinsfolk and neighbors did say of her child
    (Under the lofty elm-tree),
That a prettier never did babble and smile
    Up a-top of a proud mother's knee ;   10
And his mother did toss him, and kiss him, and call
Him her darling, and life, and her hope and her all.

But she found in the evening the child was not well
    (Under the gloomy elm-tree),
And she felt she could give all the world for to tell   15
    Of a truth what his ailing could be ;
And she thought on him last in her prayers at night,
And she look'd at him last as she put out the light.

And she found him grow worse in the dead of the night
   (Under the gloomy elm-tree),   20
And she press'd him against her warm bosom so tight,
   And she rock'd him so sorrowfully ;
And there, in his anguish, a-nestling he lay,
Till his struggles grew weak, and his cries died away.

And the moon was a-shining down into the place   25
   (Under the gloomy elm-tree),
And his mother could see that his lips and his face
   Were as white as clean ashes could be ;
And her tongue was a-tied, and her still heart did swell
Till her senses came back with the first tear that fell.   30

Never more can she feel his warm face in her breast
   (Under the leafy elm-tree),
For his eyes are a-shut, and his hands are at rest,
   And he's now from his pain a-set free ;
For his soul we do know is to heaven a-fled,   35
Where no pain is a-known, and no tears are a-shed.

Is the metre anapestic or dactyllic ? What is the rhyme-scheme?
Is the poem eminently simple in diction, or is it elaborate ? Is elaborate diction natural to the expression of deep grief? Is the poem chiefly lyrical, or chiefly narrative ?

DAVID AND ABSALOM

2 Samuel xviii.

And David sat between the two gates : and the watchman said, Methinketh the running of the foremost is like the running of Ahimaaz the son of Zadok. And the king said, He is a good man, and cometh with good tidings. And Ahimaaz called, and said unto the king, All is well. 5 And he fell down to the earth upon his face before the king, and said, Blessed be the Lord thy God, which hath delivered up the men that lifted up their hand against my lord the king.   And the king said, Is the young man Absalom safe?   And Ahimaaz answered, When Joab sent 10 the king's servant, and me thy servant, I saw a great tumult, but I knew not what it was.   And the king said unto him, Turn aside, and stand here.   And he turned aside, and stood still.   And, behold, Cushi came; and Cushi said, Tidings, my lord the king: for the Lord hath 15 avenged thee this day of all them that rose up against thee.   And the king said unto Cushi, Is the young man Absalom safe?   And Cushi answered, The enemies of my lord the king, and all that rise against thee to do thee hurt, be as that young man is.   And the king was much 20 moved, and went up to the chamber over the gate, and wept: and as he went, thus he said, O my son Absalom, my son, my son Absalom! would God I had died for thee, O Absalom, my son, my son.

From your knowledge of rhetoric, say whether the sentences are loose or periodic. Are periodic sentences natural to the expression of deep grief? Note the great number of initial *Ands;* do they lend simplicity or complexity to the tone of the narrative?

HOW'S MY BOY?

SYDNEY DOBELL

"Ho, Sailor of the sea!
How's my boy — my boy?"
"What's your boy's name, good wife,
And in what good ship sail'd he?"

"My boy John —   5
He that went to sea —
What care I for the ship, sailor?
My boy's my boy to me.

"You come back from sea,
And not know my John? 10
I might as well have ask'd some landsman
Yonder down in the town.
There's not an ass in all the parish
But he knows my John.

"How's my boy — my boy? 15
And unless you let me know
I'll swear you are no sailor,
Blue jacket or no,
Brass buttons or no, sailor,
Anchor and crown or no! 20
Sure his ship was the *Jolly Briton*" —
"Speak low, woman, speak low!"
"And why should I speak low, sailor,
About my own boy John?
If I was loud as I am proud 25
I'd sing him over the town!
Why should I speak low, sailor?"
"That good ship went down."

"How's my boy — my boy?
What care I for the ship, sailor? 30
I was never aboard her.
Be she afloat or be she aground,
Sinking or swimming, I'll be bound,
Her owners can afford her!
I say, how's my John?" 35
"Every man on board went down,
Every man aboard her."
"How's my boy — my boy?
What care I for the men, sailor?

I'm not their mother —   40
How's my boy — my boy?
Tell me of him and no other!
How's my boy — my boy?"

Is there any excuse for the irregular metre of this poem? Is the poem
chiefly lyrical or chiefly narrative ?

THE FORSAKEN MERMAN

MATTHEW ARNOLD

Come, dear children, let us away;
Down and away below!
Now my brothers call from the bay,
Now the great winds shoreward blow,
Now the salt tides seaward flow;   5
Now the wild white horses play,
Champ and chafe and toss in the spray.
Children dear, let us away!
This way, this way!
Call her once before you go —   10
Call once yet!
In a voice that she will know:
"Margaret! Margaret!"
Children's voices should be dear
(Call once more) to a mother's ear;   15
Children's voices, wild with pain —
Surely she will come again!
Call her once and come away;
This way, this way!
"Mother dear, we cannot stay!   20
The wild white horses foam and fret."
Margaret! Margaret!

Come, dear children, come away down;
Call no more!
One last look at the white-wall'd town,   25
And the little gray church on the windy shore;
Then come down!
She will not come though you call all day;
Come away, come away!

Children dear, was it yesterday   30
We heard the sweet bells over the bay?
In the caverns where we lay,
Through the surf and through the swell,
The far-off sound of a silver bell?
Sand-strewn caverns, cool and deep,   35
Where the winds are all asleep;
Where the spent lights quiver and gleam,
Where the salt weed sways in the stream,
Where the sea-beasts, ranged all round,
Feed in the ooze of their pasture-ground;   40
Where the sea-snakes coil and twine,
Dry their mail and bask in the brine;
Where great whales come sailing by,
Sail and sail, with unshut eye,
Round the world for ever and aye?   45
When did music come this way?
Children dear, was it yesterday?

Children dear, was it yesterday
(Call yet once) that she went away?
Once she sate with you and me,   50
On a red gold throne in the heart of the sea,
And the youngest sate on her knee.
She comb'd its bright hair, and she tended it well,
When down swung the sound of a far-off bell.

She sigh'd, she look'd up through the clear green sea;   55
She said: "I must go, for my kinsfolk pray
In the little gray church on the shore to-day.
'Twill be Easter-time in the world — ah me!
And I lose my poor soul, Merman! here with thee."
I said: "Go up, dear heart, through the waves;   60
Say thy prayer, and come back to the kind sea-caves!"
She smiled, she went up through the surf in the bay.
Children dear, was it yesterday?

Children dear, were we long alone?
"The sea grows stormy, the little ones moan;   65
Long prayers," I said, "in the world they say;
Come!" I said; and we rose through the surf in the bay.
We went up the beach, by the sandy down
Where the sea-stocks bloom, to the white-wall'd town;
Through the narrow paved streets, where all was still,   70
To the little gray church on the windy hill.
From the church came a murmur of folk at their prayers,
But we stood without in the cold blowing airs.
We climb'd on the graves, on the stones worn with rains,
And we gazed up the aisle through the small leaded panes.
She sate by the pillar; we saw her clear: 76
"Margaret, hist! come quick, we are here!
Dear heart," I said, "we are long alone;
The sea grows stormy, the little ones moan."
But, ah, she gave me never a look,   80
For her eyes were seal'd to the holy book!
Loud prays the priest; shut stands the door.
Come away, children, call no more!
Come away, come down, call no more!

Down, down, down!   85
Down to the depths of the sea!

She sits at her wheel in the humming town,
Singing most joyfully.
Hark what she sings: "O joy, O joy,
For the humming street, and the child with its toy! 90
For the priest, and the bell, and the holy well;
For the wheel where I spun,
And the blessed light of the sun!"
And so she sings her fill,
Singing most joyfully, 95
Till the spindle drops from her hand,
And the whizzing wheel stands still.
She steals to the window, and looks at the sand,
And over the sand at the sea;
And her eyes are set in a stare; 100
And anon there breaks a sigh,
And anon there drops a tear,
From a sorrow-clouded eye,
And a heart sorrow-laden,
A long, long sigh; 105
For the cold strange eyes of a little Mermaiden
And the gleam of her golden hair.

Come away, away, children;
Come children, come down!
The hoarse wind blows coldly; 110
Lights shine in the town.
She will start from her slumber
When gusts shake the door;
She will hear the winds howling,
Will hear the waves roar. 115
We shall see, while above us
The waves roar and whirl,
A ceiling of amber,
A pavement of pearl.

R

Singing: "Here came a mortal,   120
But faithless was she!
And alone dwell forever
The kings of the sea."

But, children, at midnight,
When soft the winds blow,   125
When clear falls the moonlight,
When spring-tides are low;
When sweet airs come seaward
From heaths starr'd with broom,
And high rocks throw mildly   130
On the blanch'd sands a gloom;
Up the still, glistening beaches,
Up the creeks we will hie,
Over banks of bright seaweed
The ebb-tide leaves dry.   135
We will gaze, from the sand-hills,
At the white, sleeping town;
At the church on the hill-side —
And then come back down.
Singing: "There dwells a loved one,   140
But cruel is she!
She left lonely forever
The kings of the sea."

This poem must not be read hastily when read aloud; let the voice linger a little after each short line, and what seems like awkward irregularity will prove a true rhythm, pleasantly varied.

Is the poem mostly narrative or mostly lyrical? Which of these words might be applied to the merman: gentle, melancholy, pathetic, treacherous, true? How does Arnold succeed in making the depths of the sea attractive? Can you remember stories in which the same regions were rendered very unlovely? What physical traits of the merman and his children are mentioned? Is there anything in Arnold's conception of the merman different from a human being, except the ability to breathe in water?

THE TOYS

COVENTRY PATMORE

My little son, who look'd from thoughtful eyes
And mov'd and spoke in quiet grown-up wise,
Having my law the seventh time disobey'd,
I struck him, and dismiss'd
With hard words and unkiss'd,   5
His Mother, who was patient, being dead.
Then, fearing lest his grief should hinder sleep,
I visited his bed,
But found him slumbering deep,
With darken'd eyelids, and their lashes yet   10
From his late sobbing wet.
And I, with moan,
Kissing away his tears, left others of my own;
For, on a table drawn beside his head,
He had put, within his reach,   15
A box of counters and a red-vein'd stone,
A piece of glass abraded by the beach,
And six or seven shells,
A bottle with bluebells
And two French copper coins, ranged there with careful
        art,   20
To comfort his sad heart.
So when that night I pray'd
To God, I wept, and said:
Ah, when at last we lie with tranced breath,
Not vexing Thee in death,   25
And Thou rememberest of what toys
We made our joys,

How weakly understood
Thy great commanded good,
Then, fatherly not less   30
Than I whom Thou hast moulded from the clay,
Thou'lt leave Thy wrath, and say,
"I will be sorry for their childishness."

AN EPISODE

JOHN ADDINGTON SYMONDS

Vasari tells that Luca Signorelli,
The morning star of Michael Angelo,
Had but one son, a youth of seventeen summers,
Who died.   That day the master at his easel
Wielded the liberal brush wherewith he painted   5
At Orvieto, on the Duomo's walls,
Stern forms of Death and Heaven and Hell and Judgment.
Then came they to him, and cried: "Thy son is dead,
Slain in a duel; but the bloom of life
Yet lingers round red lips and downy cheek."   10
Luca spoke not, but listen'd.   Next they bore
His dead son to the silent painting-room,
And left on tiptoe son and sire alone.
Still Luca spoke and groan'd not; but he rais'd
The wonderful dead youth, and smooth'd his hair,   15
Wash'd his red wounds, and laid him on a bed,
Naked and beautiful, where rosy curtains
Shed a soft glimmer of uncertain splendor
Lifelike upon the marble limbs below.

. 2. That is, the herald of Michael Angelo; Luca preceded Angelo, and
as an artist was like him in many ways. 6. *Duomo* means cáthedral;
the German word is *Dom;* our English *dome* is the same word, with a
changed meaning.

Then Luca seiz'd his palette: hour by hour   20
Silence was in the room; none durst approach:
Morn wore to noon, and noon to eve, when shyly
A little maid peep'd in, and saw the painter
Painting his dead son with unerring handstroke,
Firm and dry-ey'd before the lordly canvas.   25

What is the metre? What previous examples of it?

THE SELLING OF RHODOPÈ

WALTER SAVAGE LANDOR

Rhodopè. Never shall I forget the morning when my
father, sitting in the coolest part of the house, exchanged
his last measure of grain for a chlamys of scarlet cloth
fringed with silver. He watched the merchant out of
the door, and then looked wistfully into the corn chest. 5
I, who thought there was something worth seeing, looked
in also, and finding it empty, expressed my disappoint-
ment, not thinking, however, about the corn. A faint
and transient smile came over his countenance at the
sight of mine. He unfolded the chlamys, stretched it 10
out with both hands before me, and then cast it over my
shoulders. I looked down on the glittering fringe and
screamed with joy. He then went out; and I know not
what flowers he gathered, but he gathered many; and
some he placed in my bosom, and some in my hair. 15
But I told him with captious pride, first that I could
arrange them better, and again that I would have only
the white. However, when he had selected all the
white, and I had placed a few of them according to my

3. *chlamys* (a kind of cloak) is pronounced *clamis.*

fancy, I told him (rising in my slipper) he might crown 20
me with the remainder. The splendor of my apparel
gave me a sensation of authority. Soon as the flowers
had taken their station on my head, I expressed a dig-
nified satisfaction at the taste displayed by my father,
just as if I could have seen how they appeared! But he 25
knew that there was at least as much pleasure as pride
in it, and perhaps we divided the latter (alas! not both)
pretty equally. He now took me into the market place,
where a concourse of people was waiting for the purchase
of slaves. Merchants came and looked at me; some 30
commending, others disparaging; but all agreeing that I
was slender and delicate, that I could not live long, and
that I should give much trouble. Many would have
bought the chlamys, but there was something less salable
in the child and flowers.   35

Æsop. Had thy features been coarse, and thy voice
rustic, they would all have patted thy cheeks and found
no fault in thee.

Rhod. As it was, every one had bought exactly such
another in time past, and been a loser by it. At these 40
speeches I perceived the flowers tremble slightly on my
bosom, from my father's agitation. Although he scoffed
at them, knowing my healthiness, he was troubled inter-
nally, and said many short prayers, not very unlike
imprecations, turning his head aside. Proud was I, 45
prouder than ever, when at last several talents were
offered for me, and by the very man who, in the begin-
ning, had undervalued me the most, and prophesied the
worst of me. My father scowled at him and refused the
money. I thought he was playing a game, and began to 50
wonder what it could be, since I had never seen it
played before. Then I fancied it might be some cele-
bration because plenty had returned to the city, inso-

much that my father had bartered the last of the corn
he hoarded. I grew more and more delighted at the 55
sport. But soon there advanced an elderly man, who
said gravely: "Thou hast stolen this child: her vesture
alone is worth above a hundred drachmas. Carry her
home again to her parents, and do it directly, or Neme-
sis and the Eumenides will overtake thee." Knowing 60
the estimation in which my father had always been
holden by his fellow-citizens, I laughed again, and
pinched his ear. He, although naturally choleric, burst
forth into no resentment at these reproaches, but said
calmly, "I think I know thee by name, O guest! Surely 65
thou art Xanthus the Samian. Deliver this child from
famine."

Again I laughed aloud and heartily; and thinking it
was now my part of the game, I held out both my arms
and protruded my whole body towards the stranger. He 70
would not receive me from my father's neck, but he
asked me with benignity and solicitude if I was hungry;
at which I laughed again, and more than ever; for it
was early in the morning, soon after the first meal, and
my father had nourished me most carefully and plenti- 75 ·
fully in all the days of the famine. But Xanthus, wait-
ing for no answer, took out of a sack, which one of his
slaves carried at his side, a cake of wheaten bread and a
piece of honeycomb, and gave them to me. I held the
honeycomb to my father's mouth, thinking it the most 80
of a dainty. He dashed it to the ground; but seizing
the bread, he began to devour it ferociously. This,
also, I thought was in play; and I clapped my hands at
his distortions. But Xanthus looked on him like one

---

59. *Nemesis* was the Greek name for the avenging fate that follows
sin. The *Eumenides* were the Furies — goddesses whose duty was to hunt
down criminals.

afraid, and smote the cake from him, crying aloud, 85
"Name the price." My father now placed me in his
arms, naming a price much below what the other had·
offered, saying, "The gods are ever with thee, O Xan-
thus! therefore to thee do I consign my child." But
while Xanthus was counting out the silver, my father 90
seized the cake again, which the slave had taken up and
was about to replace in the wallet. His hunger was
exasperated by the taste and the delay. Suddenly there
arose much tumult. Turning round in the old woman's
bosom who had received me from Xanthus, I saw my 95
beloved father struggling on the ground, livid and
speechless. The more violent my cries, the more rap-
idly they hurried me away; and many were soon between
us. Little was I suspicious that he had suffered the
pangs of famine long before: alas! and he had suffered 100
them for me. Do I weep while I am telling you how
they ended? I could not have closed his eyes, I was too
young; but I might have received his last breath, the
only comfort of an orphan's bosom. Do you now think
him blamable, O Æsop? 105

Æs. It was sublime humanity: it was forbearance
and self-denial which even the immortal gods have never
shown us. He could endure to perish by those torments
which alone are both acute and slow; he could number
the steps of death and miss not one; but he could never 110
see thy tears, nor let thee see his. O weakness above
all fortitude! Glory to the man who rather bears a grief
corroding his breast, than permits it to prowl beyond,
and to prey on the tender and compassionate! Women
commiserate the brave, and men the beautiful. The 115
dominion of pity has usually this extent, no wider.
Thy father was exposed to the obloquy not only of the
malicious, but also of the ignorant and thoughtless, who

condemn in the unfortunate what they applaud in the
prosperous.   There is no shame in poverty or in slavery, 120
if we neither make ourselves poor by our improvidence
nor slaves by our venality.   The lowest and the highest
of the human race are sold: most of the intermediate
are also slaves, but slaves who bring no money into the
market.   125

Rhod.   Surely the great and powerful are never to be
purchased, are they?

Æs.   It may be a defect in my vision, but I cannot
see greatness on the earth.   What they tell me is great
and aspiring, to me seems little and crawling.   Let me 130
meet thy question with another.   What monarch gives
his daughter for nothing?   Either he receives stone
walls and unwilling cities in return, or he barters her for
a parcel of spears and horses and horsemen, waving
away from his declining and helpless age young joyous 135
life, and trampling down the freshest and sweetest
memories.   Midas, in the height of prosperity, would
have given his daughter to Sycaon, rather than to the
gentlest, the most virtuous, the most intelligent of his
subjects.   Thy father threw wealth aside, and, placing 140
thee under the protection of virtue, rose up from the
house of famine to partake in the festivals of the gods.
Release my neck, O Rhodopè! for I have other questions
to ask of thee about him.

Rhod.   To hear thee converse on him in such a 145
manner I can do even that.

Æs.   Before the day of separation was he never sor-
rowful?   Did he never by tears or silence reveal the
secret of his soul?

Rhod.   I was too infantine to perceive or imagine his 150
intention.   The night before I became the slave of
Xanthus, he sat on the edge of my bed.   I pretended

to be asleep: he moved away silently and softly. I saw
him collect in the hollow of his hand the crumbs I had
wasted on the floor, and then eat them, and then look 155
if any were remaining. I thought he did so out of
fondness for me, remembering that, even before the
famine, he had often swept up off the table the bread I
had broken, and had made me put it between his lips.
I would not dissemble very long, but said: —   160

"Come, now you have wakened me, you must sing
me asleep again, as you did when I was little."

He smiled faintly at this, and after some delay, when
he had walked up and down the chamber, thus began: —

"I will sing to thee one song more, my wakeful 165
Rhodopè! my chirping bird! over whom is no mother's
wing! That it may lull thee asleep. I will celebrate
no longer, as in the days of wine and plenteousness,
the glory of Mars, guiding in their invisibly rapid onset
the dappled steeds of Rhæsus. What hast thou to do, 170
my little one, with arrows tired of clustering in the
quiver? How much quieter is thy pallet than the tents
which whitened the plain of Simois! What knowest
thou about the river Eurotas? What knowest thou
about its ancient palace, once trodden by the assembled 175
gods, and then polluted by the Phrygians? What knowest
thou of perfidious men or of sanguinary deeds?

"Pardon me, O goddess who presidest in Cythera! I
am not irreverent to thee, but ever grateful. May she
upon whose brow I laid my hand praise and bless thee 180
for evermore.

"Ah yes! continue to hold up above the coverlet those
fresh and rosy palms clasped together; her benefits have

· 170. *Rhæsus* was a hero, mentioned in Homer's Iliad, who was famous
for his steeds, the gift of a god. 178. Mount *Cythera*, the favorite abode
of Venus.

descended on thy beauteous head, my child. The fates
also have sung beyond thy hearing, of pleasanter scenes 185
than the snow-fed Hebrus; of more than dim grottoes
and sky-bright waters. Even now a low murmur swells
upward to my ear; and not from the spindle comes the
sound, but from those who sing slowly over it, bending
all three their tremulous heads together. I wish thou 190
could'st hear it; for seldom are their voices so sweet.
Thy pillow intercepts the song perhaps, lie down again,
lie down, my Rhodopè — I will repeat what they are
saying : —

"'Happier shalt thou be, nor less glorious than even 195
she, the truly beloved, for whose return to the distaff
and the lyre, the portals of Tænarus flew open. In the
woody dells of Ismarus, and when she bathed among the
swans of Strymon, the nymphs called her Eurydice.
Thou shalt behold that fairest and that fondest one here- 200
after. But first thou must go unto the land of the lotos,
where famine never cometh, and where alone the works
of man are immortal.' O my child! the undeceiving
fates have uttered this. Other powers have visited me,
and have strengthened my heart with dreams and visions. 205
We shall meet again, my Rhodopè, in shady groves and
verdant meadows, and we shall sit by the side of those
who loved us."

He was rising: I threw my arms about his neck, and
before I would let him go, I made him promise to place 210
me, not by the side, but between them; for I thought
of her who had left us. At that time there were but
two, O Æsop! You ponder; you are about to reprove
my assurance in having thus repeated my own praises.

---

188. The *spindle* is that of the fates, the goddesses who spin the thread
of life and cut it.

I would have omitted some of the words, only that it 215
might have disturbed the measure and cadences, and
have put me out.   They are the very words my dearest
father sang; and they are the last.   Yet, shame upon
me! the nurse (the same who stood listening near, who
attended me into this country) could remember them 220
more perfectly; it is from her I have learned them since;
she often sings them, even by herself.

Æs.   So shall others.   There is much both in them
and in thee to render them memorable. . . .   The
dullest of mortals, seeing and hearing thee, would never 225
misinterpret the prophecy of the fates.   If, turning
back, I could overpass the vale of years, and could stand
on the mountain top, and could look again far before
me at the bright ascending morn, we could enjoy the
prospect together; we would walk along the summit 230
hand in hand, O Rhodopè! and we would only sigh at
last when we found ourselves below with others.

This exquisite prose will bear the closest reading.   Note its carefully
chosen poetic words, and its stately sentence-structure.

THE MERRY LARK

CHARLES KINGSLEY

The merry, merry lark was up and singing,
  And the hare was out and feeding on the lea,
And the merry, merry bells below were ringing,
  When my child's laugh rang through me.   4
Now the hare is snared and dead beside the snowyard,
  And the lark beside the dreary winter sea,
And my baby in his cradle in the churchyard
  Waiteth there until the bells bring me.

TWO SONS[1]

ROBERT BUCHANAN

I have two sons, wife —
　　Two, and yet the same;
　　One his wild way runs, wife,
　　　Bringing us to shame.
The one is bearded, sunburnt, grim, and fights across the
　　　　sea,　　　　　　　　　　　　　　　　　　　　5
The other is a little child who sits upon your knee.

　　One is fierce and cold, wife,
　　　As the wayward deep;
　　Him no arms could hold, wife,
　　　Him no breast could keep.　　　　　　　　　　　10
He has tried our hearts for many a year, not broken them;
　　　　for he
Is still the sinless little one that sits upon your knee.

　　One may fall in fight, wife —
　　　Is he not our son?
　　Pray with all your might, wife,　　　　　　　　　15
　　　For the wayward one;
Pray for the dark, rough soldier, who fights across the sea,
Because you love the little shade who smiles upon your
　　　　knee.

　　One across the foam, wife,
　　　As I speak may fall;　　　　　　　　　　　　　20
　　But this one at home, wife,
　　　Cannot die at all.
They both are only one; and how thankful should we be,
We cannot lose the darling son who sits upon your knee!

1 Reprinted by permission of Little, Brown, & Co.

SOHRAB AND RUSTUM

AN EPISODE

MATTHEW ARNOLD

And the first gray of morning filled the east,
And the fog rose out of the Oxus stream.
But all the Tartar camp along the stream
Was hushed, and still·the men were plunged in sleep;
Sohrab alone, he slept not; all night long   5
He had lain wakeful, tossing on his bed;
But when the gray dawn stole into his tent,
He rose, and clad himself, and girt his sword,
And took his horseman's cloak, and left his tent,
And went abroad into the cold wet fog,   10
Through the dim camp to Peran-Wisa's tent.

    Through the black Tartar tents he passed, which stood
Clustering like beehives on the low flat strand
Of Oxus, where the summer floods o'erflow
When the sun melts the snows in high Pamere;   15
Through the black tents he passed, o'er that low strand,
And to a hillock came, a little back
From the stream's brink — the spot where first a boat,
Crossing the stream in summer, scrapes the land.
The men of former times had crowned the top   20
With a clay fort; but that was fall'n, and now
The Tartars built there Peran-Wisa's tent,
A dome of laths, and o'er it felts were spread.
And Sohrab came there, and went in, and stood
Upon the thick piled carpets in the tent,   25
And found the old man sleeping on his bed

          11. *Wisa* — the *i* is pronounced like *e*.

Of rugs and felts, and near him lay his arms.
And Peran-Wisa heard him, though the step
Was dulled; for he slept light, an old man's sleep;
And he rose quickly on one arm, and said:— 30
"Who art thou? for it is not yet clear dawn.
Speak! is there news, or any night alarm?"
But Sohrab came to the bedside, and said:
"Thou know'st me, Peran-Wisa! it is I.
The sun is not yet risen, and the foe 35
Sleep; but I sleep not; all night long I lie
Tossing and wakeful, and I come to thee.
For so did King Afrasiab bid me seek
Thy counsel, and to heed thee as thy son,
In Samarcand, before the army marched; 40
And I will tell thee what my heart desires.
Thou know'st if, since from Ader-baijan first
I came among the Tartars and bore arms,
I have still served Afrasiab well, and shown,
At my boy's years, the courage of a man. 45
This too thou know'st, that while I still bear on
The conquering Tartar ensigns through the world,
And beat the Persians back on every field,
I seek one man, one man, and one alone—
Rustum, my father; who I hoped should greet, 50
Should one day greet, upon some well-fought field,
His not unworthy, not inglorious son.
So I long hoped, but him I never find.
Come then, hear now, and grant me what I ask.
Let the two armies rest to-day; but I 55
Will challenge forth the bravest Persian lords
To meet me, man to man; if I prevail,
Rustum will surely hear it; if I fall—
Old man, the dead need no one, claim no kin.

42. *Ader-baijan*—the *j* is pronounced like *y*.

Dim is the rumor of a common fight,   60
Where host meet host, and many names are sunk;
But of a single combat fame speaks clear."
    He spoke; and Peran-Wisa took the hand
Of the young man in his, and sighed, and said:
    "O Sohrab, an unquiet heart is thine!   65
Canst thou not rest among the Tartar chiefs,
And share the battle's common chance with us
Who love thee, but must press forever first,
In single fight incurring single risk,
To find a father thou hast never seen?   70
That were far best, my son, to stay with us
Unmurmuring; in our tents, while it is war,
And when 'tis truce, then in Afrasiab's towns.
But, if this one desire indeed rules all,
To seek out Rustum — seek him not through fight!   75
Seek him in peace, and carry to his arms,
O Sohrab, carry an unwounded son!
    But far hence seek him, for he is not here.
For now it is not as when I was young,
When Rustum was in front of every fray;   80
But now he keeps apart, and sits at home,
In Seistan, with Zal, his father old.
Whether that his own mighty strength at last
Feels the abhorred approaches of old age,
Or in some quarrel with the Persian King.   85
There go! — thou wilt not?   Yet my heart forebodes
Danger or death awaits thee on this field.
Fain would I know thee safe and well, though lost
To us; fain therefore send thee hence, in peace
To seek thy father, not seek single fights   90
In vain; — but who can keep the lion's cub
From ravening, and who govern Rustum's son?
Go, I will grant thee what thy heart desires."

So said he, and dropped Sohrab's hand, and left
His bed, and the warm rugs whereon he lay;   95
And o'er his chilly limbs his woollen coat
He passed, and tied his sandals on his feet,
And threw a white cloak round him, and he took
In his right hand a ruler's staff, no sword;
And on his head he set his sheepskin cap,   100
Black, glossy, curled, the fleece of Kara-Kul;
And raised the curtain of his tent, and called
His herald to his side, and went abroad.

    The sun by this had risen, and cleared the fog
From the broad Oxus and the glittering sands.   105
And from their tents the Tartar horsemen filed
Into the open plain; so Haman bade —
Haman, who next to Peran-Wisa ruled
The host, and still was in his lusty prime.
From their black tents, long files of horse, they streamed;   110
As when some gray November morn the files,
In marching order spread, of long-necked cranes
Stream over Casbin and the southern slopes
Of Elburz, from the Aralian estuaries,
Or some frore Caspian reed-bed, southward bound   115
For the warm Persian seaboard — so they streamed.
The Tartars of the Oxus, the King's guard,
First, with black sheepskin caps and with long spears;

94–103. This is in imitation of Homer. 111–116. This is what is called an Homeric simile. The mark of it is the poet's drifting away from the exact point of the comparison to other details where the comparison does not hold. The horses were in files, like cranes; but the horses were not moving over Casbin, etc., to the Persian seaboard. 115. *frore* means frozen. To emphasize a description of cold, Milton uses the phrase "burned frore." 116–135. This enumeration is in imitation of Homer. Poetic enumeration had much interest to the old Greek audiences, whose tribes and ancestors were included. It has some interest for modern readers, giving a notion of vast numbers, and many incidental touches of picturesqueness.

s

Large men, large steeds; who from Bokhara come
And Khiva, and ferment the milk of mares.   120
Next, the more temperate Toorkmuns of the south,
The Tukas, and the lances of Salore,
And those from Attruck and the Caspian sands;
Light men and on light steeds, who only drink
The acrid milk of camels, and their wells.   125
And then a swarm of wandering horse, who came
From far, and a more doubtful service owned;
The Tartars of Ferghana, from the banks
Of the Jaxartes, men with scanty beards
And close-set skullcaps; and those wilder hordes   130
Who roam o'er Kipchak and the northern waste,
Kalmucks and unkempt Kuzzaks, tribes who stray
Nearest the Pole, and wandering Kirghizzes,
Who come on shaggy ponies from Pamere;
These all filed out from camp into the plain.   135
And on the other side the Persians formed; —
First a light cloud of horse, Tartars they seemed,
The Ilyats of Khorassan; and behind,
The royal troops of Persia, horse and foot,
Marshalled battalions bright in burnished steel.   140
But Peran-Wisa with his herald came,
Threading the Tartar squadrons to the front,
And with his staff kept back the foremost ranks.
And when Ferood, who led the Persians, saw
That Peran-Wisa kept the Tartars back,   145
He took his spear, and to the front he came,
And checked his ranks, and fixed them where they stood.
And the old Tartar came upon the sand
Betwixt the silent hosts, and spake, and said:
   "Ferood, and ye, Persians and Tartars, hear!   150
Let there be truce between the hosts to-day.
But choose a champion from the Persian lords

To fight our champion Sohrab, man to man."
    As, in the country, on a morn in June,
When the dew glistens on the pearled ears,   155
A shiver runs through the deep corn for joy —
So, when they heard what Peran-Wisa said,
A thrill through all the Tartar squadrons ran
Of pride and hope for Sohrab, whom they loved.
    But as a troop of pedlers, from Cabool,   160
Cross underneath the Indian Caucasus,
That vast sky-neighboring mountain of milk snow;
Crossing so high, that, as they mount, they pass
Long flocks of travelling birds dead on the snow,
Choked by the air, and scarce can they themselves   165
Slake their parched throats with sugared mulberries —
In single file they move, and stop their breath,
For fear they should dislodge the o'erhanging snows —
So the pale Persians held their breath with fear.
    And to Ferood his brother chiefs came up   170
To counsel; Gudurz and Zoarrah came,
And Feraburz, who ruled the Persian hosts
Second, and was the uncle of the King;
These came and counselled, and then Gudurz said:
    "Ferood, shame bids us take their challenge up,   175
Yet champion have we none to match this youth.
He has the wild stag's foot, the lion's heart.
But Rustum came last night; aloof he sits
And sullen, and has pitched his tents apart.
Him will I seek, and carry to his ear   180
The Tartar challenge, and this young man's name.
Haply he will forget his wrath, and fight.
Stand forth the while, and take their challenge up."

160–169. A very fine Homeric simile, but without a counterpart in
Homer. 166. *sugared mulberries* of course does not mean fresh mul-
berries, though all mulberries are excessively sweet.

So spake he; and Ferood stood forth and cried:
"Old man, be it agreed as thou hast said!   185
Let Sohrab arm, and we will find a man."
He spake: and Peran-Wisa turned, and strode
Back through the opening squadrons to his tent.
But through the anxious Persians Gudurz ran,
And crossed the camp which lay behind, and reached,   190
Out on the sands beyond it, Rustum's tents.
Of scarlet cloth they were, and glittering gay,
Just pitched; the high pavilion in the midst
Was Rustum's, and his men lay camped around.
And Gudurz entered Rustum's tent, and found   195
Rustum; his morning meal was done, but still
The table stood before him, charged with food —
A side of roasted sheep, and cakes of bread,
And dark-green melons; and there Rustum sate
Listless, and held a falcon on his wrist,   200
And played with it; but Gudurz came and stood
Before him; and he looked, and saw him stand,
And with a cry sprang up and dropped the bird,
And greeted Gudurz with both hands, and said:
"Welcome! these eyes could see no better sight.   205
What news? but sit down first, and eat and drink."
But Gudurz stood in the tent door, and said:
"Not now! a time will come to eat and drink,
But not to-day; to-day has other needs.
The armies are drawn out, and stand at gaze;   210
For from the Tartars is a challenge brought
To pick a champion from the Persian lords
To fight their champion — and thou know'st his name —
Sohrab men call him, but his birth is hid.
O Rustum, like thy might is this young man's!   215
He has the wild stag's foot, the lion's heart;
And he is young, and Iran's chiefs are old,

Or else too weak; and all eyes turn to thee. .
Come down and help us, Rustum, or we lose!"
    He spoke; but Rustum answered with a smile: 220
"Go to! if Iran's chiefs are old, then I
Am older; if the young are weak, the King
Errs strangely; for the King, for Kai Khosroo,
Himself is young, and honors younger men
And lets the aged moulder to their graves.   225
Rustum he loves no more, but loves the young —
The young may rise at Sohrab's vaunts, not I.
For what care I, though all speak Sohrab's fame?
For would that I myself had such a son,
And not that one slight helpless girl I have —   230
A son so famed, so brave, to send to war,
And I to tarry with the snow-haired Zal,
My father, whom the robber Afghans vex,
And clip his borders short, and drive his herds,
And he has none to guard his weak old age.   235
There would I go, and hang my armor up,
And with my great name fence that weak old man,
And spend the goodly treasures I have got,
And rest my age, and hear of Sohrab's fame,
And leave to death the hosts of thankless kings,   240
And with these slaughterous hands draw sword no
     more."
    He spoke, and smiled; and Gudurz made reply:
"What then, O Rustum, will men say to this,
When Sohrab dares our bravest forth, and seeks
Thee most of all, and thou, whom most he seeks,   245
Hidest thy face?   Take heed lest men should say:
'Like some old miser, Rustum hoards his fame,
And shuns to peril it with younger men.' "
    And, greatly moved, then Rustum made reply:
"O Gudurz, wherefore dost thou say such words?   250

Thou knowest better words than this to say.
What is one more, one less, obscure or famed,
Valiant or craven, young or old, to me?
Are not they mortal, am not I myself?
But who for men of naught would do great deeds?   255
Come, thou shalt see how Rustum hoards his fame!
But I will fight unknown, and in plain arms;
Let not men say of Rustum, he was matched
In single fight with any mortal man."
 He spoke, and frowned; and Gudurz turned, and
  ran   260
Back quickly through the camp in fear and joy —
Fear at his wrath, but joy that Rustum came.
But Rustum strode to his tent door, and called
His followers in, and bade them bring his arms,
And clad himself in steel; the arms he chose   265
Were plain, and on his shield was no device,
Only his helm was rich, inlaid with gold,
And, from the fluted spine atop, a plume
Of horsehair waved, a scarlet horsehair plume.
So armed, he issued forth; and Ruksh, his horse,   270
Followed him like a faithful hound at heel —
Ruksh, whose renown was noised through all the earth,
The horse, whom Rustum on a foray once
Did in Bokhara by the river find
A colt beneath its dam, and drove him home,   275
And reared him; a bright bay, with lofty crest,
Dight with a saddlecloth of broidered green
Crusted with gold, and on the ground were worked
All beasts of chase, all beasts which hunters know.
So followed, Rustum left his tents, and crossed   280
The camp, and to the Persian host appeared.
And all the Persians knew him, and with shouts
Hailed; but the Tartars knew not who he was.

And dear as the wet diver to the eyes
Of his pale wife who waits and weeps on shore,   285
By sandy Bahrein, in the Persian Gulf,
Plunging all day in the blue waves, at night,
Having made up his tale of precious pearls,
Rejoins her in their hut upon the sands —
So dear to the pale Persians Rustum came.   290
    And Rustum to the Persian front advanced,
And Sohrab armed in Haman's tent, and came.
And as afield the reapers cut a swath
Down through the middle of a rich man's corn,
And on each side are squares of standing corn,   295
And in the midst a stubble, short and bare —
So on each side were squares of men, with spears
Bristling, and in the midst, the open sand.
And Rustum came upon the sand, and cast
His eyes toward the Tartar tents, and saw   300
Sohrab come forth, and eyed him as he came.
    As some rich woman, on a winter's morn,
Eyes through her silken curtains the poor drudge
Who with numb blackened fingers makes her fire —
At cockcrow, on a starlit winter's morn,   305
When the frost flowers the whitened window-panes —
And wonders how she lives, and what the thoughts
Of that poor drudge may be; so Rustum eyed
The unknown adventurous youth, who from afar
Came seeking Rustum, and defying forth   310
All the most valiant chiefs; long he perused

284. The simile is perhaps suggested by Homer, 701–708, where Paris and Hector are as dear to the eyes of their despairing comrades as a favorable wind to sailors becalmed. 286. *Bahrein* — the last syllable is like *rain*. 288. *tale* means reckoning. Thus Milton's shepherd "tells his tale" — that is, counts his sheep. Probably the King James translators did not mean by tale a "story," when they wrote, "We spend our days as a tale that is told."

His spirited air, and wondered who he was.
For very young he seemed, tenderly reared;
Like some young cypress, tall, and dark, and straight,
Which in a queen's secluded garden throws   315
Its slight dark shadow on the moonlit turf,
By midnight, to a bubbling fountain's sound —
So slender Sohrab seemed, so softly reared.
And a deep pity entered Rustum's soul
As he beheld him coming; and he stood,   320
And beckoned to him with his hand, and said:
    "O thou young man, the air of heaven is soft,
And warm, and pleasant; but the grave is cold!
Heaven's air is better than the cold dead grave.
Behold me! I am vast, and clad in iron,   325
And tried; and I have stood on many a field
Of blood, and I have fought with many a foe —
Never was that field lost, or that foe saved.
O Sohrab, wherefore wilt thou rush on death?
Be governed! quit the Tartar host, and come   330
To Iran, and be as my son to me,
And fight beneath my banner till I die!
There are no youths in Iran brave as thou."
    So he spake, mildly; Sohrab heard his voice,
The mighty voice of Rustum, and he saw   335
His giant figure planted on the sand,
Sole, like some single tower, which a chief
Hath builded on the waste in former years
Against the robbers; and he saw that head,
Streaked with its first gray hairs; — hope filled his soul, 340
And he ran forward and embraced his knees,
And clasped his hand within his own, and said:
    "Oh, by thy father's head! by thine own soul!
Art thou not Rustum? speak! art thou not he?"
    But Rustum eyed askance the kneeling youth,   345

And turned away, and spake to his own soul:
"Ah me, I muse what this young fox may mean!
False, wily, boastful, are these Tartar boys.
For if I now confess this thing he asks,
And hide it not, but say: 'Rustum is here!'   350
He will not yield indeed, nor quit our foes,
But he will find some pretext not to fight,
And praise my fame, and proffer courteous gifts,
A belt or sword perhaps, and go his way.
And on a feast-tide, in Afrasiab's hall,   355
In Samarcand, he will arise and cry:
'I challenged once, when the two armies camped
Beside the Oxus, all the Persian lords
To cope with me in single fight; but they
Shrank, only Rustum dared; then he and I   360
Changed gifts, and went on equal terms away.'
So will he speak, perhaps, while men applaud;
Then were the chiefs of Iran shamed through me."
    And then he turned, and sternly spake aloud:
"Rise! wherefore dost thou vainly question thus   365
Of Rustum? I am here, whom thou hast called
By challenge forth; make good thy vaunt, or yield!
Is it with Rustum only thou wouldst fight?
Rash boy, men look on Rustum's face and flee!
For well I know, that did great Rustum stand   370
Before thy face this day, and were revealed,
There would be then no talk of fighting more.
But being what I am, I tell thee this —
Do thou record it in thine inmost soul:
Either thou shalt renounce thy vaunt and yield,   375
Or else thy bones shall strew this sand, till winds
Bleach them, or Oxus with his summer floods,
Oxus in summer wash them all away."
    He spoke; and Sohrab answered, on his feet:

"Art thou so fierce?   Thou wilt not fright me so!   380
I am no girl, to be made pale by words.
Yet this thou hast said well, did Rustum stand
Here on this field, there were no fighting then.
But Rustum is far hence, and we stand here.
Begin! thou art more vast, more dread than I,   385
And thou art proved, I know, and I am young.
But yet success sways with the breath of heaven.
And though thou thinkest that thou knowest sure
Thy victory, yet thou canst not surely know.
For we are all, like swimmers in the sea,   390
Poised on the top of a huge wave of fate,
Which hangs uncertain to which side to fall.
And whether it will heave us up to land,
Or whether it will roll us out to sea,
Back out to sea, to the deep waves of death,   395
We know not, and no search will make us know;
Only the event will teach us in its hour."

He spoke, and Rustum answered not, but hurled
His spear; down from the shoulder, down it came,
As on some partridge in the corn a hawk,   400
That long has towered in the airy clouds,
Drops like a plummet; Sohrab saw it come,
And sprang aside, quick as a flash; the spear
Hissed, and went quivering down into the sand,
Which it sent flying wide; — then Sohrab threw   405
In turn, and full struck Rustum's shield; sharp rang,
The iron plates rang sharp, but turned the spear.
And Rustum seized his club, which none but he
Could wield; an unlopped trunk it was, and huge,

390–397. This strong simile of fate is Arnold's own. Though the
Greeks thought much on fate, the Persians thought of it still more.
408 ff. The description is suggested by Homer's description of Achilles'
spear, Iliad 19. 388 ff.

Still rough — like those which men in treeless plains   410
To build them boats fish from the flooded rivers,
Hyphasis or Hydaspes, when, high up
By their dark springs, the wind in winter time
Hath made in Himalayan forests wrack,
And strewn the channels with torn boughs — so huge   415
The club which Rustum lifted now, and struck
One stroke; but again Sohrab sprang aside,
Lithe as the glancing snake, and the club came
Thundering to earth, and leapt from Rustum's hand.
And Rustum followed his own blow, and fell   420
To his knees, and with his fingers clutched the sand;
And now might Sohrab have unsheathed his sword,
And pierced the mighty Rustum while he lay
Dizzy, and on his knees, and choked with sand;
But he looked on, and smiled, nor bared his sword,   425
But courteously drew back, and spoke, and said:
   "Thou strik'st too hard! that club of thine will float
Upon the summer floods, and not my bones.
But rise, and be not wroth! not wroth am I;
No, when I see thee, wrath forsakes my soul,   430
Thou say'st, thou art not Rustum; be it so!
Who art thou then, that canst so touch my soul.
Boy as I am, I have seen battles too —
Have waded foremost in their bloody waves,
And heard their hollow roar of dying men;   435
But never was my heart thus touched before.
Are they from Heaven, these softenings of the heart?
O thou old warrior, let us yield to Heaven!
Come, plant we here in earth our angry spears,
And make a truce, and sit upon this sand,   440
And pledge each other in red wine, like friends,
And thou shalt talk to me of Rustum's deeds.
There are enough foes in the Persian host,

Whom I may meet, and strike, and feel no pang;
Champions enough Afrasiab has, whom thou   445
Mayst fight; fight *them*, when they confront thy spear!
But oh, let there be peace 'twixt thee and me!"
    He ceased, but while he spake, Rustum had risen,
And stood erect, trembling with rage; his club
He left to lie, but had regained his spear,   450
Whose fiery point now in his mailed right hand
Blazed bright and baleful, like that autumn star,
The baleful sign of fevers; dust had soiled
His stately crest, and dimmed his glittering arms.
His breast heaved, his lips foamed, and twice his voice 455
Was choked with rage; at last these words broke way:
    "Girl! nimble with thy feet, not with thy hands!
Curled minion, dancer, coiner of sweet words!
Fight, let me hear thy hateful voice no more!
Thou art not in Afrasiab's gardens now   460
With Tartar girls, with whom thou art wont to dance;
But on the Oxus sands, and in the dance
Of battle, and with me, who make no play
Of war; I fight it out, and hand to hand.
Speak not to me of truce, and pledge, and wine!   465
Remember all thy valor; try thy feints
And cunning! all the pity I had is gone;
Because thou hast shamed me before both the hosts
With thy light skipping tricks, and thy girl's wiles."
    He spoke, and Sohrab kindled at his taunts,   470
And he too drew his sword; at once they rushed
Together, as two eagles on one prey

457-479. The fierce heat of such lines as these must not be over-
looked by those who think of Arnold as a "cold" poet.   472-473. Here is
a simile taken from Homer, but it is not Homeric in the sense mentioned
above. Neither Homer nor his modern imitator could take time to let his
mind stray from the struggle.

Come rushing down together from the clouds,
One from the east, one from the west; their shield.
Dashed with a clang together, and a din   475
Rose, such as that the sinewy woodcutters
Make often in the forest's heart at morn,
Of hewing axes, crashing trees — such blows
Rustum and Sohrab on each other hailed.
And you would say that sun and stars took part   480
In that unnatural conflict; for a cloud
Grew suddenly in heaven, and darkened the sun
Over the fighters' heads; and a wind rose
Under their feet, and moaning swept the plain,
And in a sandy whirlwind wrapped the pair.   485
In gloom they twain were wrapped, and they alone;
For both the on-looking hosts on either hand
Stood in broad daylight, and the sky was pure,
And the sun sparkled on the Oxus stream.
But in the gloom they fought, with bloodshot eyes   490
And laboring breath; first Rustum struck the shield
Which Sohrab held stiff out; the steel-spiked spear
Rent the tough plates, but failed to reach the skin,
And Rustum plucked it back with angry groan.
Then Sohrab with his sword smote Rustum's helm,   495
Nor clove its steel quite through; but all the crest
He shore away, and that proud horsehair plume,
Never till now defiled, sank to the dust;
And Rustum bowed his head; but then the gloom
Grew blacker, thunder rumbled in the air,   500
And lightnings rent the cloud; and Ruksh, the horse,
Who stood at hand, uttered a dreadful cry; —
No horse's cry was that, most like the roar

501. Do you remember the terrible cry of the wolf-hunted horses in "The Last of the Mohicans," Chapter VI.? It frightened even Hawkeye.

Of some pained desert lion, who all day
Hath trailed the hunter's javelin in his side,   505
And comes at night to die upon the sand.
The two hosts heard that cry, and quaked for fear,
And Oxus curdled as it crossed his stream.
But Sohrab heard, and quailed not, but rushed on,
And struck again; and again Rustum bowed   510
His head; but this time all the blade, like glass,
Sprang in a thousand shivers on the helm,
And in the hand the hilt remained alone.
Then Rustum raised his head; his dreadful eyes
Glared, and he shook on high his menacing spear,   515
And shouted: "Rustum!" — Sohrab heard that shout,
And shrank amazed: back he recoiled one step,
And scanned with blinking eyes the advancing form;
And then he stood bewildered; and he dropped
His covering shield, and the spear pierced his side.   520
He reeled, and, staggering back, sank to the ground;
And then the gloom dispersed, and the wind fell,
And the bright sun broke forth, and melted all
The cloud; and the two armies saw the pair —
Saw Rustum standing, safe upon his feet,   525
And Sohrab, wounded, on the bloody sand.
    Then, with a bitter smile, Rustum began:
"Sohrab, thou thoughtest in thy mind to kill
A Persian lord this day, and strip his corpse,
And bear thy trophies to Afrasiab's tent;   530
Or else that the great Rustum would come down
Himself to fight, and that thy wiles would move
His heart to take a gift, and let thee go;
And then that all the Tartar host would praise
Thy courage or thy craft, and spread thy fame,   535
To glad thy father in his weak old age.
Fool, thou art slain, and by an unknown man!

Dearer to the red jackals shalt thou be
Than to thy friends, and to thy father old."
   And, with a fearless mien, Sohrab replied: 540
"Unknown thou art; yet thy fierce vaunt is vain.
Thou dost not slay me, proud and boastful man!
No! Rustum slays me, and this filial heart.
For were I matched with ten such men as thee,
And I were that which till to-day I was,   545
They should be lying here, I standing there.
But that belovéd name unnerved my arm —
That name, and something, I confess, in thee,
Which troubles all my heart, and made my shield
Fall; and thy spear transfixed an unarmed foe.   550
And now thou boastest, and insult'st my fate.
But hear thou this, fierce man, tremble to hear:
The mighty Rustum shall avenge my death!
My father, whom I seek through all the world,
He shall avenge my death, and punish thee!"   555
   As when some hunter in the spring hath found
A breeding eagle sitting on her nest,
Upon the craggy isle of a hill lake,
And pierced her with an arrow as she rose,
And followed her to find her where she fell   560
Far off; — anon her mate comes winging back
From hunting, and a great way off descries
His huddling young left sole; at that, he checks
His pinion, and with short uneasy sweeps
Circles above his eyry, with loud screams   565
Chiding his mate back to her nest; but she
Lies dying, with the arrow in her side,
In some far stony gorge out of his ken,

556–575. Arnold has not forgotten the eagle and its poetic possibilities;
now the time has come for him to let his fancy run, and how good is the
result! This simile is not in Homer.

A heap of fluttering feathers — never more
Shall the lake glass her, flying over it;   570
Never the black and dripping precipices
Echo her stormy scream as she sails by —
As that poor bird flies home, nor knows his loss,
So Rustum knew not his own loss, but stood
Over his dying son, and knew him not.   575
    But, with a cold incredulous voice, he said:
"What prate is this of fathers and revenge?
The mighty Rustum never had a son."
    And, with a failing voice, Sohrab replied:
"Ah yes, he had! and that lost son am I.   580
Surely the news will one day reach his ear,
Reach Rustum, where he sits, and tarries long,
Somewhere, I know not where, but far from here;
And pierce him like a stab, and make him leap
To arms, and cry for vengeance upon thee.   585
Fierce man, bethink thee, for an only son!
What will that grief, what will that vengeance be?
Oh, could I live till I that grief had seen!
Yet him I pity not so much, but her,
My mother, who in Ader-baijan dwells   590
With that old king, her father, who grows gray
With age, and rules over the valiant Koords.
Her most I pity, who no more will see
Sohrab returning from the Tartar camp,
With spoils and honor, when the war is done.   595
But a dark rumor will be bruited up,
From tribe to tribe, until it reach her ear;
And then will that defenceless woman learn
That Sohrab will rejoice her sight no more,
But that in battle with a nameless foe,   600
By the far-distant Oxus, he is slain."
    He spoke; and as he ceased, he wept aloud,

Thinking of her he left, and his own death.
He spoke; but Rustum listened, plunged in thought.
Nor did he yet believe it was his son   605
Who spoke, although he called back names he knew;
For he had had sure tidings that the babe,
Which was in Ader-baijan born to him,
Had been a puny girl, no boy at all —
So that sad mother sent him word, for fear   610
Rustum should seek the boy, to train in arms.
And so he deemed that either Sohrab took,
By a false boast, the style of Rustum's son;
Or that men gave it him, to swell his fame.
So deemed he: yet he listened, plunged in thought;   615
And his soul set to grief, as the vast tide
Of the bright rocking Ocean sets to shore
At the full moon; tears gathered in his eyes;
For he remembered his own early youth,
And all its bounding rapture; as, at dawn,   620
The shepherd from his mountain lodge descries
A far, bright city, smitten by the sun,
Through many rolling clouds — so Rustum saw
His youth; saw Sohrab's mother, in her bloom;
And that old king, her father, who loved well   625
His wandering guest, and gave him his fair child
With joy; and all the pleasant life they led,
They three, in that long-distant summer time —
The castle, and the dewy woods, and hunt
And hound, and morn on those delightful hills   630
In Ader-baijan.   And he saw that youth,
Of age and looks to be his own dear son,
Piteous and lovely, lying on the sand,

620–624. The tone of this exquisite simile is more modern than Homer
and yet is antique in its bright simplicity.

T

Like some rich hyacinth which by the scythe
Of an unskilful gardener has been cut,   635
Mowing the garden grassplots near its bed,
And lies, a fragrant tower of purple bloom,
On the mown, dying grass — so Sohrab lay,
Lovely in death, upon the common sand.
And Rustum gazed on him with grief, and said: 640
    "O Sohrab, thou indeed art such a son ·
Whom Rustum, wert thou his, might well have loved!
Yet here thou errest, Sohrab, or else men
Have told thee false — thou art not Rustum's son.
For Rustum had no son; one child he had —   645
But one — a girl; who with her mother now
Plies some light female task, nor dreams of us —
Of us she dreams not, nor of wounds, nor war."
    But Sohrab answered him in wrath; for now
The anguish of the deep-fixed spear grew fierce,   650
And he desired to draw forth the steel,
And let the blood flow free, and so to die —
But first he would convince his stubborn foe;
And, rising sternly on one arm, he said:
    "Man, who art thou who dost deny my words?   655
Truth sits upon the lips of dying men,
And falsehood, while I lived, was far from mine.
I tell thee, pricked upon this arm I bear
The seal which Rustum to my mother gave,
That she might prick it on the babe she bore."   660
    He spoke; and all the blood left Rustum's cheeks,
And his knees tottered, and he smote his hand
Against his breast, his heavy mailed hand,

634–639. Homer likens a slain youth to a drooping poppy, but he would
have thought it fanciful and over-elaborate to call a hyacinth "a tower of
purple bloom." How good "common sand" is, contrasted with the deli-
cate fairness of the dead boy!

That the hard iron corselet clanked aloud;
And to his heart he pressed the other hand,   665
And in a hollow voice he spake, and said:
  "Sohrab, that were a proof which could not lie!
If thou show this, then art thou Rustum's son."
  Then, with weak hasty fingers, Sohrab loosed
His belt, and near the shoulder bared his arm,   670
And showed a sign in faint vermilion points
Pricked; as a cunning workman, in Pekin,
Pricks with vermilion some clear porcelain vase,
An emperor's gift — at early morn he paints,
And all day long, and, when night comes, the lamp   675
Lights up his studious forehead and thin hands —
So delicately pricked the sign appeared
On Sohrab's arm, the sign of Rustum's seal.
It was that griffin, which of old reared Zal,
Rustum's great father, whom they left to die,   680
A helpless babe, among the mountain rocks;
Him that kind creature found and reared, and loved —
Then Rustum took it for his glorious sign.
And Sohrab bared that image on his arm,
And himself scanned it long with mournful eyes,   685
And then he touched it with his hand, and said:
  "How say'st thou? Is that sign the proper sign
Of Rustum's son, or of some other man's?"
  He spoke; but Rustum gazed, and gazed, and stood
Speechless; and then he uttered one sharp cry: 690
"O boy — thy father!" — and his voice choked there.
And then a dark cloud passed before his eyes,
And his head swam, and he sank down to earth.
But Sohrab crawled to where he lay, and cast

669-678. This lovely simile has a phrase or two from Homer, and is
Homeric in its straying from the point; but the beautiful conception is
Arnold's own.

His arms about his neck, and kissed his lips, 695
And with fond faltering fingers stroked his cheeks,
Trying to call him back to life; and life
Came back to Rustum, and he oped his eyes,
And they stood wide with horror; and he seized
In both his hands the dust which lay around, 700
And threw it on his head, and smirched his hair, —
His hair, and face, and beard, and glittering arms;
And strong convulsive groanings shook his breast,
And his sobs choked him; and he clutched his sword,
To draw it, and forever let life out. 705
But Sohrab saw his thought, and held his hands,
And with a soothing voice he spake, and said:
"Father, forbear! for I but meet to-day
The doom which at my birth was written down
In heaven, and thou art heaven's unconscious hand. 710
Surely my heart cried out that it was thou,
When first I saw thee; and thy heart spoke too,
I know it! but fate trod those promptings down
Under its iron heel; fate, fate engaged
The strife, and hurled me on my father's spear. 715
But let us speak no more of this! I find
My father; let me feel that I have found!
Come, sit beside me on this sand, and take
My head betwixt thy hands, and kiss my cheeks,
And wash them with thy tears, and say: 'My son!' 720
Quick! quick! for numbered are my sands of life,
And swift; for like the lightning to this field
I came, and like the wind I go away —
Sudden, and swift, and like a passing wind.
But it was writ in heaven that this should be." 725
So said he, and his voice released the heart
Of Rustum, and his tears broke forth; he cast
His arms round his son's neck, and wept aloud,

And kissed him.   And awe fell on both the hosts,
When they saw Rustum's grief; and Ruksh, the horse,   730
With his head bowing to the ground and mane
Sweeping the dust, came near, and in mute woe
First to the one then to the other moved
His head, as if inquiring what their grief
Might mean; and from his dark, compassionate eyes,   735
The big warm tears rolled down, and caked the sand.
But Rustum chid him with stern voice, and said:
    "Ruksh, now thou grievest; but, O Ruksh, thy feet ·
Should first have rotted on their nimble joints,
Or ere they brought thy master to this field!"   740
    But Sohrab looked upon the horse, and said:
"Is this, then, Ruksh?   How often, in past days,
My mother told me of thee, thou brave steed,
My terrible father's terrible horse! and said,
That I should one day find thy lord and thee.   745
Come, let me lay my hand upon thy mane!
O Ruksh, thou art more fortunate than I;
For thou hast gone where I shall never go,
And snuffed the breezes of my father's home.
And thou hast trod the sands of Seistan,   750
And seen the River of Helmund, and the Lake
Of Zirrah; and the aged Zal himself
Has often stroked thy neck, and given thee food,
Corn in a golden platter, soaked with wine,
And said: 'O Ruksh! bear Rustum well,' — but I   755
Have never known my grandsire's furrowed face,
Nor seen his lofty house in Seistan,
Nor slaked my thirst at the clear Helmund stream;
But lodged among my father's foes, and seen
Afrasiab's cities only, Samarcand,   760
Bokhara, and lone Khiva in the waste,
And the black Toorkmun tents; and only drunk

The desert rivers, Moorghab and Tejend,
Kohik, and where the Kalmuks feed their sheep,
The northern Sir; and this great Oxus stream,   765
The yellow Oxus, by whose brink I die."
    Then, with a heavy groan, Rustum bewailed:
"Oh, that its waves were flowing over me!
Oh, that I saw its grains of yellow silt
Roll tumbling in the current o'er my head!"   770
    But, with a grave mild voice, Sohrab replied:
"Desire not that, my father! thou must live.
For some are born to do great deeds, and live,
As some are born to be obscured, and die.
Do thou the deeds I die too young to do,   775
And reap a second glory in thine age;
Thou art my father, and thy gain is mine.
But come! thou seest this great host of men
Which follow me; I pray thee, slay not these!
Let me entreat for them; what have they done?   780
They followed me, my hope, my fame, my star.
Let them all cross the Oxus back in peace.
But me thou must bear hence, not send with them,
But carry me with thee to Seistan,
And place me on a bed, and mourn for me,   785
Thou, and the snow-haired Zal, and all thy friends.
And thou must lay me in that lovely earth,
And heap a stately mound above my bones,
And plant a far-seen pillar over all.
That so the passing horseman on the waste   790
May see my tomb a great way off, and cry:
'Sohrab, the mighty Rustum's son, lies there,
Whom his great father did in ignorance kill!'
And I be not forgotten in my grave."
    And, with a mournful voice, Rustum replied: 795
"Fear not! as thou hast said, Sohrab, my son,

So shall it be; for I will burn my tents,
And quit the host, and bear thee hence with me,
And carry thee away to Seistan,
And place thee on a bed, and mourn for thee,   800
With the snow-headed Zal, and all my friends.
And I will lay thee in that lovely earth,
And heap a stately mound above thy bones,
And plant a far-seen pillar over all,
And men shall not forget thee in thy grave.   805
And I will spare thy host; yea, let them go!
Let them all cross the Oxus back in peace!
What should I do with slaying any more?
For would that all that I have ever slain
Might be once more alive; my bitterest foes,   810
And they who were called champions in their time,
And through whose death I won that fame I have —
And I were nothing but a common man,
A poor, mean soldier, and without renown,
So thou mightest live too, my son, my son!   815
Or rather would that I, even I myself,
Might now be lying on this bloody sand,
Near death, and by an ignorant stroke of thine,
Not thou of mine! and I might die, not thou;
And I, not thou, be borne to Seistan;   820
And Zal might weep above my grave, not thine;
And say: 'O son, I weep thee not too sore,
For willingly, I know, thou met'st thine end!'
But now in blood and battles was my youth,
And full of blood and battles is my age,   825
And I shall never end this life of blood."
    Then, at the point of death, Sohrab replied:
"A life of blood indeed, thou dreadful man!
But thou shalt yet have peace; only not now,
Not yet! but thou shalt have it on that day   830

When thou shalt sail in a high-masted ship,
Thou and the other peers of Kai Khosroo,
Returning home over the salt blue sea,
From laying thy dear master in his grave."
   And Rustum gazed in Sohrab's face, and said: 835
"Soon be that day, my son, and deep that sea!
Till then, if fate so wills, let me endure."
   He spoke; and Sohrab smiled on him, and took
The spear, and drew it from his side, and eased
His wound's imperious anguish; but the blood   840
Came welling from the open gash, and life
Flowed with the stream; — all down his cold white
      side
The crimson torrent ran, dim now and soiled,
Like the soiled tissue of white violets
Left, freshly gathered, on their native bank,   845
By children whom their nurses call with haste
Indoors from the sun's eye; his head drooped low,
His limbs grew slack; motionless, white, he lay —
White, with eyes closed; only when heavy gasps,
Deep heavy gasps quivering through all his frame,   850
Convulsed him back to life, he opened them,
And fixed them feebly on his father's face;
Till now all strength was ebbed, and from his limbs
Unwillingly the spirit fled away,
Regretting the warm mansion which it left,   855
And youth, and bloom, and this delightful world.
   So, on the bloody sand, Sohrab lay dead;
And the great Rustum drew his horseman's cloak
Down o'er his face, and sate by his dead son.
As those black granite pillars, once high-reared   860
By Jemshid in Persepolis, to bear
His house, now 'mid their broken flight of steps
Lie prone, enormous, down the mountain side—

So in the sand lay Rustum by his son.

And night came down over the solemn waste,   865
And the two gazing hosts, and that sole pair,
And darkened all; and a cold fog, with night,
Crept from the Oxus. Soon a hum arose,
As of a great assembly loosed, and fires
Began to twinkle through the fog; for now   870
Both armies moved to camp, and took their meal;
The Persians took it on the open sands
Southward, the Tartars by the river marge;
And Rustum and his son were left alone.

But the majestic river floated on,   875
Out of the mist and hum of that low land,
Into the frosty starlight, and there moved,
Rejoicing, through the hushed Chorasmian waste,
Under the solitary moon; — he flowed
Right for the polar star, past Orgunjé,   880
Brimming, and bright, and large; then sands begin
To hem his watery march, and dam his streams,
And split his currents; that for many a league
The shorn and parcelled Oxus strains along
Through beds of sand and matted rushy isles —   885
Oxus, forgetting the bright speed he had
In his high mountain cradle in Pamere,
A foiled circuitous wanderer — till at last
The longed-for dash of waves is heard, and wide
His luminous home of waters opens, bright   890
And tranquil, from whose floor the new-bathed stars
Emerge, and shine upon the Aral Sea.

875–892. It is not fanciful to say that this superb passage is an allegory of human life. It is pure allegory, not mixed; that is, no definite word, like *life*, gives us the clue. Is "Pilgrim's Progress" a pure allegory, or mixed?

Has the poem high seriousness? Is it musical? Is it strong in emotional power? in description? in dramatic climax?

Plan of Summary. — Reviewing the chapter, (1) enumerate the kinds of metre, designating them by the number of accents and by the predominant foot. Then (2) say which poem is most noticeable for melody; (3) which for beauty of suggested sights; (4) which for pleasure of suggested sounds; (5) which for pleasure of suggested activity; (6) which for pleasure of suggested odors or tastes; (7) which is most easily understood; (8) which moves the reader most deeply; (9) which shows most skill in character drawing; (10) which has the best unity; (11) which, your critical judgment tells you, is the best piece of work; (12) which you like the best, — without regard to its deserved rank, or its fame.

CHAPTER VII

THE MORNING LANDSCAPE

THE outdoor world is man's strength, medicine, delight. It seems to him most beautiful when it interprets for him his happiest feelings — as we gather from Thomas Ashe's poem called *Sympathy*. When he feels jolly all things seem jolly ; Sympathy, p. 293.

> The sun dances up in the sky,
> The moon dances down in the dews.

When he feels sad, nature seems sad also. To the poet the sea-wind yesterday suggested liberty ; to-day it sounds like a fettered soul trying to speak. Doubtless it would be better for man to study nature for its own sake, and learn what it has to say to him ; but, as a matter of fact, man's view of nature is deeply colored by his own moods. Watson's Changed Voices, p. 294.

The outdoor world engages all human beings. It satisfies the curiosity of the child, whose business it is to get acquainted with the wonderful place in which he finds himself. All animals interest him, for he must learn which are naturally his friends and comrades, which his enemies. All physical laws interest him, for nature must teach him that some things are heavy, others light ; some dull, others sharp ; some cold, others hot ; some poisonous, others wholesome. If he does not learn these laws, he will be, as Professor Huxley puts it, "untimely ended."

Nature is the place to which the grown man looks for rest and calm after the struggles of the city. He slips into the woods to be quieted in soul. He goes up into the mountain to seek serenity, 'for here he looks down upon the warring world and sees that after all it is not to be taken too seriously. The mountain teaches him firmness and faith. And when the stars come out, the man that yesterday tired his eyes over a ledger now soothes them with gazing into infinite miles of rest.

Midway between childhood and manhood is youth, and early youth is the age which loves nature in her fresh and happy moods. Since the world is freshest and happiest in the morning, we may speak in this chapter of nature's cheerful phases under the head of the "Morning Landscape." For the morning landscape is full of exhilaration, and cries out with the joy of activity. "The sun cometh forth from his chamber, and rejoiceth as a strong man to run a race." This is the time of day when hard tasks are play. Every breath seems to reach the finger-tips. Flowers have no heavy sweetness like that of house-blown roses in a room; they are aromatic now. It is the hour of daffodil and brier-rose and clover-dew. The streams are not sluggish and lazy, for the slowest is alive with sun. Let us review the morning moods of the year.

As youth is the morning of life, so, said the Greek, is springtime the youth of the year. The farther south we go, the earlier this youth begins. In Italy it is spring in January. Browning's little heroine, Pippa, is a factory girl, who has but one holiday in the year, and that is New Year's. She leaps from her bed determined to make the most of the time. Wherever she goes she sings merrily, and her songs are overheard by others, and quite unknown to Pippa they save many a life from its evil instincts. The first song that she carols captures in eight lines the whole springtime.

Pippa Passes, p. 295.

In England in January there are no larks in the heaven nor snails on the thorn; but a little later there is green in the mountains. Among the Westmoreland hills Words-

worth wrote his stanzas on March. No flowers yet, but March, p. 295.
sunny grass in the field. Cattle are grazing — forty feeding
like one — and everybody is at work, from the baby to the
grandsire.

Presently, both in England and America, the crocus
appears. Mr. Thomas Bailey Aldrich, in a graceful sonnet,
has found words for the feeling of surprise and joy that
springs up at sight of the first crocus. He likens himself
to Crusoe discovering the footprints in the sand. In the
mother country the crocus blooms in far greater profusion
than in America. Tennyson, remembering the look of
these delicate blossoms that mantle the greensward, wrote
one of the finest similes in English : —

> And at her feet the crocus brake like fire ! [1]

Before March is over in England the daffodils arrive ;
not in patches beside the door, but in the fields by the
thousand. Shakspere calls them

> Daffodils
> That come before the swallows dare, and take
> The winds of March with beauty.

It was on one of his long Westmoreland walks that, " wan-
dering lonely as a cloud," Wordsworth saw a host of these I wandered Lonely as a Cloud, p. 296.
golden flowers, beside the lake, beneath the trees. A very
simple matter, surely ; yet Wordsworth received such delight
from that glance that those daffodils have become a posses-
sion of thousands. They gladdened the poet still more
when his memory ran back to them as he lay within doors.
The dweller in cities understands what this means, as he
thinks back on his summer vacation.

The first poet to praise an American flower was Bryant, The Yellow Violet, p. 297.
in his musical lines on the *Yellow Violet*. This hardiest

---

[1] From *Œnone*, describing the goddess Venus. Flowers were fabled to
spring up sometimes where a goddess trod.

little blossom of its family appears in April, on the very edge of the lingering snowbank.   Bryant cannot help moralizing (to himself) about it.   He is ashamed that in May he should forget the flower he welcomed so joyfully a month before.

The Rho-
dora,
p. 298.
Less musical than Bryant's song about the violet, but more profound, are Emerson's lines on the *Rhodora*.   Some one had asked him "whence is the flower," and the wise poet answered that "if eyes were made for seeing, then beauty is it own excuse for being."   No one knows why or how Heaven made the rhodora.   It exists, and it is beautiful to look upon.

Warble for
Lilac-
Time,
p. 299.
Walt Whitman, whom some critics think a true maker of poetry and others think merely a gatherer of poetic material, has a spring poem of reminiscence.   He calls it *Warble for Lilac-Time*.   He details his memories of spring, — the crisp February days, the sugar-making, the vapors, the haze, the sound of frogs and birds, the melted snow, the yellow-green willow sprouts, then the flowers of April and May, — till he makes those jocund days live again.   To remember just what spring was like, most people have to await its return. Not so Walt Whitman.

The Crow,
p. 300.
One bird, familiar alike to the American and the English spring, even Whitman does not mention, fond as he is of the grotesque.   The crow has been sung but little, but he would be greatly missed if he appeared no more in the morning landscape.   Mr. Canton pictures him as an old ungodly rogue, whose feathers, torn by shot, show black against the blue sky.   He wears funereal garb, but he grins behind it. Suspicious that the frost is not yet gone, and still more suspicious of his enemy the farmer, the crow perches alert on the tip of an ash tree.   As his rakish eye looks round, he drinks in the glad morning's sun and air.

In the spring morning landscape of England the lark plays a real part.   We have no skylark in America, but we are so familiar with the bird in poetry that it seems like one of our own possessions. Still, he who hears it for the first time in the English sky has a new experience. He looks aloft, but it is poised invisible in upper air. In Shakspere's phrase, the lark is singing at heaven's gates. Hark, Hark! the Lark! p. 301.

This is the moment when the earliest sunshine creeps through the lattice, plays upon the wall, and wakens the sleeper. He turns upon his side, and watches the light in its lambent beauty. This glory, that every morning comes stealing back, and that on every delicate morning seems almost divine, is the theme of Tennyson-Turner's sonnet, *The Lattice at Sunrise.* Mr. Norman Gale thinks of the same moment as that when God returns from his other cares to look at the world ; it is the light of his countenance that we see. Longfellow, in one of his boyish poems, finds in the spring sunrise on the hills the perfect look of joy, un-dimmed by tears. The Lattice at Sunrise, p. 302. Dawn and Dark, p. 302. Sunrise on the Hills, p. 303.

With spring come the showers, and with these the rainbow. To Wordsworth, perhaps the greatest poet of nature, the rainbow always gave a thrill at the heart. In his poem he declares that he feels the pleasure as keenly in manhood as he did in childhood. He wishes that the day may never come when he shall cease to be stirred in the same way ; that the best joys of his boyhood may last into manhood ; that, so to speak, the child may be the father of the man. My Heart leaps up when I Behold, p. 304.

The early summer comes, with what Lowell calls " the perfect days," and Emerson calls " the charméd days." Bryant, in a poem on June, enters into the spirit of this weather, but not with such jubilance as Lowell does in his praise of June, at the opening of Sir Launfal. Bryant hoped that his time to die might be in this month of months. It is interesting to know that his wish was granted. In June of 1878 it could at last be said of him,— Twas One of the Charméd Days, p. 305. June, p. 305.

His part in all the pomp that fills
The circuit of the summer hills,
Is — that his grave is green.

Intrinsically the dandelion is a very beautiful blossom, and
To the
Dandelion,
p. 307. if rare would be costly.   Lowell's *Dandelion* is the flower of
everybody.   Lowell reads everything lovely into it, says it
stands to him for the warm land of flowers, calls it his
tropics and his Italy.   He delights beyond expression to
find the first blooms.   They remind him of the beauty that
might be lighted on in the natures of ordinary people, if it
were looked for.

Emerson is another poet who, forsaking the rose and the
nightingale, sings of commoner flowers and birds.   Note
some of his flowers, page 311.   Of the birds, he likes best
the chickadee, the snow-bird.

Here was this atom in full breath,
Hurling defiance at vast death.

The
Humble-
Bee, p. 309. It remained for Emerson to celebrate the bumblebee,
which gets back from him its proper but less descriptive
name, *The Humble-Bee.*   Emerson dubs him a philosopher,
because, though burly and dozing, he knows enough to sip
only what is sweet.   Clean and savory flowers furnish
forth his meal, and nothing else does he regard — all else
was picture as he passed.   Emerson grows enthusiastic, and
declares that he asks no better clime than that the humble-
bee loves.   As Lowell called a common flower his tropics,
so Emerson calls his burly bee an animated torrid zone.
For Emerson, the New England of this yellow-breeched
philosopher is good enough ; let others sail for Porto Rique
— that is the way the poet's fancy takes liberties with
geographic names.

The bee is perhaps the most steadily cheerful creature in
the landscape, but he is not the most joyful.   The bird is the

one being that seems capable of rapturous happiness. The bird is therefore one of the poet's keenest delights, and never has the poet neglected to write of it. For the present, one or two instances must suffice. Let these instances be extremes — " the bird which is most like a bee" (as the poet Forceythe Willson says), and the bird which is most like a beast of prey.

Eight quaint lines by the late Emily Dickinson convey an impression of the humming-bird. He comes like a resonant streak of emerald and red, whirring the blossoms down as he passes. He is probably the morning mail from Africa. In contrast to this revolving wheel of color, consider Tennyson's little picture of the statuesque king of birds. How he catches the genius of the eagle in what he calls *A Fragment!* A few terse lines, if they are the work of a Tennyson, suffice for an eagle : he is too sudden and too secret to be pursued in a long poem up to his hidden eyry. He wheels unceasingly " with clang of wings," as Shelley says ; he is glassed in the lake — how Arnold's lines (p. 271) seize that moment ; he clasps the crag, near the sun, in the blue ; he watches ; he falls on his prey like a thunderbolt.

The Humming-Bird, p. 311.

The Eagle, a Fragment, p. 312.

Both these birds are embodiments of swift, exulting strength, the one all delicacy, the other all grandeur. We must look to other poems for the joy of bird-song : to those of Bryant and Mr. Robert Burns Wilson on the bobolink, those of Mr. George Meredith and Mr. William Watson on the lark, those of Walt Whitman and Mr. Maurice Thompson on the mocking-bird, and that of Lowell on the cat-bird. Meantime, a little prose rhapsody of Ruskin will give us whatever impression prose can give of the fragility, the power, the grace, the passionate sweetness and strength of voice, the cloud-like, shadow-like, sky-like beauty of the bird.

The Bird, p. 312.

Midsummer comes, the song of birds is still, and the parched plains long for the cool water of rivers. " The dry

U

Song of the
Chatta-
hoochee,
p. 313.
fields burn, and the mills are to turn," sings the Chatta-
hoochee, in Sidney Lanier's poem. The poet Lanier was
also a musician, one of the best flute-players of his time, a
fact which accounts for the musical quality of his verse.
And, indeed, unless one has much music in him, he cannot
write the music of a stream. Tennyson has caught the
chatter of the brook in his song, *The Brook*. Mr. Maurice
Thompson has suggested the flow of the lowland creek, in
his *Death of the White Heron*.

> Bubble, bubble flows the stream,
> Like an old song through a dream.

Lanier has turned into verse the swift rush of the mountain
river.

And now, in our pursuit of the advancing year, we have
reached the dog-days. To many of us these bring sugges-
tions of a desire for the seashore. Let us make a digres-
sion, take a holiday, and demand of the poets a breath of
salt air. First, remembering that we are looking for the
cheerful side of nature, we may even dare to enjoy the ·
railway journey shoreward, although Mr. Ruskin objects so
strongly to the railway. It is almost incredible that Mr.
Ruskin never felt the exultation of becoming, so to speak, a
part of the landscape, as the train thundered over hill, down
The Rail-
way Train,
p. 315.
vale. Noise and smoke are occasionally as natural as sun-
shine and the luminous quiet of evening ; the railroad train
is a jubilant storm. Nor is it always ugly in the landscape.
Miss Dickinson very naturally likes to see it " step around a
pile of mountains."

And now we may imagine ourselves to have passed that
line of mystery, the horizon behind which lies the sea.
There it stretches, the universe of water, always pulsing and
always resounding. The wind that blows from it is the very
breath of life to the sick man. Wind and wave alike are full

of dark possibilities, but if no man loved to dare the wind
and the wave, it would speak ill for our race and its future.
For many years the English race has approved Barry Corn-
wall's lines beginning with the buoyant cry : —

> The sea! the sea! the open sea!
> The blue, the fresh, the ever free!

The Sea,
p. 316.

The seaside has not usually given the poets an inspiration
so cheerful as this of Barry Cornwall's. The never ceasing
minor music of the surge has often saddened the poet's
heart. But even Tennyson sometimes finds delight by the
sea, for here as elsewhere he is moved to exclamation at the
beauty of the world. For example, he stands in wonder
beside a shell, small and pure as a pearl. He dreams of the
little living will that made it stir on the shore. He is aston-
ished at its structure, which cannot bear a finger-tap, but
which has resisted the shock and pressure of seas that break
the three-decker's oaken spine.

The Shell,
p. 317.

The spring and the summer are usually spoken of as the
glad time of the year. When the north wind begins to blow
human spirits are supposed to sink. But a stout heart
rather enjoys the rough north wind and its promise of
healthful cold. On this subject, Mr. W. E. Henley has a
poem that is even exultant. The wind, he says, comes
roaring from his spacious arctic fastnesses, and like a giant
hunter storms down upon the sea; but the wrinkled sea,
Old Indefatigable, merely laughs with delight.

With summer go the flowers. For that matter, some fade
every day in the year. The seventeenth-century poet
Herrick laments, —

> Fair Daffodils, we weep to see
> You haste away so soon:
> As yet the early-rising Sun
> Has not attain'd his Noon.

But that is not the normal way in which to regard flowers and the morning. Mr. Lang sees the grass falling asleep beneath the lullaby the scythe sings to it. That is a normal view. In a wise little book[1] recently written are the following words : —

Scythe Song, p. 318.

The people of Japan are passionately fond of flowers. A great many of their holidays are fixed by the blossoming of trees and shrubs. These festivals are known as flower-viewings, when everybody is expected to be out of doors enjoying the rich colors of the landscape. Thus, at a time of year when we are celebrating Washington's birthday, perhaps with the thermometer at zero and snow all over the ground, the Japanese have their plum viewing; the plum blossom being the first to put forth after the snow is gone. This happens commonly in February. In April is the cherry-viewing, in May it is the peonies which cause the schools to close, in August the lotus, in November the chrysanthemum, and these are only a part.

Blossoms do not last forever in Japan any more than in any other country, and no doubt the people are sorry to see them drop and fade away, especially when the fruit is worthless (as in the case of the Japanese plum tree). Still, the Japanese do not have fast-days or mourning-days when the flower-viewing is over, but go cheerfully about their work till the next bloomtime comes. They know that

> Leaves have their time to fall
> And flowers to wither at the north wind's breath.

Sweet Day, so Cool, p. 319.

That contemporary of Herrick whom they called Holy George Herbert felt as keenly as any one the passing of the sweet rose, and of the sweet day, so cool, so calm, so bright. Yet the change did not sadden him, for, in his own quaint words, "the sweet and virtuous soul, like seasoned timber, never gives."

Even when autumn comes, it is not necessary to regard the fall of the leaves as a grievous thing. Bryant calls November "the melancholy days, the saddest of the year." Mr. Frank Stanton, a southern dialect poet, protests : —

The Death of the Flowers, p. 320.

[1] Wendell P. Garrison's "Parables for School and Home." Longmans, Green, & Co.

These ain't the " melancholy days " — there's lots o' fun in sight;
The cool and bracin' mornin's, an' the big oak fires at night.

In a finer vein Whittier has the same protest in his poem
called *A Day*. Listening in November to the squirrel drop-
ping nutshells from the shagbark trees, and to the soft
whisper of the dark green hemlocks, the poet finds a gra-
cious beauty in the scene. He folds to his heart the mem-
ory of " each lovely thing the sweet day yields," and, not
disconsolate, waits with the calm patience of the woods for
the leaf and blossom of spring. Bryant himself felt that
November is not always to be thought of as melancholy.
In a poem to November he says : — November,
p. 321.

> Yet one rich smile and we will try to bear
> The piercing winter frost, and winds, and biting air.

November is distinctly a less agreeable month than Decem-
ber, at least in north temperate latitudes. Snow is a cheer-
ful thing, for what Emerson calls its " frolic architecture " The Snow-
gives to the landscape the charm of strangeness, and mer- Storm,
rily shuts human beings indoors " in a tumultuous privacy p. 322.
of storm." Whittier's most poetic poem is the long idyl
which details the cosey delights of being snow-bound. A
young English poet of our own day, Mr. A. C. Benson, wel-
comes the rude, rough December because it compels the Winter
cheerful indoor life. This is the time of harvests ; not those Harvests,
of golden grain, but those of song. In music and book and p. 323.
school are pleasures as real as those of woods and waters.

SYMPATHY

THOMAS ASHE

Is nature all so beautiful?
The human feeling makes it so:
The sounds we love, the flowers we cull,
Are hallowed with man's joy or woe.

The lit le speedwell's tender blue   5
Is not so pure and delicate,
As the simple wish in you
That will its tardy advent wait.

The wishing for the green of trees
Is fresher than the leaves that come: 10
The blowing of a scented breeze
Is sweetest round a happy home.

The ripple of a tranquil bay,
The water-lisp in curve or creek,
Are softest on the welcome day   15
We trust to find some friend we seek.

CHANGED VOICES

WILLIAM WATSON

Last night the sea-wind was to me
A metaphor of liberty,
    And every wave along the beach
A starlit music seemed to be.

To-day the sea-wind is to me   5
A fettered soul that would be free,
    And dumbly striving after speech
The tides yearn landward painfully.

To-morrow how shall sound for me
The changing voice of wind and sea?   10
    What tidings shall be borne of each?
What rumor of what mystery?

SONG FROM *PIPPA PASSES*

Robert Browning

The year's at the spring,
And day's at the morn;
Morning's at seven;
The hillside's dew-pearl'd;
The lark's on the wing;   5
The snail's on the thorn;
God's in His heaven —
All's right with the world.

There is a charming buoyancy, elasticity, springiness about the move-
ment of the poem, as if Pippa were dancing down the path. In what ways
does Browning secure this effect?

MARCH

William Wordsworth

The cock is crowing,
The stream is flowing,
The small birds twitter,
The lake doth glitter,
The green field sleeps in the sun: 5
The oldest and youngest
Are at work with the strongest;
The cattle are grazing,
Their heads never raising;
There are forty feeding like one!   10

Like an army defeated,
The snow hath retreated,
And now doth fare ill
On the top of the bare hill;
The ploughboy is whooping anon, anon.   15
There's joy in the mountains;
There's life in the fountains;
Small clouds are sailing,
Blue sky prevailing;
The rain is over and gone!   20

I WANDERED LONELY AS A CLOUD

WILLIAM WORDSWORTH

I wandered lonely as a cloud
That floats on high o'er vales and hills,
When all at once I saw a crowd,
A host of golden daffodils;
Beside the lake, beneath the trees,   5
Fluttering and dancing in the breeze.

Continuous as the stars that shine
And twinkle on the milky way,
They stretch in never ending line
Along the margin of a bay: 10
Ten thousand saw I at a glance,
Tossing their heads in sprightly dance.

The waves beside them danced; but they
Out-did the sparkling waves in glee:
A poet could not but be gay   15
In such a jocund company:
I gazed — and gazed — but little thought
What wealth the show to me had brought.

For oft, when on my couch I lie
    In vacant or in pensive mood,   20
They flash upon that inward eye
    Which is the bliss of solitude;
And then my heart with pleasure fills,
And dances with the daffodils.

The best way to appreciate the fresh charm of this poem is to learn it.
If, as is said, Mrs. Wordsworth composed the last stanza, she was more
Wordsworthian than her husband.

THE YELLOW VIOLET

WILLIAM CULLEN BRYANT

When beechen buds begin to swell,
    And woods the bluebird's warble know,
The yellow violet's modest bell
    Peeps from the last year's leaves below.

Ere russet fields their green resume,   5
    Sweet flower, I love, in forest bare,
To meet thee, when thy faint perfume
    Alone is in the virgin air.

Of all her train, the hands of Spring
    First plant thee in the watery mould,   10
And I have seen thee blossoming
    Beside the snow-bank's edges cold.

Thy parent sun, who bade thee view
    Pale skies, and chilling moisture sip,
Has bathed thee in his own bright hue,   15
    And streaked with jet thy glowing lip.

Yet slight thy form, and low thy seat,
  And earthward bent thy gentle eye,
Unapt the passing view to meet,
  When loftier flowers are flaunting nigh.   20

Oft, in the sunless April day,
  Thy early smile has stayed my walk,
But 'midst the gorgeous blooms of May,
  I passed thee on thy humble stalk.

So they, who climb to wealth, forget   25
  The friends in darker fortunes tried.
I copied them — but I regret
  That I should ape the ways of pride.

And when again the genial hour
  Awakes the painted tribes of light,   30
I'll not o'erlook the modest flower
  That made the woods of April bright.

Select from this poem the two lines (consecutive or not) that seem to
you the most musical, and tell what vowels and consonants make them so.

THE RHODORA:

ON BEING ASKED, WHENCE IS THE FLOWER?

RALPH WALDO EMERSON

In May, when sea-winds pierced our solitudes,
I found the fresh Rhodora in the woods,
Spreading its leafless blooms in a damp nook,
To please the desert and the sluggish brook.
The purple petals, fallen in the pool,   5
Made the black water with their beauty gay;
Here might the redbird come his plumes to cool,
And court the flower that cheapens his array.

Rhodora! if the sages ask thee why
This charm is wasted on the earth and sky,   10
Tell them, dear, that if eyes were made for seeing,
Then Beauty is its own excuse for being:
Why thou wert there, O rival of the rose!
I never thought to ask, I never knew;
But, in my simple ignorance, suppose   15
The self-same Power that brought me there brought you.

WARBLE FOR LILAC-TIME [1]

WALT WHITMAN

Warble me now for joy of lilac-time (returning in remi-
    niscence),
Sort me, O tongue and lips, for Nature's sake, souvenirs of
    earliest summer,
Gather the welcome signs (as children with pebbles or
    stringing shells),
Put in April and May, the hylas croaking in the ponds, the
    elastic air,
Bees, butterflies, the sparrow with its simple notes,   5
Bluebird and darting swallow, nor forget the high-hole
    flashing his golden wings,
The tranquil sunny haze, the clinging smoke, the vapor,
Shimmer of waters with fish in them, the cerulean above,
All that is jocund and sparkling, the brooks running,
The maple woods, the crisp February days and the sugar-
    making,   10
The robin where he hops, bright-eyed, brown-breasted,

---

[1] Reprinted by permission of Small, Maynard, & Co.

4. *hylas* are frogs. How can air be called elastic? 5. Can anything better
be said of a sparrow ? 8. *cerulean*, blue. 11. Is the robin red-breasted ?

With musical clear call at sunrise, and again at sunset,
Or flitting among the trees of the apple orchard, building
the nest of his mate,
The melted snow of March, the willow sending forth its
yellow-green sprouts,
For spring-time is here!·the summer is here! and what is
this in it and from it?   15

Thou, soul, unloos'd — the restlessness after I know not what;
Come, let us lag here no longer, let us be up and away!
O if one could but fly like a bird!
O to escape, to sail forth as in a ship!
To glide with thee, O soul, o'er all, in all, as a ship o'er
the waters;   20
Gathering these hints, the preludes, the blue sky, the grass,
the morning drops of dew,
The lilac-scent, the bushes with dark green heart-shaped
leaves,
Wood-violets, the little delicate pale blossoms called inno-
cence,
Samples and sorts not for themselves alone, but for their
atmosphere,
To grace the bush I love — to sing with the birds,   25
A warble for joy of lilac-time, returning in reminiscence.

What senses does the poem appeal to ?   What emotions does it stir ?

THE CROW

WILLIAM CANTON

With rakish eye and plenished crop,
    Oblivious of the farmer's gun,
Upon the naked ash tree top
    The Crow sits basking in the sun.

An old ungodly rogue, I wot!   5
 For, perched in black against the blue,
His feathers, torn with beak and shot,
 Let woful glints of April through.

The year's new grass, and, golden-eyed,
 The daisies sparkle underneath,   10
And chestnut trees on either side
 Have opened every ruddy sheath.

But doubtful still of frost and snow
 The ash alone stands stark and bare,
And on its topmost twig the Crow   15
 Takes the glad morning's sun and air.

HARK! HARK! THE LARK

WILLIAM SHAKSPERE

Hark, hark! the lark at heaven's gate sings,
 And Phœbus 'gins arise,
His steeds to water at those springs
 On chaliced flowers that lies;
And winking Mary-buds begin   5
 To ope their golden eyes;
With everything that pretty bin
 My lady sweet, arise:
  Arise, arise.

7. *bin* is an old form for *is*.
The best thing to do with these nine charming lines is to sing them to
Schubert's music.

THE LATTICE AT SUNRISE

CHARLES TENNYSON-TURNER

As on my bed at dawn I mus'd and pray'd,
I saw my lattice prank'd upon the wall,
The flaunting leaves and flitting birds withal —
A sunny phantom interlaced with shade;
"Thanks be to heaven," in happy mood I said,   5
"What sweeter aid my matins could befall
Than the fair glory from the East hath made?
What holy sleights hath God, the Lord of all,
To bid us feel and see! we are not free
To say we see not, for the glory comes   10
Nightly and daily, like the flowing sea;
His lustre pierceth through the midnight glooms
And, at prime hour, behold! He follows me
With golden shadows to my secret rooms."

8. *sleights*, of course, means subtle devices.   Is the paradox pleasing?

DAWN AND DARK[1]

NORMAN GALE

God with his million cares
Went to the left or right,
Leaving our world; and the day
Grew light.

[1] Reprinted by permission of G. P. Putnam's Sons, the original American publishers of "Orchard Songs."

Back from a sphere He came   5
     Over a starry lawn,
Looked at our world; and the dark
     Grew dawn.

Is this poem a pleasant and uplifting fancy, or is it a "conceit" — that is, is the fancy rather far-fetched? In deciding, do not be too much influenced by your conviction that God never leaves His world. Of course He does not. The question is, May we find pleasure in fancying that He goes and returns?

SUNRISE ON THE HILLS

HENRY WADSWORTH LONGFELLOW

I stood upon the hills, when heaven's wide arch
Was glorious with the sun's returning march,
And woods were brightened, and soft gales
Went forth to kiss the sun-clad vales.
The clouds were far beneath me; — bathed in light,   5
They gathered mid-way round the wooded height,
And, in their fading glory, shone
Like hosts in battle overthrown,
As many a pinnacle, with shifting glance,
Through the gray mist thrust up its shattered lance,   10
And rocking on the cliff was left
The dark pine blasted, bare, and cleft.
The veil of cloud was lifted, and below
Glowed the rich valley, and the river's flow
Was darkened by the forest's shade,   15
Or glistened in the white cascade;
Where upward, in the mellow blush of day,
The noisy bittern wheeled his spiral way.

I heard the distant waters dash,
I saw the current whirl and flash, —   20
And richly, by the blue lake's silver beach,
The woods were bending with a silent reach.
Then o'er the vale, with gentle swell,
The music of the village bell
Came sweetly to the echo-giving hills;   25
And the wild horn, whose voice the woodland fills,
Was ringing to the merry shout,
That faint and far the glen sent out,
Where, answering to the sudden shot, thin smoke,
Through thick-leaved branches, from the dingle broke.   30

If thou art worn and hard beset
With sorrows, that thou wouldst forget,
If thou wouldst read a lesson, that will keep
Thy heart from fainting and thy soul from sleep,
Go to the woods and hills! — No tears   35
Dim the sweet look that Nature wears.

MY HEART LEAPS UP WHEN I BEHOLD

WILLIAM WORDSWORTH

My heart leaps up when I behold
    A rainbow in the sky:
So was it when my life began;
So is it now I am a man;
So be it when I shall grow old,   5
    Or let me die!
The Child is father of the Man;
And I could wish my days to be
Bound each to each by natural piety.

What line in this poem is an epigram, and has become famous as such ?

'TWAS ONE OF THE CHARMÉD DAYS

RALPH WALDO EMERSON

'Twas one of the charméd days,
When the genius of God doth flow,
The wind may alter twenty ways,
A tempest cannot blow;
It may blow north, it still is warm;   5
Or south, it still is clear;
Or east, it smells like a clover-farm;
Or west, no thunder fear.

JUNE

WILLIAM CULLEN BRYANT

I gazed upon the glorious sky
    And the green mountains round;
And thought, that when I came to lie
    Within the silent ground,
'Twere pleasant, that in flowery June,   5
When brooks sent up a cheerful tune,
    And groves a joyous sound,
The sexton's hand, my grave to make,
The rich, green mountain turf should break.

A cell within the frozen mould,   10
    A coffin borne through sleet,
And icy clods above it rolled,
    While fierce the tempests beat —
Away! — I will not think of these —
Blue be the sky and soft the breeze,   15
    Earth green beneath the feet,
And be the damp mould gently pressed
Into my narrow place of rest.
    x

There, through the long, long summer hours
    The golden light should lie,   20
And thick young herbs and groups of flowers
    Stand in their beauty by.
The oriole should build and tell
His love-tale, close beside my cell;
    The idle butterfly   25
Should rest him there, and there be heard
The housewife bee and humming-bird.

And what if cheerful shouts, at noon,
    Come from the village sent,
Or songs of maids, beneath the moon,   30
    With fairy laughter blent?
And what if, in the evening light,
Betrothéd lovers walk in sight
    Of my low monument?
I would the lovely scene around   35
Might know no sadder sight or sound.

I know, I know I should not see
    The season's glorious show,
Nor would its brightness shine for me,
    Nor its wild music flow;   40
But if, around my place of sleep,
The friends I love should come to weep,
    They might not haste to go.
Soft airs and song, and light, and bloom,
Should keep them lingering by my tomb.   45

These to their softened hearts should bear
    The thought of what has been,
And speak of one who cannot share
    The gladness of the scene;

Whose part, in all the pomp that fills 50
The circuit of the summer hills,
  Is — that his grave is green;
And deeply would their hearts rejoice
To hear, again, his living voice.

50–52. These lines were much admired by Edgar Poe, whose ear for music in poetry was very true.

.

TO THE DANDELION

JAMES RUSSELL LOWELL

Dear common flower, that grow'st beside the way,
Fringing the dusty road with harmless gold,
  First pledge of blithesome May,
Which children pluck, and, full of pride uphold,
  High-hearted buccaneers, o'erjoyed that they 5
An Eldorado in the grass have found,
  Which not the rich earth's ample round
May match in wealth, thou art more dear to me
Than all the prouder summer-blooms may be.

Gold such as thine ne'er drew the Spanish prow 10
Through the primeval hush of Indian seas,
  Nor wrinkled the lean brow
Of age, to rob the lover's heart of ease;
  'Tis the Spring's largess, which she scatters now
To rich and poor alike, with lavish hand, 15
  Though most hearts never understand
To take it at God's value, but pass by
The offered wealth with unrewarded eye.

6. *Eldorado*, a fabled land rich in gold — "golden land."

Thou art my tropics and mine Italy;
To look at thee unlocks a warmer clime;   20
    The eyes thou givest me
Are in the heart, and heed not space or time:
  Not in mid June the golden-cuirassed bee
Feels a more summer-like warm ravishment
    In the white lily's breezy tent,   25
  His fragrant Sybaris, than I, when first
From the dark green thy yellow circles burst.

Then think I of deep shadows on the grass,
Of meadows where in sun the cattle graze,
    Where, as the breezes pass,   30
The gleaming rushes lean a thousand ways,
  Of leaves that slumber in a cloudy mass,
Or whiten in the wind, of waters blue
    That from the distance sparkle through
Some woodland gap, and of a sky above,   35
Where one white cloud like a stray lamb doth move.

My childhood's earliest thoughts are linked with thee;
The sight of thee calls back the robin's song,
    Who, from the dark old tree
Beside the door, sang clearly all day long,   40
  And I, secure in childish piety,
Listened as if I heard an angel sing
    With news from heaven, which he could bring
Fresh every day to my untainted ears
When birds and flowers and I were happy peers.   45

How like a prodigal doth nature seem,
When thou, for all thy gold, so common art!
    Thou teachest me to deem
More sacredly of every human heart,

26. *Sybaris*, a town in ancient Italy, famous for its luxury.

Since each reflects in joy its scanty gleam   50
Of heaven, and could some wondrous secret show,
    Did we but pay the love we owe,
And with a child's undoubting wisdom look
On all these living pages of God's book.

What is the rhyme-scheme? How many lines in a stanza? Which
stanza recalls to the poet certain pictures of his boyhood, which certain
sounds? Is it natural that so trifling a thing as a flower should recall so
much to one? The first three stanzas are eminently worth learning.

THE HUMBLE-BEE

RALPH WALDO EMERSON

Burly, dozing humble-bee,
Where thou art is clime for me.
Let them sail for Porto Rique,
Far-off heats through seas to seek;
I will follow thee alone,   5
Thou animated torrid zone!
Zigzag steerer, desert cheerer,
Let me chase thy waving lines;
Keep me nearer, me thy hearer,
Singing over shrubs and vines.   10

Insect lover of the sun,
Joy of thy dominion!
Sailor of the atmosphere;
Swimmer through the waves of air;
Voyager of light and noon;   15
Epicurean of June!

16. *Epicurean* should be accented on the second *e*, though to do so
here will require breaking this vowel into two syllables. The Epicureans
were a school of Greek philosophers who believed that death ends all.
Can you infer how the word came to be applied to those who are fond
of dainty food?

Wait, I prithee, till I come
Within earshot of thy hum, —
All without is martyrdom.

When the south wind, in May days,   20
With a net of shining haze
Silvers the horizon wall,
And, with softness touching all,
Tints the human countenance
With the color of romance,   25
And infusing subtle heats
Turns the sod to violets,
Thou, in sunny solitudes,
Rover of the underwoods,
The green silence dost displace   30
With thy mellow, breezy bass.

Hot midsummer's petted crone,
Sweet to me thy drowsy tone
Tells of countless sunny hours,
Long days, and solid banks of flowers;   35
Of gulfs of sweetness without bound
In Indian wildernesses found;
Of Syrian peace, immortal leisure,
Firmest cheer, and bird-like pleasure.

Aught unsavory or unclean   40
Hath my insect never seen;
But violets and bilberry bells,
Maple sap and daffodels,
Grass with green flag half-mast high,

19. This is what is called hyperbole, — a poetic exaggeration. 25. There is no particular *color of romance*. What does Emerson mean? 26. Is the sod actually turned into violets? 38. *Syrian* is a pleasant word, and the poet probably uses it in the larger sense of Oriental; the Orientals are always leisurely; they are not prompt, and cannot understand our Western notions of the value of time.

Succory to match the sky, 45
Columbine with horn of honey,
Scented fern, and agrimony,
Clover, catchfly, adder's-tongue,
And brier-roses, dwelt among;
All beside was unknown waste, 50
All was picture as he passed.

Wiser far than human seer,
Yellow-breeched philosopher!
Seeing only what is fair,
Sipping only what is sweet, 55
Thou dost mock at fate and care,
Leave the chaff and take the wheat.
When the fierce northwestern blast
Cools sea and land so far and fast,
Thou already slumberest deep; 60
Woe and want thou canst outsleep;
Want and woe, which torture us,
Thy sleep makes ridiculous.

50–51. In Shakspere's time (not Emerson's) *waste*, like *vast*, rhymed with *passed*. 56–57. Is the metaphor a trifle mixed? 62–63. Note Emerson's epigrammatic power.

THE HUMMING–BIRD [1]

EMILY DICKINSON

A route of evanescence
  With a revolving wheel;
A resonance of emerald,

[1] From " Poems," Second Series, Copyright, 1891, by Roberts Bros.; now published by Little, Brown, & Co., Boston, and reprinted by their permission and that of Miss Lavinia N. Dickinson.

1. Here *route* is used in the old sense, of *rush*. 3. Is this line truthful to the impression the bird gives? 2, 4. Would it have been better not to rhyme these lines?

A rush of cochineal ;
And every blossom on the bush   5
    Adjusts its tumbled head, —
The mail from Tunis, probably,
    An easy morning's ride.

THE EAGLE

FRAGMENT

ALFRED, LORD TENNYSON

He clasps the crag with hookéd hands ;
Close to the sun in lonely lands,   .
Ringed with the azure world, he stands.

The wrinkled sea beneath him crawls ;
He watches from his mountain walls,   5
And like a thunderbolt he falls.

THE BIRD

JOHN RUSKIN

The bird is little more than a drift of the air brought
into form by plumes ; the air is in all its quills, it breathes
through its whole frame and flesh, and glows with air in
its flying, like a blown flame : it rests upon the air, sub-
dues it, surpasses it, outraces it, — *is* the air, conscious 5
of itself, conquering itself, ruling itself.

Also, into the throat of the bird is given the voice of
the air.   All that in the wind itself is weak, wild, useless
in sweetness, is knit together in its song.   As we may

imagine the wild form of the cloud closed into the 10
perfect form of the bird's wings, so the wild voice
of the cloud into its ordered and commanded voice;
unwearied, rippling through the clear heaven in its glad-
ness, interpreting all intense passion through the soft
spring nights, bursting into acclaim and rapture of choir 15
at daybreak, or lisping and twittering among the boughs
and hedges through heat of day, like little winds that
only make the cowslip bells shake, and ruffle the petals
of the wild rose.

Also, upon the plumes of the bird are put the colors 20
of the air: on these the gold of the cloud, that cannot
be gathered by any covetousness; the rubies of the
clouds, the vermilion of the cloud-bar, and the flame
of the cloud-crest, and the snow of the cloud, and its
shadow, and the melted blue of the deep wells of the sky 25
— all these, seized by the creating spirit, and woven into
films and threads of plume; with wave on wave following
and fading along breast, and throat, and opened wings,
infinite as the dividing of the foam and the sifting of the
sea-sand. 30

SONG OF THE CHATTAHOOCHEE [1]

SIDNEY LANIER

Out of the hills of Habersham,
Down through the valleys of Hall,
I hurry amain to reach the plain,
Run the rapid and leap the fall,
Split at the rock and together again, 5

[1] Reprinted by permission of Charles Scribner's Sons.

Accept my bed, or narrow or wide,
And flee from folly on every side,
With a lover's pain to attain the plain
  Far from the hills of Habersham,
  Far from the valleys of Hall.   10

All down the hills of Habersham,
  All through the valleys of Hall,
The rushes cried, " Abide, abide,"
The wilful waterweeds held me thrall,
The loving laurel turned my tide,   15
The ferns and the fondling grass said, " Stay,"
The dewberry dipped for to work delay,
And the little reeds sighed, " Abide, abide,"
  Here in the hills of Habersham,
  Here in the valleys of Hall.   20

High o'er the hills of Habersham,
  Veiling the valleys of Hall,
The hickory told me manifold
Fair tales of shade ; the poplar tall
Wrought me her shadowy self to hold ;   25
The chestnut, the oak, the walnut, the pine,
Overleaning, with flickering meaning and sign,
Said : " Pass not so cold, these manifold
  Deep shades of the hills of Habersham,
  These glades in the valleys of Hall."   30

And oft in the hills of Habersham,
  And oft in the valleys of Hall,
The white quartz shone, and the smooth brook stone
Did bar me of passage with friendly brawl ;
And many a luminous jewel lone   35

(Crystals clear or a-cloud with mist,
Ruby, garnet, or amethyst)
Made lures with the lights of streaming stone
  In the clefts of the hills of Habersham,
  In the beds of the valleys of Hall.   40

But oh ! not the hills of Habersham,
  And oh ! not the valleys of Hall
Avail ; I am fain for to water the plain.
Downward the voices of Duty call ;
Downward to toil and be mixed with the main.   45
The dry fields burn, and the mills are to turn,
And a myriad flowers mortally yearn,
And the lordly main from beyond the plain
  Calls o'er the hills of Habersham,
  Calls through the valleys of Hall.   50

The poem is distinctly worth learning. The swift melody of it is obvious.
Is the melody obtained at the expense of thought and of pictures, or is there
a happy blending of poetic qualities ?

THE RAILWAY TRAIN [1]

EMILY DICKINSON

I like to see it lap the miles,
  And lick the valleys up,
And stop to feed itself at tanks ;
  And then, prodigious, step

Around a pile of mountains,   5
  And, supercilious, peer
In shanties by the sides of roads ;
  And then a quarry pare

[1] From " Poems," Second Series, Copyright, 1891, by Roberts Brothers ;
now published by Little, Brown, & Co., Boston, and reprinted by their per-
mission and that of Miss Lavinia N. Dickinson.

To fit its sides, and crawl between,
    Complaining all the while   10
In horrid, hooting stanza;
    Then chase itself down hill

And neigh like Boanerges;
    Then, punctual as a star,
Stop — docile and omnipotent —   15
    At its own stable door.

13. *Boanerges,* " sons of thunder."
For what do you praise, for what adversely criticise, this poem?

THE SEA

BARRY CORNWALL

The sea! the sea! the open sea!
The blue, the fresh, the ever free!
Without a mark, without a bound,
It runs the earth's wide regions round;
It plays with the clouds; it mocks the skies,   5
Or like a cradled creature lies.

I'm on the sea! I'm on the sea!
I am where I would ever be,
With the blue above and the blue below,
And silence wheresoe'er I go;   10
If a storm should come and awake the deep,
What matter? *I* shall ride and sleep.

I love, oh! how I love to ride
On the fierce, foaming, bursting tide,
When every mad wave drowns the moon,   15

Or whistles aloud his tempest tune,
And tells how goeth the world below,
And why the southwest blasts do blow.

I never was on the dull, tame shore,
But I loved the great sea more and more,   20
And back I flew to her billowy breast,
Like a bird that seeks its mother's nest ;
And a mother she *was* and *is* to me,
For I was born on the deep blue sea !

And I have lived, in calm and strife,   25
Full fifty summers a sailor's life,
With wealth to spend and power to range,
But never have sought or sighed for change ;
And Death, whenever he comes to me,
Shall come on the wild and boundless sea.   30

THE SHELL

ALFRED, LORD TENNYSON

See what a lovely shell,
Small and pure as a pearl,
Lying close to my foot,
Frail, but a work divine,
Made so fairily well   5
With delicate spine and whorl,
How exquisitely minute,
A miracle of design !

What is it ? A learned man
Could give it a clumsy name.   10
Let him name it who can,
The beauty would be the same.

The tiny cell is forlorn,
Void of the little living will
That made it stir on the shore.   15
Did he stand at the diamond door
Of his house in a rainbow frill?
Did he push, when he was uncurl'd,
A golden foot or a fairy horn
Thro' his dim water-world?   20

Slight, to be crush'd with a tap
Of my finger-nail on the sand,
Small, but a work divine,
Frail, but of force to withstand,
Year upon year, the shock   25
Of cataract seas that snap
The three-decker's oaken spine
Athwart the ledges of rock,
Here on the Breton strand !

Write the rhyme-scheme of each stanza.   Why is the second the short-
est? Are short lines better than long for a poem on a tiny shell? Do they
lend a certain sense of care, as if the poet paused in time, even held his
breath, as he touched it?

SCYTHE SONG

Andrew Lang

Mowers, weary and brown and blithe,
    What is the word methinks ye know,
Endless over-word that the scythe
    Sings to the blades of the grass below?
Scythes that swing in the grass and clover,   5
    Something, still, they say as they pass ;
What is the word that, over and over,
    Sings the scythe to the flowers and grass?

Hush, ah hush, the scythes are saying,
  Hush, and heed not, and fall asleep ; 10
Hush, they say to the grasses swaying,
  Hush, they sing to the clover deep !
Hush, — 'tis the lullaby Time is singing, —
  Hush, and heed not, for all things pass,
Hush, ah hush ! and the scythes are swinging 15
  Over the clover, over the grass !

Is there in this poem onomatopœia, that is, deliberate imitation, by means of words, of some sound in nature ?

SWEET DAY, SO COOL

George Herbert

Sweet day, so cool, so calm, so bright,
The bridal of the earth and sky,
The dew shall weep thy fall to-night ;
        For thou must die.

Sweet rose, whose hue, angry and brave, 5
Bids the rash gazer wipe his eye,
Thy root is ever in its grave,
        And thou must die.

Sweet spring, full of sweet days and roses,
A box where sweets compacted lie, 10
My music shows ye have your closes,
        And all must die.

Only a sweet and virtuous soul,
Like season'd timber, never gives ;
But though the whole world turn to coal, 15
        Then chiefly lives.

5, 6. Is this a conceit ?

THE DEATH OF THE FLOWERS

WILLIAM CULLEN BRYANT

The melancholy days are come, the saddest of the year,
Of wailing winds, and naked woods, and meadows brown
    and sere.
Heaped in the hollows of the grove the withered leaves lie
    dead ;
They rustle to the eddying gust, and to the rabbit's tread.
The robin and the wren are flown, and from the shrubs the
    jay,   5
And from the wood-top calls the crow, through all the
    gloomy day.

Where are the flowers, the fair young flowers, that lately
    sprang and stood
In brighter light and softer airs, a beauteous sisterhood?
Alas ! they all are in their graves, the gentle race of flowers
Are lying in their lowly beds, with the fair and good of
    ours.   10
The rain is falling where they lie, but the cold November
    rain,
Calls not, from out the gloomy earth, the lovely ones again.

The wind-flower and the violet, they perished long ago,
And the brier-rose and the orchis died amid the summer
    glow ;
But on the hill the goldenrod, and the aster in the wood, 15
And the yellow sunflower by the brook in autumn beauty
    stood,
Till fell the frost from the clear cold heaven, as falls the
    plague on men,
And the brightness of their smile was gone, from upland,
    glade, and glen.

And now, when comes the calm mild day, as still such days
    will come,
To call the squirrel and the bee from out their winter home ;
When the sound of dropping nuts is heard, though all the
    trees are still, 21
And twinkle in the smoky light the waters of the rill,
The south wind searches for the flowers whose fragrance late
    he bore,
And sighs to find them in the wood and by the stream no
    more.

And then I think of one who in her youthful beauty died, 25
The fair, meek blossom that grew up and faded by my side :
In the cold moist earth we laid her, when the forest cast the
    leaf,
And we wept that one so lovely should have a life so brief :
Yet not unmeet it was that one, like that young friend of
    ours,
So gentle and so beautiful, should perish with the flowers. 30

NOVEMBER

WILLIAM CULLEN BRYANT

Yet one smile more, departing, distant sun !
    One mellow smile through the soft vapory air,
Ere, o'er the frozen earth, the loud winds run,
    Or snows are sifted o'er the meadows bare.
One smile on the brown hills and naked trees, 5
    And the dark rocks whose summer wreaths are cast,
And the blue Gentian flower, that, in the breeze,
    Nods lonely, of her beauteous race the last.
Yet a few sunny days, in which the bee
    Shall murmur by the hedge that skirts the way, 10

Y

The cricket chirp upon the russet lea,
    And man delight to linger in thy ray.
Yet one rich smile, and we will try to bear
The piercing winter frost, and winds, and darkened air.

THE SNOW-STORM

RALPH WALDO EMERSON

Announced by all the trumpets of the sky,
Arrives the snow, and, driving o'er the fields,
Seems nowhere to alight : the whited air
Hides hills and woods, the river, and the heavens,
And veils the farmhouse at the garden's end.   5
The sled and traveller stopped, the courier's feet
Delayed, all friends shut out, the housemates sit
Around the radiant fireplace, enclosed
In a tumultuous privacy of storm.

Come see the north wind's masonry.   10
Out of an unseen quarry evermore
Furnished with tile, the fierce artificer
Curves his white bastions with projected roof
Round every windward stake, or tree, or door.
Speeding, the myriad-handed, his wild work   15
So fanciful, so savage, nought cares he
For number or proportion.   Mockingly,
On coop or kennel he hangs Parian wreaths ;
A swan-like form invests the hidden thorn ;
Fills up the farmer's lane from wall to wall,   20
Maugre the farmer's sighs ; and, at the gate,

3. Is this line faithful to the appearance of nature? 1-9. These lines
would be worth learning, were it only for the condensation of phrase in the
ninth.   18. Parian marble was the whitest and finest known to the ancients.
Our shops are full of a cheap imitation stone that unfortunately goes by
this famous name.   21. *Maugre* is an old French word, meaning *in spite of.*

A tapering turret overtops the work.
And when his hours are numbered, and the world
Is all his own, retiring, as he were not,
Leaves, when the sun appears, astonished Art   25
To mimic in slow structures, stone by stone,
Built in an age, the mad wind's night-work,
The frolic architecture of the snow.

WINTER HARVESTS[1]

ARTHUR CHRISTOPHER BENSON

Pipe, winds of winter,
    O'er the hill's cold brow.
Shatter and splinter
    The dying, dying bough;

Brim the icy river,   5
    Let the dead reeds shake;
Make the wild swan shiver
    In her northern lake.

O'er the empty cover
    Bid the brown hawk swing,   10
Send the wailing plover,
    Southward to the spring.

I do not fear thee,
    Wind, harsh and shrill,
Rather let me hear thee   15
    Thunder in the hill.

[1] Reprinted from " Lord Vyet and Other Poems," by permission of Mr. John Lane.

Rude, rough December,
   Thine be all the earth,
So the ruddy ember
   Rustle on the hearth.   20

When the shadow beckons,
   Home, and bar the door;
Then the poet reckons
   All his summer store;

Coins his gathered gladness   25
   Into ringing rhyme,
Hugs his merry madness,
   'Tis his harvest time.

Plan of Summary. — Reviewing the chapter, (1) enumerate the kinds of metre, designating them by the number of accents, and by the predominant foot. Then (2) say which poem is most noticeable for melody; (3) which for beauty of suggested sights; (4) which for pleasure of suggested sounds; (5) which for pleasure of suggested activity; (6) which for pleasure of suggested odors or tastes; (7) which is most easily understood; (8) which moves the reader most deeply; (9) which shows most skill in character drawing; (10) which has the best unity; (11) which, your critical judgment tells you, is the best piece of work; (12) which you like the best, without regard to its deserved rank, or its fame.

CHAPTER VIII

THE GENTLEMAN

THE word which stands at the head of this chapter is a curious example of how language changes its meaning. *Gentile* is from Latin *gentilis*, "belonging to the same clan." The early Christians fell into the Jewish habit of calling all but themselves gentiles. Christianity first spread among the peasants, the poor of the earth. As time went on and almost all the poor embraced the new religion, the only gentiles left were the rich nobles. After a while, therefore, *gentile* meant little more than *nobleman*. Finally even these gentiles became Christians, their native breeding developed into a nobler and finer behavior, and *gentile* came to mean *gentle* in the modern sense. In the sixteenth century the playwright Dekker could speak of Christ as the first gentleman without suggesting *gentile* to any one. Yet it remains true that men are often called gentlemen merely because they happen to be high born.

With such a history the gentleman has long been before the world of letters. In Shakspere the necessity of being really gentle if high born is often asserted; it is the French doctrine of *noblesse oblige*. In our own time John Ruskin has found it impossible to write on art without defining to himself the difference between gentlemanliness and vulgarity, for some artists have the one quality and some the other. In the course of a chapter on Vulgarity, in his "Modern Painters," Ruskin analyzes at some length the nature of the gentleman. Like Shakspere he throws great weight on good breeding, even in the sense that a horse

Of Vulgarity, p. 329.

325

The
Young
Montagu,
p. 343.
or dog is well bred.   Blood will tell, even in a chimney-sweep; an old story to this effect has been rehearsed by Charles Lamb.   And Perdita, in Shakspere's *Winter's Tale*, proves by her acts that if a shepherd lass is a princess in disguise she behaves like the king's daughter.   It is only by being of pure race that a man can develop into the fineness of fibre and feeling which distinguishes the courtier from the clown.   Sensitiveness to impression, — this is a prime condition of gentlemanly conduct, and this is exactly what the badly bred peasant lacks.   The peasant's skin is thick, callous.   To be thin-skinned, in the better sense, is what makes men alive to the rights of their fellows.

Tact,
p. 345.
"Tact" means sense of touch; and tact, according to Emerson, will work wonders when all else fails.

Breeding shows itself in the unerring emphasis that the gentleman lays upon the really important matters of courtesy.   An ill-bred man is often punctilious about some absurd form, thinking that the observance of this shows
Two Gen-
tlemen at
Petersburg,
p. 346.
great knowledge of how things should be done.   Not so the two gentlemen whom Mr. Eggleston tells about. Though officers of opposing armies, the one was severely honorable in surrendering a captain who had offended against the letter of the truce-law, the other equally honorable in refusing to punish this captain for a mere inadvertence.

The real test of gentlemanliness lies deeper than forms. One may obey all the forms and yet be counted what the English call a "cad," that is, an unmanly, selfish, egotistic
The
Gentleman,
p. 349.
bore.   According to Cardinal Newman, it is almost a definition of a gentleman to say that he is one who never inflicts pain.   Kindliness and consideration are qualities that depend on a knowledge neither of etiquette nor of the newest fashions in dress.

That a man may be boorish in satins or in shirt-sleeves

is exhibited in two selections in this chapter. Shakspere's
delicate irony impales, like a fly on a pin, the exquisite
who came to Hotspur in the battlefield, and smiled and
talked and took snuff while dead men were carried by.
Mr. Eggleston tells a delightful story of how the Southern
cavalry leader, Stuart, enforced his objections to a sol-
dier's appearing in shirt-sleeves at table before ladies.
Contrast with Shakspere's fop and Mr. Eggleston's slouches
a true gentleman of the battlefield, Bret Harte's John
Burns of Gettysburg. The old beau was dressed in the
style of a hundred years since, and yet as he stood immov-
able there, picking the rebels off, the gleam of his old
white hat afar rallied the very boys who had mocked
him.

A Fop,
p. 351.

A Breach
of Eti-
quette,
p. 353.

In war or peace, the gentleman is often a hero. His
sense of humane courtesy may be so highly developed that
the gentleman must some day choose between obeying it
and losing his life. This is the sublime alternative which
Mr. Henry Newbolt celebrates in a poem on Craven, the
hero of Mobile Bay. When only one of two men can pass
through a door alive, because there is only a second of
time to do it in, the man that says "After you" (as Cap-
tain Craven did) must pay for it with his life. The other
man may be as brave at heart; but it is the trained gen-
tleman who speaks first and ends the situation.

Certain forms of gentlemanliness which may almost be
called heroic, are found among savage or half-civilized
races. The Arab will protect with his life the guest who
has eaten his salt. The North American Indian, as
Franklin has pointed out, will not under any provocation
interrupt another when speaking. In China the laws of
Confucius forbid a son to approach his father closely
without permission.

Remarks
concerning
the Savages
of North
America,
p. 355.

According to Dr. Theodore Munger, the foundation of

the gentlemanly character is truth.[1] Thus, the story told by Sarah Williams, of how the warrior Omàr kept his word to a guest, when to do so was against all traditions of war, belongs here rather than in the preceding chapter on war. The Persian captive was brought before the victor Omàr and told that he must die. The captive thirsted for a cup of wine. It was brought him, but he hesitated to drink it, fearing poison. This touched the victor's pride, and he assured the Persian that his life was safe from poison; nay, it was safe from all harm until he should have slaked his thirst. The Persian smiled and poured the wine upon the ground. At this ruse a shout arose that he should be slain. But Omàr rose to the occasion. "Hold! if there be a sacred thing, it is the warrior's word."

Omàr and the Persian, p. 362.

One mark of the gentleman is freedom from envy. He is alert to recognize merit even in the friend who outstrips him in a race. The "rooter" who cheers when the other team makes a false play does an ungentlemanly thing. The critic who, as Pope says of Addison, "damns with faint praise" the work of his rival reveals the vulgarity of envy. How vigorously Mr. Theodore Watts-Dunton scores this evil in his allegory of the Octopus!

The Octopus of the Golden Isle, p. 364.

Between Shakspere's time and Tennyson's, English literature has many portraits of gentlemen. In the early eighteenth century, Steele sketched the character of Sir Roger de Coverley, and his friend Addison completed the picture. Sir Roger is the ideal country gentleman who has a care for all his dependents. Goldsmith, a little later, created Beau Tibbs, the gentleman whose cheerful good manners never fail, though he may owe his family a meal. Early in our own century, Scott gave us his Lord Evandale, his Guy Mannering, and many another prince of courtesy.

---

[1] "On the Threshold."

Tennyson wrote a long cycle of poems on the death of his friend Hallam, whose exceptional breeding was remarked by all who knew him — by Gladstone, for instance. The one hundred and eleventh poem of *In Memoriam* concerns Arthur's gentlemanliness. The poet declares that the man who is churlish in spirit cannot hide the fact, though he be by blood a king. But Hallam was finer in grain than anything he could do; was more than all the gentleness he seemed to be. Whatever he did, he seemed perfectly natural, wholly himself. Yet he joined in all the social life around him, to which he brought the flower of noble manners without touch of narrowness or spite. And thus he bore without abuse the grand old name of gentleman.

The Churl in Spirit, p. 365.

To Thackeray the name of gentleman seemed one of the noblest. His Colonel Newcome is one of the gracious figures that cannot be spared from literature. Thackeray closed one of his books with a poem called *The End of the Play*. The author represents himself as an actor after a performance. He bids his audience good night, remembering that they, too, have parts to play, in real life. He wishes them well, but, whatever may betide, wishes them to be superior to their fate. The race is not always to the swift, any more in life than in school. Not all can win, but all can accept their fate like gentlemen.

The End of the Play, p. 366.

OF VULGARITY

JOHN RUSKIN

1. Two great errors, coloring, or rather discoloring, severally, the minds of the higher and lower classes, have sown wide dissension, and wider misfortune, through the society of modern days. These errors are in our modes of interpreting the word "gentleman."

5

Its primal, literal, and perpetual meaning is "a man of pure race"; well bred, in the sense that a horse or dog is well bred.

The so-called higher classes, being generally of purer race than the lower, have retained the true idea, and the convictions associated with it; but are afraid to speak it out, and equivocate about it in public; this equivocation mainly proceeding from their desire to connect another meaning with it, and a false one; — that of "a man living in idleness on other people's labor"; — with which idea, the term has nothing whatever to do.

The lower classes, denying vigorously, and with reason, the notion that a gentleman means an idler, and rightly feeling that the more any one works, the more of a gentleman he becomes, and is likely to become, — have nevertheless got little of the good they otherwise might, from the truth, because, with it, they wanted to hold a falsehood, — namely, that race was of no consequence. It being precisely of as much consequence in man as it is in any other animal.

2. The nation cannot truly prosper till both these errors are finally got quit of. Gentlemen have to learn that it is no part of their duty or privilege to live on other people's toil. They have to learn that there is no degradation in the hardest manual, or the humblest servile, labor, when it is honest. But that there *is* degradation, and that deep, in extravagance, in bribery, in indolence, in pride, in taking places they are not fit for, or in coining places for which there is no need. It does not disgrace a gentleman to become an errand boy, or a day laborer; but it disgraces him much to become a knave, or a thief. And knavery is not the less knavery because it involves large interests, nor theft the less theft because it is countenanced by usage, or accom-

panied by failure in undertaken duty. It is an incom- 40
parably less guilty form of robbery to cut a purse out of
a man's pocket, than to take it out of his hand on the
understanding that you are to steer his ship up channel,
when you do not know the soundings.

3. On the other hand, the lower orders, and all orders, 45
have to learn that every vicious habit and chronic disease
communicates itself by descent; and that by purity of
birth the entire system of the human body and soul may
be . gradually elevated, or by recklessness of birth,
degraded; until there shall be as much difference 50
between the well-bred and ill-bred human creature
(whatever pains be taken with their education) as
between a wolf-hound and the vilest mongrel cur. And
the knowledge of this great fact ought to regulate the
education of our youth, and the entire conduct of the 55
nation.

4. Gentlemanliness, however, in ordinary parlance,
must be taken to signify those qualities which are usually
the evidence of high breeding, and which, so far as they
can be acquired, it should be every man's effort to 60
acquire; or, if he has them by nature, to preserve and
exalt. Vulgarity, on the other hand, will signify quali-
ties usually characteristic of ill-breeding which, accord-
ing to his power, it becomes every person's duty to
subdue. We have briefly to note what these are. 65

5. A gentleman's first characteristic is that fineness
of structure in the body, which renders it capable of the
most delicate sensation; and of structure in the mind
which renders it capable of the most delicate sympa-
thies — one may say, simply, "fineness of nature." 70
This is, of course, compatible with heroic bodily strength
and mental firmness; in fact, heroic strength is not
conceivable without such delicacy. Elephantine strength

may·drive its way through a forest and feel no touch of
the boughs;.but the white skin of Homer's Atrides 75
would have felt a bent rose-leaf, yet subdue its feeling
in glow of battle, and behave itself like iron. I do not
mean to call an elephant a vulgar animal; but if you
think about him carefully you will find that his non-
vulgarity consists in such gentleness as is possible to 80
elephantine nature; not in his insensitive hide, nor in
his clumsy foot; but in the way he will lift his foot if
a child lies in his way; and in his sensitive trunk, and
still more sensitive mind, and capability of pique on
points of honor. 85

6. And, though rightness of moral conduct is ulti-
mately the great purifier of race, the sign of nobleness
is not in this rightness of moral conduct, but in sensi-
tiveness. When the make of the creature is fine, its
temptations are strong, as well as its perceptions; it is 90
liable to all kinds of impressions from without in their
most violent form; liable therefore to be abused and
hurt by all kinds of rough things which would do a
coarser creature little harm, and thus to fall into fright-
ful wrong if its fate will have it so. Thus David, 95
coming of gentlest as well as royalest race, of Ruth as
well as of Judah, is sensitiveness through all flesh and
spirit; not that his compassion will restrain him from
murder when his terror urges him to it; nay, he is
driven to the murder all the more by his sensitiveness 100
to the shame which otherwise threatens him. But when
his own story is told him under a disguise, though only
a lamb is now concerned, his passion about it leaves
him no time for thought. "The man shall die " — note
the reason — " because he had no pity." He is so eager 105
and indignant that it never occurs to him as strange that
Nathan hides the name. This is true gentleman. A

vulgar man would assuredly have been cautious, and asked "who it was?"

7. Hence it will follow that one of the probable signs [110] of high-breeding in men generally, will be their kindness and mercifulness; these always indicating more or less fineness of make in the mind; and miserliness and cruelty the contrary; hence that of Isaiah: "The vile person shall no more be called liberal, nor the churl said [115] to be bountiful." But a thousand things may prevent this kindness from displaying or continuing itself; the mind of the man may be warped so as to bear mainly on his own interests, and then all his sensibilities will take the form of pride, or fastidiousness, or revengefulness; [120] and other wicked, but not ungentlemanly tempers; or, further, they may run into utter sensuality and covetousness, if he is bent on pleasure, accompanied with quite infinite cruelty when the pride is wounded, or the passions thwarted; — until your gentleman becomes [125] Ezzelin, and your lady, the deadly Lucrece; yet still gentleman and lady, quite incapable of making anything else of themselves, being so born.

8. A truer sign of breeding than mere kindness is therefore sympathy; a vulgar man may often be kind in [130] a hard way, on principle, and because he thinks he ought to be; whereas, a highly bred man, even when cruel, will be cruel in a softer way, understanding and feeling what he inflicts, and pitying his victim. Only we must carefully remember that the quality of sym- [135] pathy a gentleman feels can never be judged of by its outward expression, for another of his chief characteristics is apparent reserve. I say "apparent" reserve;

---

126. *Ezzelin*, a character in Byron's *Lara*, treacherous, revengeful, and cruel. *Lucrece*, Lucretia Borgia, an Italian duchess of the early sixteenth century, famous as a poisoner.

for the sympathy is real, but the reserve not: a perfect
gentleman is never reserved, but sweetly and entirely 140
open, so far as it is good for others, or possible that he
should be.   In a great many respects it is impossible
that he should be open except to men of his own kind.
To them, he can open himself, by a word, or syllable,
or a glance; but to men not of his kind he cannot open 145
himself, though he tried it through an eternity of clear
grammatical speech.   By the very acuteness of his sym-
pathy he knows how much of himself he can give to
anybody; and he gives that much frankly; — would
always be glad to give more if he could, but is obliged, 150
nevertheless, in his general intercourse with the world,
to be a somewhat silent person; silence is to most
people, he finds, less reserved than speech.   Whatever
he said, a vulgar man would misinterpret: no words
that he could use would bear the same sense to the vul- 155
gar man that they do to him; if he used any, the vulgar
man would go away saying, "He had said so and so,
and meant so and so" (something assuredly he never
meant); but he keeps silence, and the vulgar man goes
away saying, "He didn't know what to make of him." 160
Which is precisely the fact, and the only fact which he
is anywise able to announce to the vulgar man con-
cerning himself.

9. There is yet another quite as efficient cause of the
apparent reserve of a gentleman.   His sensibility being 165
constant and intelligent, it will be seldom that a feeling
touches him, however acutely, but it has touched him
in the same way often before, and in some sort is touch-
ing him always.   It is not that he feels little, but that he
feels habitually; a vulgar man having some heart at the 170
bottom of him, if you can by talk or by sight fairly force
the pathos of anything down to his heart, will be excited

about it and demonstrative; the sensation of pity being strange to him, and wonderful. But your gentleman has walked in pity all day long; the tears have never 175 been out of his eyes: you thought the eyes were bright only; but they were wet. You tell him a sorrowful story, and his countenance does not change; the eyes can but be wet still; he does not speak neither, there being, in fact, nothing to be said, only something to be 180 done; some vulgar person, beside you both, goes away saying, "How hard he is!" Next day he hears that the · hard person has put good end to the sorrow he said nothing about; — and then he changes his wonder and, exclaims, "How reserved he is!" 185

10. Self-command is often thought a characteristic of high-breeding: and to a certain extent it is so, at least it is one of the means of forming and strengthening character; but it is rather a way of imitating a gentleman than a characteristic of him; a true gentleman has no 190 need of self-command; he simply feels rightly on all occasions: and desiring to express only so much of his feeling as it is right to express, does not need to command himself. Hence perfect ease is indeed characteristic of him; but perfect ease is inconsistent with 195 self-restraint. Nevertheless gentlemen, so far as they fail of their own ideal, need to command themselves, and do so; while, on the contrary, to feel unwisely, and to be unable to restrain the expression of the unwise feeling is vulgarity; and yet even then, the vulgarity, 200 at its root, is not in the mistimed expression, but in the unseemly feeling; and when we find fault with a vulgar person for "exposing himself," it is not his openness, but clumsiness; and yet more the want of sensibility to his own failure, which we blame; so that still the vul- 205 garity resolves itself into want of sensibility. Also, it

is to be noted that great powers of self-restraint may be attained by very vulgar persons, when it suits their purposes.

11. Closely, but strangely, connected with this open- 210 ness is that form of truthfulness which is opposed to cunning, yet not opposed to falsity absolute. And herein is a distinction of great importance.

Cunning signifies especially a habit or gift of over-reaching, accompanied with enjoyment and a sense of 215 superiority. It is associated with small and dull conceit, and with an absolute want of sympathy or affection. Its essential connection with vulgarity may be at once exemplified by the expression of the butcher's dog in Landseer's "Low Life." Cruikshank's "Noah Clay- 220 pole," in the illustrations to "Oliver Twist," in the interview with the Jew, is, however, still more characteristic. It is the intensest rendering of vulgarity absolute and utter with which I am acquainted.

The truthfulness which is opposed to cunning ought, 225 perhaps, rather to be called the desire of truthfulness; it consists more in unwillingness to deceive than in not deceiving, — an unwillingness implying sympathy with and respect for the person deceived; and a fond observance of truth up to the possible point, as in a good 230 soldier's mode of retaining his honor through a *ruse-de-guerre*. A cunning person seeks for opportunities to deceive; a gentleman shuns them. A cunning person triumphs in deceiving; a gentleman is humiliated by his success, or at least by so much of the success as is 235 dependent merely on the falsehood, and not on his intellectual superiority.

12. The absolute disdain of all lying belongs rather to Christian chivalry than to mere high breeding; as

231. *ruse-de-guerre*, French for *ruse of war*.

connected merely with this latter, and with general 240
refinement and courage, the exact relations of truthful-
ness may be best studied in the well-trained Greek
mind. The Greeks believed that mercy and truth were
co-relative virtues — cruelty and falsehood co-relative
vices. But they did not call necessary severity, cruelty; 245
nor necessary deception, falsehood. It was needful
sometimes to slay men, and sometimes to deceive them.
When this had to be done, it should be done well and
thoroughly; so that to direct a spear well to its mark, or
a lie well to its end, was equally the accomplishment of 250
a perfect gentleman. Hence, in the pretty diamond-
cut-diamond scene between Pallas and Ulysses, when
she receives him on the coast of Ithaca, the goddess
laughs delightedly at her hero's good lying, and gives
him her hand upon it; showing herself then in her 255
woman's form, as just a little more than his match.
"Subtle would he be, and stealthy, who should go
beyond thee in deceit, even were he a god, thou many-
witted! What! here in thine own land, too, wilt thou
not cease from cheating? Knowest thou not me, Pallas 260
Athena, maid of Jove, who am with thee in all thy
labors, and gave thee favor with the Phæacians, and
keep thee, and have come now to weave cunning with
thee?" But how completely this kind of cunning was
looked upon as a part of a man's power, and not as a 265
diminution of faithfulness, is perhaps best shown by the
single line of praise in which the high qualities of his
servant are summed up by Chremulus in the Plutus —
"Of all my house servants, I hold you to be the faith-
fullest, and the greatest cheat (or thief)." 270

13. Thus, the primal difference between honorable
and base lying in the Greek mind lay in honorable pur-
pose. A man who used his strength wantonly to hurt

z

others was a monster; so, also, a man who used his cunning wantonly to hurt others.   Strength and cunning 275 were to be used only in self-defence, or to save the weak, and then were alike admirable.   This was their first idea.   Then the second, and perhaps the more essential, difference between noble and ignoble lying in the Greek mind, was that the honorable lie — or, if we 280 may use the strange, yet just expression, the true lie — knew and confessed itself for such — was ready to take the full responsibility of what it did.   As the sword answered for its blow, so the lie for its snare.   But what the Greeks hated with all their heart was the false lie; 285 the lie that did not know itself, feared to confess itself, which slunk to its aim under a cloak of truth, and sought to do liars' work, and yet not take liars' pay, excusing itself to the conscience by quibble and quirk.   Hence the great expression of Jesuit principle by Euripides, 290 "The tongue has sworn, but not the heart," was a subject of execration throughout Greece, and the satirists exhausted their arrows on it — no audience was ever tired hearing (τὸ Εὐριπίδειον ἐκεῖνο) "that Euripidean thing" brought to shame.   295

14. And this is especially to be insisted on in the early education of young people.   It should be pointed out to them with continual earnestness that the essence of lying is in deception, not in words; a lie may be told by silence, by equivocation, by the accent on a syllable, 300 by a glance of the eye attaching a peculiar significance to a sentence; and all these kinds of lies are worse and

---

290. *Jesuit.* The Society of Jesus, founded by Loyola in the sixteenth century, did a great deal of good and a great deal of harm. *Jesuitical* is sometimes used to mean hypocritical, because the Jesuits believed that lying is excusable if it accomplishes good. *Euripides*, a Greek tragic poet, born 480 B.C.

baser by many degrees than a lie plainly worded; so
that no form of blinded conscience is so far sunk as that
which comforts itself for having deceived, because the 305
deception was by gesture or silence, instead of utterance;
and, finally, according to Tennyson's deep and tren-
chant line, "A lie which is half a truth is ever the worst
of lies."

15. Although, however, ungenerous cunning is usually 310
so distinct an outward manifestation of vulgarity, that
I name it separately from insensibility, it is in truth
only an effect of insensibility, producing want of affec-
tion to others, and blindness to the beauty of truth.
The degree in which political subtlety in men such as 315
Richelieu, Machiavel, or Metternich, will efface the
gentleman, depends on the selfishness of political pur-
pose to which the cunning is directed, and on the base
delight taken in its use. The command, "Be ye wise
as serpents, harmless as doves," is the ultimate expres- 320
sion of this principle, misunderstood usually because
the word "wise" is referred to the intellectual power
instead of the subtlety of the serpent. The serpent has
very little intellectual power, but according to that
which it has, it is yet, as of old, the subtlest of the beasts 325
of the field.

16. Another great sign of vulgarity is also, when
traced to its root, another phase of insensibility, namely,
the undue regard to appearances and manners, as in the
households of vulgar persons, of all stations, and the 330
assumption of behavior, language, or dress unsuited to
them, by persons in inferior stations of life. I say

316. *Richelieu*, born 1585, was the famous cardinal who ruled France
under Louis XIII. *Machiavel*, Machiavelli, b. 1469, was a Florentine
writer on the art of politics. *Metternich*, b. 1773, was the diplomatist on
whom Francis I. of Austria depended.

"undue" regard to appearances, because in the undue-
ness consists, of course, the vulgarity. It is due and
wise in some sort to care for appearances, in another 335
sort undue and unwise. Wherein lies the difference?

At first one is apt to answer quickly: the vulgarity is
simply in pretending to be what you are not. But that
answer will not stand. A queen may dress like a wait-
ing maid, — perhaps succeed, if she chooses, in passing 340
for one; but she will not, therefore, be vulgar; nay, a
waiting maid may dress like a queen, and pretend to
be one, and yet need not be vulgar, unless there is
inherent vulgarity in her. In Scribe's very absurd but
very amusing "Reine d'un jour," a milliner's girl sustains 345
the part of a queen for a day. She several times amazes
and disgusts her courtiers by her straightforwardness;
and once or twice very nearly betrays herself to her
maids of honor by an unqueenly knowledge of sewing;
but she is not in the least vulgar, for she is sensitive, 350
simple, and generous, and a queen could be no more.

17. Is the vulgarity, then, only in trying to play a
part you cannot play, so as to be continually detected?
No; a bad amateur actor may be continually detected
in his part, but yet continually detected to be a gentle- 355
man: a vulgar regard to appearances has nothing in it
necessarily of hypocrisy. You shall know a man not to
be a gentleman by the perfect and neat pronunciation of
his words: but he does not pretend to pronounce accu-
rately; he *does* pronounce accurately, the vulgarity is in 360
the real (not assumed) scrupulousness.

18. It will be found on further thought, that a vulgar
regard for appearances is, primarily, a selfish one,
resulting, not out of a wish to give pleasure (as a wife's
wish to make herself beautiful for her husband), but out 365
of an endeavor to mortify others, or attract for pride's

sake; — the common "keeping up appearances" of society, being a mere selfish struggle of the vain with the vain. But the deepest stain of the vulgarity depends on this being done, not selfishly only, but stupidly, with- 370 out understanding the impression which is really produced nor the relations of importance between oneself and others, so as to suppose that their attention is fixed upon us, when we are in reality ciphers in their eyes — all which comes of insensibility. Hence pride simple 375 is not vulgar (the looking down on others because of their true inferiority to us), nor vanity simple (the desire of praise), but conceit simple (the attribution to ourselves of qualities we have not), is always so. In cases of over-studied pronunciation, etc., there is insensi- 380 bility, first, in the person's thinking more of himself than of what he is saying; and, secondly, in his not having musical fineness of ear enough to feel that his talking is uneasy and strained.

19. Finally, vulgarity is indicated by coarseness of 385 language or manners, only so far as this coarseness had been contracted under circumstances not necessarily producing it. The illiterateness of a Spanish or Calabrian peasant is not vulgar, because they had never an opportunity of acquiring letters; but the illiterateness 390 of an English school-boy is. . . .

20. So also of personal defects, those only are vulgar which imply insensibility or dissipation.

There is no vulgarity in the emaciation of Don Quixote, the deformity of the Black Dwarf, or the corpulence of 395 Falstaff; but much in the same personal characters, as they are seen in Uriah Heep, Quilp, and Chadband.

---

395. *The Black Dwarf* is a character in Scott's novel of the same name. 397. *Uriah Heep, Quilp*, and *Chadband* are vulgar characters drawn by Dickens.

21. One of the most curious minor questions in this matter is respecting the vulgarity of excessive neatness, complicating itself with inquiries into the distinction [400] between base neatness, and the perfectness of good execution in the fine arts. It will be found on final thought that precision and exquisiteness of arrangement are always noble; but become vulgar only when they arise from an equality (insensibility) of temperament, [405] which is incapable of fine passion, and is set ignobly, and with a dullard mechanism, on accuracy in vile things. In the finest Greek coins, the letters of the inscriptions are purposely coarse and rude, while the relievi are wrought with inestimable care. But in an [410] English coin, the letters are the best done, and the whole is unredeemably vulgar. In a picture of Titian's, an inserted inscription will be complete in the lettering, as all the rest is; because it costs Titian very little more trouble to draw rightly than wrongly, and in him, there- [415] fore, impatience with the letters would be vulgar, as in the Greek sculptor of the coin, patience would have been. For the engraving of a letter accurately is difficult work, and his time must have been unworthily thrown away.

22. All the different impressions connected with [420] negligence or foulness depend, in like manner, on the degree of insensibility implied. Disorder in a drawing-room is vulgar, in an antiquary's study, not; the black battle-stain on a soldier's face is not vulgar, but the dirty face of a housemaid is. [425]

And lastly, courage, so far as it is a sign of race, is peculiarly the mark of a gentleman or a lady: but it becomes vulgar if rude or insensitive, while timidity is not vulgar, if it be a characteristic of race or fineness of make. A fawn is not vulgar in being timid, nor a [430] crocodile "gentle" because courageous.

23. Without following the inquiry into further detail, we may conclude that vulgarity consists in a deadness of the heart and body, resulting from prolonged, and especially from inherited conditions of "degeneracy," 435 or literally "un-racing"; — gentlemanliness being another word for an intense humanity. And vulgarity shows itself primarily in dulness of heart, not in rage or cruelty, but in inability to feel or conceive noble character or emotion. This is its essential, pure, and 440 most fatal form. Dulness of bodily sense and general stupidity, with such forms of crime as peculiarly issue from stupidity, are its material manifestation.

THE YOUNG MONTAGU

CHARLES LAMB

Yet must I confess, that from the mouth of a true sweep a display (even to ostentation) of those white and shining ossifications, strikes me as an agreeable anomaly in manners, and an allowable piece of foppery. It is, as when 5

> A sable cloud
> Turns forth her silver lining on the night.

It is like some remnant of gentry not quite extinct; a badge of better days; a hint of nobility — and, doubtless, under the obscuring darkness and double night of their 10 forlorn disguisement, oftentimes lurketh good blood and gentle conditions, derived from lost ancestry and a lapsed pedigree. The premature apprenticements of these tender victims give but too much encouragement, I fear, to clandestine and almost infantile abductions; the seeds 15 of civility and true courtesy, so often discernible in these young grafts (not otherwise to be accounted for), plainly hint at some forced adoptions; many noble Rachels, mourning for their children even in our days, countenance the fact; the tales of fairy-spiriting may shadow 20 a lamentable verity, and the recovery of the young Montagu be but a solitary instance of good fortune out of many irreparable and hopeless *defiliations.*

In one of the state beds at Arundel Castle, a few years since — under a ducal canopy — (that seat of the How- 25 ards is an object of curiosity to visitors, chiefly for its beds, in which the late duke was especially a connoisseur) — encircled with curtains of delicatest crimson, with starry coronets inwoven — was discovered by chance, after all methods of search had failed, at noonday, fast asleep, 30 a lost chimney-sweeper. The little creature, having somehow confounded his passage among the intricacies of those lordly chimneys, by some unknown aperture had alighted upon this magnificent chamber; and, tired with his tedious explorations, was unable to resist the delicious invitement 35 to repose which he there saw exhibited; so creeping between the sheets very quietly, laid his black head upon the pillow, and slept like a young Howard.

Such is the account given to the visitors at the Castle. But I cannot help seeming to perceive a confirmation of 40 what I have just hinted at in this story. A high instinct was at work in the case, or I am mistaken. Is it probable that a poor child of that description, with whatever weariness he might be visited, would have ventured, under such a penalty as he would be taught to expect, to uncover the 45 sheets of a duke's bed, and deliberately to lay himself down between them, when the rug or the carpet presented an obvious couch, still far above his pretensions — is this probable, I would ask, if the great power of

23. *defiliations*, a word of Lamb's impromptu coinage, to mean the loss of children by kidnapping.

nature, which I contend for, had not been manifested 50
within him, prompting to the adventure? Doubtless this
young nobleman (for such my mind misgives me that he
must be) was allured by some memory, not amounting to
full consciousness, of his condition in infancy, when he
was used to be lapped by his mother, or his nurse, in just 55
such sheets as he there found, into which he was now
but creeping back as into his proper *lucunabula* and
resting-place. By no other theory than by this sentiment
of a ·preëxistent state (as I may call it) can I explain a
deed so venturous, and indeed upon any other system so 60
indecorous, in this tender, but unseasonable, sleeper.

Is the diction modern or archaic ?   Lamb's favorite authors were those
of Shakspere's time, and he was fond of a partly serious, partly playful, use
of pompous terms, in imitation of the prose writers of the sixteenth and
seventeenth centuries.

TACT

RALPH WALDO EMERSON

What boots it, thy virtue,
　What profit thy parts,
While one thing thou lackest, —
　The art of all arts?

The only credentials,　　　　　　　　　　　5
　Passport to success ;
Opens castle and parlor, —
　Address, man, Address.

The maiden in danger
　Was saved by the swain ;　　　　　　　10
His stout arm restored her
　To Broadway again.

2. *Parts* is an old expression for natural abilities. 5, 7. Note the ellip-
sis ; *address* is (credentials), then *address* (opens).

The maid would reward him, —
   Gay company come, —
They laugh, she laughs with them;   **15**
   He is moonstruck and dumb.

This clinches the bargain;
   Sails out of the bay;
Gets the vote in the senate,
   Spite of Webster and Clay.   **20**

Has for genius no mercy,
   For speeches no heed;
It lurks in the eyebeam,
   Its leaps to its deed.

Church, market, and tavern,   **25**
   Bed and board, it will sway.
It has no to-morrow,
   It ends with to-day.

18. Perhaps this means that but for the tact that clinches bargains, there would be no commerce; every ship that sets sail means so much tact. **23.** Is this true? Can the eye say things that the tongue cannot? **24.** That is, tact comes in play when something must be done quickly, as when danger is averted by a tactful answer made instantly.

TWO GENTLEMEN AT PETERSBURG

GEORGE CARY EGGLESTON

At that point where the great mine was blown up at Petersburg, the lines of the two armies were within fifty yards of each other.

In the fearful slaughter that ensued, the space between the rival breastworks was literally piled high with dead   5 men, lying one on top of the other. Only in one other place, namely, at Cold Harbor, was there ever so much of slaughter within so small a space.

It was evident, apart from all considerations of decency, that for the comfort of both sides some arrangement must be made for the burial of these dead men. Neither side could have lived long in its works otherwise.

Accordingly, a cartel was arranged between General Grant and General Lee. It was stipulated that there should be a cessation of hostilities for a specified number of hours for the purpose of burying the dead.

It was arranged that two lines should be formed twelve feet apart in the middle of the space between the works; that one line should be composed of Federal sentinels, the other of Confederates; that the space between these two lines should be a neutral ground, accessible to both sides; but that no person from either side should cross the line established by the other side. It was agreed that the dead men who had fallen within the Confederate line should be dragged to the neutral ground by Confederate soldiers, and there delivered to Federal troops to be carried within their lines for burial.

There were no Confederate dead there, of course. All of our men who had been killed were killed within our own works. So every corpse on our side of the neutral ground was dragged by a rope to that common space and there delivered to its official friends.

It was specially stipulated in the cartel that no officer or soldier on either side should take advantage of the truce to appropriate property of any kind lying upon the field, whether upon the one or the other side of the neutral ground. Swords, pistols, sashes, everything of the kind must, by agreement, be left precisely where they were.

Many of us, of course, went out to the neutral ground 40
to look over the situation.   There was a certain grue-
some delight even in standing upon ground, where for
a month or more it had been impossible for a twig or
a blade of grass to grow without instant decapitation, and
where for months to come it would be equally impossible 45
for anything having material substance to exist.   The very
turf itself had been literally skinned from the surface of
the earth by a continuous scything of bullets.   For a
month it had been impossible for any soldier on either
·side even to shoot over the breastworks, for he who tried 50
to do so was sure to be instantly destroyed.   The fire on
either side had to be through carefully sand-bag-guarded
port-holes.   And even the port-holes had to be protected
by hanging blankets behind them to conceal the sky, lest
their darkening by a human head should invite a hail- 55
storm of alert and waiting bullets.

Of course every man who, during the truce, wandered
over this perilous space for an hour, must have been
impressed, if he had any imagination at all, with the
historical interest of the occasion.   Every one desired 60
naturally to carry away some memento of the event.
Only one man yielded to this impulse, and he did so
thoughtlessly.   He was a captain of Confederate
infantry.

He saw lying on the ground a star that had been cut 65
by a bullet from some officer's coat collar.

It was a worthless bawble, valuable only as a souvenir.
He picked it up and pocketed it.   Instantly he was
arrested by the Confederate guards and taken before the
officer in command of the Confederate line.   70

That officer immediately and with great dignity went
to the Federal commander and said : "I desire under
the terms of the cartel to surrender this officer to you

for such punishment as a court-martial of your army may
see fit to inflict. He has violated the cartel." 75

"What has he done?" asked the Federal officer.

"He has taken possession of property left upon the
field, contrary to the terms of the truce."

"Would you mind telling me," asked the Federal offi-
cer, "the exact nature and extent of his offence?" 80

A little explanation followed, the Confederate com-
mander remaining stern and uncompromising in his
determination to deliver the man for punishment, asking
no favors or mercies for him, and offering no apologies
for that which he deemed a breach of honor. 85

When the Federal officer had learned the exact facts
of the situation, he made the usual military salute and
said to the Confederate commander: "I thank you.
You have been very honorable and very punctilious, but
the officer's fault has been merely one of inadvertence. 90
I beg to return him to you with the assurance that we
have no desire to punish so brave a man as he must be,
in order to hold his commission in your army, for an act
that involved no intention of wrong."

Here were two brave men — two gentlemen — met. 95
Naturally they understood each other.

Examine the paragraphing of this story, and say what paragraphs might
be combined.

THE GENTLEMAN

JOHN HENRY, CARDINAL NEWMAN

Hence it is that it is almost a definition of a gentle-
man to say he is one who never inflicts pain. This
description is both refined and, as far as it goes, accurate.
He is mainly occupied in merely removing the obstacles
which hinder the free and unembarrassed action of those 5

about him; and he concurs with their movements rather than takes the initiative himself. His benefits may be considered as parallel to what are called comforts or conveniences in arrangements of a personal nature: like an easy-chair or a good fire, which do their part in dispelling cold and fatigue, though nature provides both means of rest and animal heat without them. The true gentleman in like manner carefully avoids whatever may cause a jar or a jolt in the minds of those with whom he is cast;—all clashing of opinion, or collision of feeling, all restraint, or suspicion, or gloom, or resentment; his great concern being to make every one at their ease and at home. He has his eyes on all his company; he is tender towards the bashful, gentle towards the distant, and merciful towards the absurd; he can recollect to whom he is speaking; he guards against unseasonable allusions, or topics which may irritate; he is seldom prominent in conversation, and never wearisome. He makes light of favors while he does them, and seems to be receiving when he is conferring. He never speaks of himself except when compelled, never defends himself by a mere retort, he has no ears for slander or gossip, is scrupulous in imputing motives to those who interfere with him, and interprets everything for the best. He is never mean or little in his disputes, never takes unfair advantage, never mistakes personalities or sharp sayings for arguments, or insinuates evil which he dare not say out. From a long-sighted prudence, he observes the maxim of the ancient sage, that we should ever conduct ourselves towards our enemy as if he were one day to be our friend. He has too much good sense to be affronted at insults, he is too well employed to remember injuries, and too indolent to bear malice. He is patient, forbearing, and resigned, on philosophical principles; he sub-

mits to pain, because it is inevitable, to bereavement, 40
because it is irreparable, and to death, because it is
his destiny. If he engages in controversy of any kind,
his disciplined intellect preserves him from the blun-
dering discourtesy of better, perhaps, but less educated
minds; who, like blunt weapons, tear and hack instead 45
of cutting clean, who mistake the point in argument,
waste their strength on trifles, misconceive their adver-
sary, and leave the question more involved than they find
it. He may be right or wrong in his opinion, but he is
too clear-headed to be unjust; he is as simple as he 50
is forcible, and as brief as he is decisive. Nowhere
shall we find greater candor, consideration, indulgence:
he throws himself into the minds of his opponents, he
accounts for their mistakes.

A FOP

WILLIAM SHAKSPERE

Hotspur. My liege, I did deny no prisoners.
But I remember, when the fight was done,
When I was dry with rage, and extreme toil,
Breathless and faint, leaning upon my sword,
Came there a certain lord, neat, trimly dressed,   5
Fresh as a bridgroom; and his chin, new reaped,
Showed like a stubble-land at harvest-home;
He was perfumèd like a milliner;
And 'twixt his finger and his thumb he held
A pouncet-box, which ever and anon   10
He gave his nose, and took't away again; —

---

3. Note the old accent of *ex'treme*. 6–7. Is this a humorous hyperbole?
9. *pouncet-box*, a box for powder or perfume.

Who therewith angry, when it next came there,
Took it in snuff: — and still he smiled and talked;
And, as the soldiers bore dead bodies by,
He called them untaught knaves, unmannerly,   15
To bring a slovenly unhandsome corse
Betwixt the wind and his nobility.
With many holiday and lady terms
He questioned me; among the rest demanded
My prisoners, in your majesty's behalf.   20
I then, all smarting, with my wounds being cold,
To be so pestered with a popinjay,
Out of my grief and my impatience,
Answered neglectingly, I know not what;
He should, or he should not; — for he made me mad   25
To see him shine so brisk, and smell so sweet,
And talk so like a waiting-gentlewoman,
Of guns, and drums, and wounds (God save the mark!),
And telling me, the sovereign'st thing on earth
Was parmaceti, for an inward bruise;   30
And that it was great pity, so it was,
That villanous saltpetre should be digged
Out of the bowels of the harmless earth,
Which many a good tall fellow had destroyed
So cowardly; and but for these vile guns,   35
He would himself have been a soldier.

---

13. *To take in snuff* means, of course, to be angry; but see how Shak-
spere pleases his whim by using the words at once in their original and
in their derived sense, when he is talking of the original function. 25. Is
mad correctly intended, or does the good Shakspere nod? That is, does
mad here really mean *out of his mind with rage*, or has Shakspere been
caught napping? 28. *God save the mark!* is a sarcastic exclamation, as
if Hotspur should say, "This popinjay talks about wounds! Heaven
preserve us! What does he know about wounds?" Philologists are not
sure of the origin of the expression (which is still common). Perhaps it
originally referred to the target, in shooting.

This bald unjointed chat of his, my lord,
I answered indirectly, as I said;
And I beseech you, let not his report
Come current for an accusation, 40
Betwixt my love and your high majesty.

Henry IV.

37. The *unjointed* is clear: the fop's talk was rambling, incoherent.
Bald is harder, but probably means merely that the popinjay spoke his
mind rather too freely and rudely. *Bald* expressions are those which lack
the covering of courtesy.

A BREACH OF ETIQUETTE

GEORGE CARY EGGLESTON

We had marched nearly all night, in order to join Jeb
Stuart at the time appointed. This was in the early
summer of 1861.

We regarded ourselves with more or less of self-pity,
as sleep-sacrificing heroes, who were clearly entitled to 5
a full day's rest.

Jeb Stuart didn't look at it in that way at all. He
was a soldier, while we were just beginning to learn how
to be soldiers. These things make a difference.

We hadn't got our tents pitched when he ordered us out 10
for a scouting expedition under his personal command.

Our army lay at Winchester. The enemy was at Mar-
tinsburg, twenty-two miles away. Stuart, with his four
or five hundred horsemen, lay at Bunker Hill, about
half-way between but a little nearer to the enemy than to 15
his supports. That was always Stuart's way.

In our scouting expedition that day, we had two or
three " brushes " with the enemy — " just to get us used
to it," Stuart said.

Finally we went near to Martinsburg, and came upon 20

2A

a farmhouse. The farm gave no appearance of being a large one, or one more than ordinarily prosperous, yet we saw through the open door a dozen or fifteen "farm hands" eating dinner, all of them in their shirt-sleeves.

Stuart rode up, with a few of us at his back, to make 25 inquiries, and we dismounted. Just then a slip of a girl, — not over fourteen, I should say, — accompanied by a thick-set, young bull-dog, with an abnormal development of teeth, ran up to us.

She distinctly and unmistakably "sicked" that dog upon 30 *us.* But as the beast assailed us, the young girl ran after him and restrained his ardor by throwing her arms around his neck.   As she did so, she kept repeating in a low but very insistent tone to us: "Make 'em put their coats on! Make 'em put their coats on!   Make 'em put their coats 35 on!"

Stuart was a peculiarly ready person.   He said not one word to the young girl as she led her dog away, but with a word or two he directed a dozen or so of us to follow him with cocked carbines into the dining room. 40 There he said to the "farm hands": "Don't you know that a gentleman never dines without his coat?   Aren't you ashamed of yourselves?   And ladies present, too! Get up and put on your coats, every man jack of you, or I'll riddle you with bullets in five seconds." 45

They sprang first of all into the hallway, where they had left their arms; but either the bull-dog or the four-teen-year-old girl had taken care of that.   The arms were gone.   Then seeing the carbines levelled, they made a hasty search of the hiding-places in which they 50 had bestowed their coats.   A minute later they appeared as fully uniformed, but helplessly unarmed Pennsylvania volunteers.

They were prisoners of war at once, without even an

opportunity to finish that good dinner. As we left the 55
house the young girl came up to Stuart and said: "Don't
say anything about it; but the dog wouldn't have bit
you. He knows which side *we're* on in this war."

As we rode away, this young girl — she of the bull-dog
— cried out: "To think the wretches made us give 'em 60
dinner! And in their shirt-sleeves, too!"

Criticise the paragraphing of this story, and suggest improvements.

REMARKS CONCERNING THE SAVAGES OF NORTH AMERICA

BENJAMIN FRANKLIN

Savages we call them, because their manners differ
from ours, which we think the perfection of civility;
they think the same of theirs.

Perhaps, if we could examine the manners of different
nations with impartiality, we should find no people so 5
rude as to be without any rules of politeness; or none
so polite as not to have some remains of rudeness.

The Indian men, when young, are hunters and war-
riors; when old, counsellors; for all their government is
by the counsel or advice of the sages. There is no 10
force, there are no prisons, no officers to compel obedi-
ence or inflict punishment. Hence they generally study
oratory, the best speaker having the most influence.
The Indian women till the ground, dress the food, nurse
and bring up the children, and preserve and hand down 15
to posterity the memory of public transactions. These
employments of men and women are accounted natural
and honorable. Having few artificial wants, they have
abundance of leisure for improvement by conversation.
Our laborious manner of life, compared with theirs, 20

they esteem slavish and base and the learning on which we value ourselves they regard as frivolous and useless. An instance of this occurred at the treaty of Lancaster, in Pennsylvania, anno 1744, between the government of Virginia and the Six Nations. After the principal business was settled, the commissioners from Virginia acquainted the Indians by a speech, that there was at Williamsburg a college, with a fund for educating Indian youth; and that, if the chiefs of the Six Nations would send down half a dozen of their sons to that college, the government would take care that they should be well provided for, and instructed in all the learning of the white people. It is one of the Indian rules of politeness not to answer a public proposition the same day that it is made; they think this would be treating it as a light matter, and that they show it respect by taking time to consider it, as of a matter important. They therefore deferred their answer till the day following, when their speaker began by expressing their deep sense of the kindness of the Virginia government in making them that offer; "for we know," says he, "that you highly esteem the kind of learning taught in those colleges, and that the maintenance of our young men, while with you, would be very expensive to you. We are convinced, therefore, that you mean to do us good by your proposal, and we thank you heartily. But you, who are wise, must know that different nations have different conceptions of things; and you will therefore not take it amiss if our ideas of this kind of education happen not to be the same with yours. We have had some experience of it. Several of our young people were formerly brought up at the colleges of the northern provinces; they were instructed in all your sciences; but, when they came back to us, they were bad runners,

ignorant of every means of living in the woods, unable 55
to bear either cold or hunger, knew neither how to build
a cabin, take a deer, nor kill an enemy, spoke our
language imperfectly; were therefore neither fit for
hunters, warriors, nor counsellors; they were therefore
totally good for nothing. We are however not the less 60
obliged by your kind offer, though we decline accepting
it; and, to show our grateful sense of it, if the gentle-
men of Virginia will send us a dozen of their sons, we
will take great care of their education, instruct them in
all we know, and make *men* of them." 65

Having frequent occasions to hold councils, they have
acquired great order and decency in conducting them.
The old men sit in the foremost ranks, the warriors in
the next, and the women and children in the hindmost.
The business of the women is to take exact notice of 70
what passes, imprint it in their memories (for they have
no writing), and communicate it to their children.
They are the records of the council, and they preserve the
tradition of the stipulations in treaties a hundred years
back; which, when we compare with our writings, we 75
always find exact. He that would speak rises. The
rest observe a profound silence. When he has finished
and sits down, they leave him five or six minutes to
recollect that, if he has omitted anything he intended to
say, or has anything to add, he may rise again and deliver 80
it. To interrupt another, even in common conversation,
is reckoned highly indecent. How different this is from
the conduct of a polite British House of Commons,
where scarce a day passes without some confusion that
makes the speaker hoarse calling *to order;* and how 85
different from the mode of conversation in many polite
companies of Europe, where, if you do not deliver your
sentence with great rapidity, you are cut off in the

middle of it by the impatient loquacity of those you
converse with, and never suffered to finish it!   90

The politeness of these savages in conversation is
indeed carried to excess, since it does not permit them
to contradict or deny the truth of what is asserted in
their presence.   By this means they indeed avoid dis-
putes; but then it becomes difficult to know their 95
minds, or what impression you make upon them.   The
missionaries who have attempted to convert them to
Christianity all complain of this as one of the great
difficulties of their mission.   The Indians hear with
patience the truths of the Gospel explained to them, 100
and give their usual tokens of assent and approbation.
You would think they were convinced.   No such matter.
It is mere civility.

A Swedish minister, having assembled the chiefs of
the Susquehanna Indians, made a sermon to them, ac- 105
quainting them with the principal historical facts on
which our religion is founded, such as the fall of our
first parents by eating an apple, the coming of Christ to
repair the mischief, his miracles and suffering, etc.
When he had finished, an Indian orator stood up to 110
thank him.   "What you have told us," says he, "is all
very good.   It is indeed bad to eat apples.   It is better
to make them all into cider.   We are much obliged by
your kindness in coming so far to tell us those things
which you have heard from your mothers.   In return, I 115
will tell you some of those we have heard from ours.
'In the beginning, our fathers had only the flesh of ani-
mals to subsist on, and if their hunting was unsuccessful
they were starving.   Two of our young hunters, having
killed a deer, made a fire in the woods to boil some 120
parts of it.   When they were about to satisfy their
hunger, they beheld a beautiful young woman descend

from the clouds and seat herself on that hill which you
see yonder among the Blue Mountains. They said to
each other, "It is a spirit, that perhaps has smelt our 125
broiling venison and wishes to eat of it; let us offer some
to her." They presented her with the tongue; she was
pleased with the taste of it, and said: "Your kindness
shall be rewarded; come to this place after thirteen
moons, and you will find something that will be of great 130
benefit in nourishing you and your children to the latest
generations." They did so, and, to their surprise, found
plants they had never seen before, but which, from that
ancient time, have been constantly cultivated among us
to our great advantage. Where her right hand had 135
touched the ground, they found maize; where her left
had touched it, they found kidney-beans.'" The
good missionary, disgusted with this idle tale, said:
"What I delivered to you were sacred truths; but what
you tell me is mere fable, fiction, and falsehood." The 140
Indian, offended, replied: "My brother, it seems your
friends have not done you justice in your education;
they have not well instructed you in the rules of com-
mon civility. You saw that we, who understand and
practise those rules, believed all your stories; why do 145
you refuse to believe ours?"

When any of them come into our towns, our people are
apt to crowd them, gaze upon them, and incommode
them where they desire to be private; this they esteem
great rudeness, and the effect of the want of instruction 150
in the rules of civility and good manners. "We have,"
say they, "as much curiosity as you, and when you come
into our towns we wish for opportunities of looking at
you; but for this purpose we hide ourselves behind
bushes where you are to pass, and never intrude ourselves 155
into your company."

Their manner of entering one another's village has likewise its rules. It is reckoned uncivil in travelling strangers to enter a village abruptly without giving notice of their approach. Therefore, as soon as they arrive 160 within hearing they stop and hollow, remaining there until invited to enter. Two old men usually come out to them and lead them in. There is in every village a vacant dwelling, called *the strangers' house*. Here they are placed, while the old men go round from hut to hut 165 acquainting the inhabitants that strangers are arrived, who are probably hungry and weary; and every one sends them what he can spare of victuals, and skins to repose on. When the strangers are refreshed, pipes and tobacco are brought, and then, but not before, conversation 170 begins, with inquiries who they are, whither bound, what news, etc.; and it usually ends with offers of service, if the strangers have occasion for guides, or any necessaries for continuing their journey; and nothing is exacted for the entertainment.   175

The same hospitality, esteemed among them as a principal virtue, is practised by private persons, of which Conrad Weiser, our interpreter, gave me the following instance. He had been naturalized among the Six Nations, and spoke well the Mohawk language. In 180 going through the Indian country to carry a message from our governor to the council at Onondaga, he called at the habitation of Canassetego, an old acquaintance, who embraced him, spread furs for him to sit on, and placed before him some boiled beans and venison, and 185 mixed some rum and water for his drink. When he was well refreshed, and had lit his pipe, Canassetego began to converse with him; asked him how he had fared the many years since they had seen each other, whence he then came, what occasioned the journey, etc. Conrad 190

answered all his questions; and when the discourse
began to flag, the Indian, to continue it, said: "Con-
rad, you have lived long among the white people, and
know something of their customs. I have been some-
times at Albany, and have observed that once in seven 195
days they shut up their shops and assemble all in the
great house. Tell me what it is for? What do they do
there?" "They meet there," says Conrad, "to hear and
learn *good things*." "I do not doubt," says the Indian,
"that they tell you so — they have told me the same; 200
but I doubt the truth of what they say, and I will tell
you my reasons. I went lately to Albany to sell my
skins and buy blankets, knives, powder, rum, etc. You
know I used generally to deal with Hans Hanson; but
I was a little inclined this time to try some other mer- 205
chants. However, I called first upon Hans, and asked
him what he would give for beaver. He said he could
not give any more than four shillings a pound; 'but,'
says he, 'I cannot talk on business now: this is the day
when we meet together to learn *good things*, and I am 210
going to meeting.' So I thought to myself, 'Since I
cannot do any business to-day, I may as well go to the
meeting too,' and I went with him. There stood up a
man in black, and began to talk to the people very
angrily. I did not understand what he said, but, per- 215
ceiving that he looked much at me and at Hanson, I
imagined he was angry at seeing me there; so I went
out, sat down near the house, struck fire and lit my pipe,
waiting till the meeting should break up. I thought,
too, that the man had mentioned something of beaver, 220
and I suspected it might be the subject of their meet-
ing. So, when they came out, I accosted my merchant.
'Well, Hans,' says I, 'I hope you have agreed to give
more than four shillings a pound.' 'No,' says he; 'I

cannot give so much; I cannot give more than three 225
shillings and sixpence.'   I then spoke to several dealers,
but they all sung the same song, — three and sixpence,
— three and sixpence.   This made it clear to me that
my suspicion was right; and that, whatever they pre-
tended of meeting to learn *good things*, the real purpose 230
was to consult how to cheat Indians in the price of
beaver.   Consider but a little, Conrad, and you must
be of my opinion.   If they met so often to learn *good
things*, they would certainly have learned some before
this time.   But they are still ignorant.   You know our 235
practice.   If a white man, in travelling through our
country, enters one of our cabins, we all treat him as I
do you: we dry him if he is wet, we warm him if he
is cold, and give him meat and drink, that he may allay
his thirst and hunger, and we spread soft furs for him 240
to rest and sleep on.   We demand nothing in return.
But, if I go into a white man's house at Albany and ask
for victuals and drink, they say, 'Where is your
money?' and if I have none, they say, 'Get out, you
Indian dog!'   You see they have not learned those little 245
good things that we need no meetings to be instructed
in, because our mothers taught them to us when we were
children; and therefore it is impossible their meetings
should be, as they say, for any such purpose, or have
any such effect; they are only to contrive *the cheating of* 250
Indians in the price of beaver.''

OMÀR AND THE PERSIAN

SARAH WILLIAMS

The victor stood beside the spoil, and by the grinning dead:
"The land is ours, the foe is ours, now rest, my men," he
    said.

But while he spoke there came a band of foot-sore, panting
    men :
"The latest prisoner, my lord, we took him in the glen,
And left behind dead hostages that we would come again." 5

The victor spoke: "Thou, Persian dog! hast cost more
    lives than thine.
That was thy will, and thou shouldst die full thrice, if I
    had mine.
Dost know thy fate, thy just reward?" The Persian bent
    his head,
"I know both sides of victory, and only grieve," he said,
"Because there will be none to fight 'gainst thee when I am
    dead.   10

"No Persian faints at sight of Death, — we know his face
    too well, —
He waits for us on mountain side, in town, or shelter'd
    dell;
But I crave a cup of wine, thy first and latest boon,
For I have gone three days athirst, and fear lest I may
    swoon,
Or even wrong mine enemy, by dying now, too soon."   15

The cup was brought; but ere he drank the Persian
    shudder'd white.
Omàr replied, "What fearest thou? The wine is clear and
    bright;
We are no poisoners, not we, nor traitors to a guest,
No dart behind, nor dart within, shall pierce thy gallant
    breast;
Till thou hast drain'd the draught, O foe, thou dost in
    safety rest."   20
The Persian smil'd, with parched lips, upon the foemen
    round,

Then pour'd the precious liquid out, untasted, on the
    ground.
"Till that is drunk, I live," said he, "and while I live, I
    fight;
So, see you to your victory, for 'tis undone this night;
Omàr the worthy, battle fair is but thy godlike right."   25

Upsprang a wrathful army then, — Omàr restrain'd them
    all,
Upon no battlefield had rung more clear his martial call,
The dead men's hair beside his feet as by a breeze was
    stirr'd,
The farthest henchman in the camp the noble mandate
    heard:
"Hold! if there be a sacred thing, it is the warrior's
    word."   30

THE OCTOPUS OF THE GOLDEN ISLES[1]

THEODORE WATTS-DUNTON

" What! Will they even strike at *me ?* "

Round many an Isle of Song, in seas serene,
   With many a swimmer strove the poet-boy,
   Yet strove in love: their strength, I say, was joy
To him, my friend — dear friend of godlike mien!
But soon he felt beneath the billowy green   5
   A monster moving — moving to destroy:
   Limb after limb became the tortured toy
Of coils that clung and lips that stung unseen.

[1] Reprinted from "The Coming of Love, and Other Poems," by permission of Mr. John Lane.

"*And can'st thou strike ev'n me ?* " the swimmer said,
    As rose above the waves the deadly eyes,   10
    Arms flecked with mouths that hissed in hellish wise,
Quivering in hate around a hateful head. —
    I saw him fight old Envy's sorceries:
I saw him sink: the man I loved is dead!

Does this sonnet, like the former one by the same author, break naturally into the octave and the sestet, devoting each to a distinct phase of the theme?

THE CHURL IN SPIRIT

ALFRED, LORD TENNYSON

The churl in spirit, up or down
    Along the scale of ranks, thro' all,
    To him who grasps a golden ball,
By blood a king, at heart a clown;

The churl in spirit, howe'er he veil   5
    His want in forms for fashion's sake,
    Will let his coltish nature break
At seasons thro' the gilded pale:

For who can always act? but he,
    To whom a thousand memories call,   10
    Not being less but more than all
The gentleness he seem'd to be,

Best seem'd the thing he was, and join'd
    Each office of the social hour
    To noble manners, as the flower   15
And native growth of noble mind;

3. The student will perhaps remember statues of Roman emperors holding in the hand a sphere, signifying the earth.

Nor ever narrowness or spite,
   Or villain fancy fleeting by,
   Drew in the expression of an eye,
Where God and Nature met in light;   20

And thus he bore without abuse
   The grand old name of gentleman,
   Defamed by every charlatan,
And soil'd with all ignoble use.

In what other poem appeared the same rhyme-scheme? Tennyson made this stanza famous.

THE END OF THE PLAY

WILLIAM MAKEPEACE THACKERAY

The play is done — the curtain drops,
   Slow falling to the prompter's bell;
A moment yet the actor stops,
   And looks around, to say farewell.
It is an irksome word and task;   5
   And, when he's laugh'd and said his say,
He shows, as he removes the mask,
   A face that's anything but gay.

One word, ere yet the evening ends:
   Let's close it with a parting rhyme,   10
And pledge a hand to all young friends,
   As fits the merry Christmas time;
On life's wide scene you, too, have parts,
   That fate ere long shall bid you play;
Good-night! — with honest gentle hearts   15
   A kindly greeting go alway!

Good-night! — I'd say the griefs, the joys,
 Just hinted in this mimic page,
The triumphs and defeats of boys,
 Are but repeated in our age;   20
I'd say your woes were not less keen,
 Your hopes more vain, than those of men,
Your pangs or pleasures of fifteen
 At forty-five played o'er again.

I'd say we suffer and we strive   25
 Not less nor more as men than boys,
With grizzled beards at forty-five,
 As erst at twelve in corduroys.
And if, in time of sacred youth,
 We learn'd at home to love and pray, 30
Pray Heaven that early love and truth
 May never wholly pass away.

And in the world, as in the school,
 I'd say how fate may change and shift,—
The prize be sometimes with the fool, 35
 The race not always to the swift;
The strong may yield, the good may fall,
 The great man be a vulgar clown,
The knave be lifted over all,
 The kind cast pitilessly down.   40

Who knows the inscrutable design?
 Blessed be He who took and gave!
Why should your mother, Charles, not mine,
 Be weeping at her darling's grave?

27. How old was Thackeray when he died? See the Chronological
Table.

We bow to Heaven that will'd it so,   45
    That darkly rules the fate of all,
That sends the respite or the blow,
    That's free to give or to recall.

So shall each mourn, in life's advance,
    Dear hopes, dear friends, untimely kill'd,   50
Shall grieve for many a forfeit chance,
    And longing passion unfulfill'd.
Amen! — whatever fate be sent,
    Pray God the heart may kindly glow,
Although the head with cares be bent,   55
    And whiten'd with the winter snow.

Come wealth or want, come good or ill,
    Let young and old accept their part,
And bow before the awful will,
    And bear it with an honest heart.   60
Who misses or who wins the prize —
    Go, lose or conquer as you can;
But if you fail, or if you rise,
    Be each, pray God, a gentleman.

A gentleman, or old or young!   65
    (Bear kindly with my humble lays);
The sacred chorus first was sung
    Upon the first of Christmas days;
The shepherds heard it overhead —
    The joyful angels rais'd it then: 70
Glory to heaven on high, it said,
    And peace on earth to gentle men!

My song, save this, is little worth;
  I lay the weary pen aside,
And wish you health, and love, and mirth,   75
  As fits the solemn Christmas-tide.
As fits the holy Christmas birth,
  Be this, good friends, our carol still:
Be peace on earth, be peace on earth,
  To men of gentle will.   80

Plan of Summary. — Reviewing the chapter, (1) enumerate the kinds of metre, designating them by the number of accents and by the predominant foot. Then (2) say which poem is most noticeable for melody; (3) which for beauty of suggested sights; (4) which for pleasure of suggested sounds; (5) which for pleasure of suggested activity; (6) which for pleasure of suggested odors or tastes; (7) which is most easily understood; (8) which moves the reader most deeply; (9) which shows most skill in character drawing; (10) which has the best unity; (11) which, your critical judgment tells you, is the best piece of work; (12) which you like the best, — without regard to its deserved rank, or its fame.

2 B

CHAPTER IX

WIT AND HUMOR[1]

It is an interesting question to ask ourselves why we laugh. Certainly it is not always because the thing laughed at is funny. People in an audience will guffaw at a joke so poor as to deserve tears; they would not smile if they saw the same stale jest in the morning paper. When people are tired or nervously weak, they laugh at nothing, and we call them hysterical; of this order are the giggling boy and the giggling girl. When a student is at work over an algebraic problem, he sees nothing funny in the mathematical puzzle he is trying to solve. He is very serious indeed, poring with knitted brows over the task. Yet presently when the answer is found, and particularly if it is found in an unexpected way, the brows unbend and a smile breaks out upon the face. Still the answer is not amusing.

The student smiled when the nervous tension of searching for the answer was relaxed. The answer came as a pleasant surprise. Similarly the audience laughed at the poor joke because the tension of expectation ceased. A pleasant relaxing of attention or a pleasant surprise usually produces a smile.

What we call the sense of the ridiculous has in it a great deal of this surprise element. When Patrick Henry exclaimed, "Cæsar had his Brutus, Charles the First his Cromwell, and George the Third — may profit by their example!" he saved himself by a stroke of wit from being

[1] For several anecdotes in this chapter the editor is indebted to Walter Jerrold's "Bon Mots of the Nineteenth Century."

370

called a traitor. We may be sure his hearers laughed. So did the attendants who, having repeatedly dipped the invalid Charles Lamb into cold water, learned at last that, if they had given the stammering patient time, he would have said, "I was to be di-di-di-dipped only *once*." When Bret Harte's soldier said, "I was with Grant," — the old farmer thought himself. face to face with a comrade of his son. He was ridiculously surprised when the stranger, having eaten a good dinner at the farmer's expense, explained that he had worked for Grant some years before the war.

Lamb's Salt Dips, p. 376.

There is nothing so surprising, and therefore so funny, as to find a thing quite out of its place. If one should see a cow jumping over the moon he would feel that the situation was unnatural for the cow and for the moon. What is called wit consists largely in seeing things or imagining things out of place. What is called a pun is putting the wrong word into a given place because it sounds like the word which really belongs there. Good puns are rare. Two of the three in the following anecdote, told by Mr. Walter Jerrold, are good, the other poor.

As an "elaborately dressed young lady stepped out on the hotel piazza to admire the sunset, a friend whispered to Oliver Wendell Holmes, 'The young lady is in evening dress.'

"'The *close* of the day, my dear sir,' remarked Holmes.

"'That's Holmes' pun,' was the reply.

"'I'm worsted,' added the poet."

The intentional pun is not so funny as the unintentional. Sheridan's Mrs. Malaprop was an adept in the latter species. She wouldn't wish a daughter of hers to become a progeny of learning, but would have her instructed in geometry, that she might know something of contagious countries.

Mrs. Malaprop on Education for Girls, p. 378.

Very like punning is the kind of surprise produced by intentional bad spelling. It is rather a low form of wit, but now and then a man like Artemus Ward could make it irresistible. His "amoosin' grate show" of one kangaroo was droll enough until every country newspaper began to imitate the method of the fun. Thackeray makes use of bad spelling to burlesque the sentimental love-poetry of his day. The conventional love-lorn youth, apostrophizing the heartless fair who has jilted him for rank and wealth, is displaced in Thackeray's poem by a footman. The latter says exactly what the lover would say, but he spells the words in footman style. He makes a single slip in his use of adjectives: instead of saying "weeping eyes" he says "weeping lips." A careful reader finds that the best thing in the poem.

When
Moonlike
ore the
Hazure
Seas,
p. 378.

Now and then the pun is used with great effect for purposes of satire. When Mr. Kipling was a very young man he poured forth great numbers of magazine stories. His fertility did not escape the satire of the late James Kenneth Stephen, who longed for the day "When the Rudyards cease from kipling." Douglas Jerrold said to a writer, "Why, Chorley, your hair's red; your waistcoat's red; your necktie's red; — in fact everything about you is red except your books." One of the most effective forms of satirical wit is irony. This may be illustrated by Mr. Gilbert's congratulation of an Englishman for condescending to be born an Englishman.

Lapsus
Cálami,
p. 379.

He is an
English-
man,
p. 380.

Wit has often been directed against dull poetry. Alexander Pope, in the early eighteenth century, wrote a long poem called *The Dunciad*, in which he flayed all his poetaster rivals, singling out one — Shadwell — as the prince of the dunces. In our own day, Lowell has plied his wit upon American writers in his *Fable for Critics*. In this poem he has a fling against even himself: —

There is Lowell, who's striving Parnassus to climb
With a whole bale of *isms* tied together with rhyme.

He might get on alone, spite of brambles and boulders,
But he can't with that bundle he has on his shoulders.
The top of the hill he will ne'er come nigh reaching
Till he learns the distinction 'twixt singing and preaching;
His lyre has some chords that would ring pretty well;
But he'd rather by half make a drum of the shell,
And rattle away till he's old as Methusalem,
At the head of a march to the last new Jerusalem.

Here Lowell is remembering the morals he drew from the dandelion, from Sir Launfal, and from many other poetic themes.   Lowell felt, with Dr. Garnett, that poetry with a deliberate moral — didactic, or preaching poetry — is not poetry at all; a mule is a mule, no matter what he carries on his back.   Lowell wrote a bright satire on didactic poetry, pretending that it originated with the goddess Minerva, who put Jove himself to sleep with it.

The Didactic Poem, p. 380.

Wit is the keenest of weapons.   It is, indeed, often cruel and heartless.   Napoleon said that "a victory could no more be made without sacrificing men than an omelette without eggs."   Similarly the joker thinks that somebody must pay the expense of his jokes.   When, however, the biter is bitten, we rejoice; severe repartee is the sweetest of morsels to everybody save one.   "A Vienna lady visiting England remarked to Lord Dudley, 'What wretchedly bad French you all speak in London!'   'It is true, madame,' he answered, 'we have not enjoyed the advantage of having the French twice in our capital.'"   Even when there is no reasonable justification of the retort, the mere fact of its wittiness will sometimes take the place of reason.   "At the East India House the head of the office once reproved Lamb for the excessive irregularity of his attendance.   'Really, Mr. Lamb, you come very late!' observed the official.   'Y-yes,' replied Lamb, with his habitual stammer; 'b-but consi-sider how ear-early I go!'"

It is in rude stages of civilization that the wit which has
no personal sting is thought to be no wit. Thus, all savage
tribes find personal deformity funny. When Shakspere
wished to make a study of insanity, in Hamlet, he found
that his audience — an audience of only three hundred
years ago — regarded insanity as comic. To this day a
drunken man is laughed at even when, having passed the
early stages of his drunken fit, he lies in the gutter, a shame
to his race. D'Orsay, the famous dandy, "was irritated
at receiving anonymously some offensive verses sealed with
a wafer and thimble. These verses caused great laughter
at the Beau's expense; D'Orsay, however, had a shrewd
idea as to their author, a would-be dandy, deeply marked
by small-pox; and meeting him at a club he called out to
him, 'The next time, *mon cher*, that you write an anony-
mous letter, don't seal it with the end of your nose.'"
There can be no doubt that D'Orsay's joke was a bit funny.
The trouble is that he lacked the gentlemanly sympathy
which would have prevented the funny side of the case from
presenting itself to his mind. The true gentleman, as Dr.
Theodore Munger says, "simply does not see deformity" ; [1]
or, if he does, he reasons to himself that it is only by the
grace of God that he himself is free from the same. For
that matter, every one probably has something like de-
formity. Our eyes are bad, or our blood is pale, or some-
where in our system there is a disease slowly developing.
We can very properly laugh at the physical inadequacy of
our race. Little man takes his gun and goes forth to hunt
the red deer and the wild-fowl; meantime some "fearful
wild-fowl" like the microbe of malaria starts out in millions
to hunt little man. If looked at in a certain way, even
little man is something of a joke.

[1] "On the Threshold."

Several distinctions are usually made between wit and humor. For example wit originates bright, sharp expressions, while humor merely appreciates them. General Grant liked a good story, but he rarely tried to tell one. Another distinction is that wit often spends itself in word-play, while humor spreads itself over a general situation. For example, Charles Lamb, having dined very heartily with a company, and afterwards squeezed into a coach with them, sat appreciating the pervading humor of the situation. When presently some one without shouted, "All full within?" Lamb's wit burst forth. "I can't answer for the others, but that last piece of pudding did the business for me."

Wit and humor are alike in enjoying an exaggeration of the truth, but this form of the ridiculous is chiefly a matter of humor. Americans are supposed to supply this kind of joke; but some of the best things in British humor are of the same order. Lamb declared of a certain man, "He'd throw a d-damp upon a-a-a funeral!" "Lamb said that on one occasion he met Coleridge in the street. Coleridge took hold of his friend by the button of his coat and began telling something in his long-drawn-out manner, discussing perhaps one of those questions of 'fate, free-will, foreknowledge absolute,' of which he was so fond. Elia,[1] who was on his way to the India House, had no time for discussion, so he took out his penknife, cut the button off his coat, and, leaving it in Coleridge's hand, continued his way. On his return some hours later, says Elia, he found Coleridge still holding the button, and holding forth to his imagined auditor." It is hard to say which are the calmer and drier, the exaggerations of Dr. Holmes or those of the Rev. Dr. Sydney Smith, the one a Yankee, the other an

---

[1] Elia (pronounced *El'lia*) was Lamb's literary name, or pseudonym.

Englishman.   Dr. Holmes tells the story of the wonderful
The Height
of the
Ridiculous,
p. 381. one-hoss shay that was built so evenly well as to be logically
unable to wear out.   Again, he says that for years he has
not dared to write "as funny as he can," since the time
when his doing so almost cost the life of a servant.
Elsewhere he adapts the old legend of a headsman whose
victims had to sneeze in order to know whether they were
already decapitated.   Sydney Smith tells of the wonders
of Ceylon, where musk is so strong as to infect bottled
The Pro-
ductions of
Ceylon,
p. 382. wine, and a leaf of the talipot tree shelters ten soldiers.

The most important of the distinctions between wit and
humor is the following.   Humor is closely allied to pathos,
wit is usually not.   Humor is a feeling, more than an in-
tellectual perception; wit is a cold, intellectual process.
Dickens is a great humorist; he makes us laugh and cry in
the same breath.   His street boys are funny things, but
they touch our hearts.   Charles Lamb was both wit and
humorist, but we value his puns far less than the skilful
mixture of comic and pathetic in his praise of chimney-
sweepers (cf. page 343).   Dr. Holmes, like Lamb, knew
the secret of making the lips smile while there is a lump in
The Last
Leaf,
p. 384. the throat.   The exquisite humor of *The Last Leaf* proves
this.

LAMB'S SALT DIPS

WALTER JERROLD

Lamb had been medically advised to take a course of
sea-bathing; and, accordingly, at the door of his bath-
ing machine, whilst he stood shivering with the cold,
two stout fellows laid hold of him, one at each shoulder,
like heraldic supporters; they waited for the word of   5
command from their principals, who began the following
oration to them : —

"Hear me, men! Take notice of this — I am to be dipped." What more he would have said is unknown, for having reached the word "dipped," he commenced such a rolling fire of di-di-di-di, that when at length he descended *à plomb* upon the full word *dipped*, the two men, rather tired of the long suspense, became satisfied that they had reached what lawyers call the "operative clause" of the sentence; and both exclaiming, "Oh yes, sir, we are quite aware of that," down they plunged him into the sea.

On emerging, Lamb sobbed so much from the cold that he found no voice suitable to his indignation; from necessity he seemed tranquil; and again addressing the men, who stood respectfully listening, he began thus: —

"Men! is it possible to obtain your attention?"

"Oh, surely, sir, by all means."

"Then listen; — once more I tell you I am to be di-di-di-di-," and then, with a burst of indignation, "dipped, I tell you."

"Oh, decidedly, sir," rejoined the men, "decidedly," and down the stammerer went for a second time.

Petrified with cold and wrath, once more Lamb made a feeble attempt at explanation : —

"Grant me pa-pa-patience! Is it mum-um-murder you me-me-ean? Again, and again I tell you I'm to be di-di-di-dipped," now speaking furiously, with the tone of an injured man.

"Oh yes, sir," the men replied, "we know that; we fully understood it;" and, for the third time, down went Lamb into the sea.

"O limbs of Satan!" he said, on coming up for the third time, "it's now too late; I tell you that I am — no, that I was — by medical direction, to be di-di-di-dipped only *once*."

MRS. MALAPROP ON EDUCATION FOR GIRLS

RICHARD BRINSLEY SHERIDAN

Sir Anthony Absolute. Why, Mrs. Malaprop, in moderation now, what would you have a woman know?

Mrs. Malaprop. Observe me, Sir Anthony, I would by no means wish a daughter of mine to be a progeny of learning; I don't think so much learning becomes a 5 young woman; for instance, I would never let her meddle with Greek or Hebrew, or algebra, or simony, or fluxions, or paradoxes, or such inflammatory branches of learning — neither would it be necessary for her to handle any of your mathematical, astronomical, dia- 10 bolical instruments. But, Sir Anthony, I would send her, at nine years old, to a boarding-school in order to learn a little ingenuity and artifice. Then, sir, she should have a supercilious knowledge in accounts; and as she grew up, I would have her instructed in geometry, 15 that she might know something of contagious countries. But above all, Sir Anthony, she should be mistress of orthodoxy, that she might not mis-spell and mis-pronounce words so shamefully as girls usually do; and likewise that she might reprehend the true meaning of 20 what she is saying. This, Sir Anthony, is what I would have a woman know, — and I don't think there is a superstitious article in it.

WHEN MOONLIKE ORE THE HAZURE SEAS

WILLIAM MAKEPEACE THACKERAY

When moonlike ore the hazure seas
  In soft effulgence swells,
When silver jews and balmy breaze
  Bend down the Lily's bells;

When calm and deap, the rosy sleap   5
   Has lapt your soal in dreems,
R Hangeline! R lady mine!
   Dost thou remember Jeames?

I mark thee in the Marble All,
   Where England's loveliest shine —   10
I say the fairest of them hall
   Is Lady Hangeline.
My soul, in desolate eclipse,
   With recollection teems —
And then I hask, with weeping lips,   15
   Dost thou remember Jeames?

Away! I may not tell thee hall
   This soughring heart endures —
There is a lonely sperrit-call
   That Sorrow never cures;   20
There is a little, little Star,
   That still above me beams;
It is the Star of Hope — but ar!
   Dost thou remember Jeames?

LAPSUS CALAMI

TO R. K.

JAMES KENNETH STEPHEN

Will there never come a season
Which shall rid us from the curse
Of a prose which knows no reason
And an unmelodious verse:
When the world shall cease to wonder   5
At the genius of an ass,
And a boy's eccentric blunder
Shall not bring success to pass:

When mankind shall be delivered
From the clash of magazines,   10
And the inkstand shall be shivered
Into countless smithereens:
When there stands a muzzled stripling,
Mute, beside a muzzled bore:
When the Rudyards cease from kipling   15
And the Haggards ride no more.

HE IS AN ENGLISHMAN

WILLIAM SCHWENK GILBERT

He is an Englishman,
    For he himself has said it,
    And it's greatly to his credit
That he is an Englishman.
    For he might have been a Roosian,   5
    A French, or Turk, or Proosian,
Or perhaps Ital-i-an;
    But in spite of all temptations
    To belong to other nations,
He remains an Englishman.   10

THE DIDACTIC POEM

RICHARD GARNETT

Soulless, colorless strain, thy words are the words of
    wisdom.
Is not a mule a mule, bear he a burden of gold?

THE HEIGHT OF THE RIDICULOUS

OLIVER WENDELL HOLMES

I wrote some lines once on a time
   In wondrous merry mood,
And thought, as usual, men would say
   They were exceeding good.

They were so queer, so very queer,   5
   I laughed as I would die;
Albeit, in the general way,
   A sober man am I.

I called my servant, and he came;
   How kind it was of him,   10
To mind a slender man like me,
   He of the mighty limb!

"These to the printer," I exclaimed,
   And, in my humorous way,
I added (as a trifling jest),   15
   "There'll be the devil to pay."

He took the paper, and I watched,
   And saw him peep within;
At the first line he read, his face
   Was all upon the grin.   20

He read the next; the grin grew broad,
   And shot from ear to ear.
He read the third; a chuckling noise
   I now began to hear.

The fourth; he broke into a roar;   25
   The fifth; his waistband split;
The sixth; he burst five buttons off,
   And tumbled in a fit.

Ten days and nights, with sleepless eye,
   I watched that wretched man,   30
And since, I never dare to write
   As funny as I can.

THE PRODUCTIONS OF CEYLON

SYDNEY SMITH

Ceylon produces the elephant, the buffalo, tiger, elk, wild hog, rabbit, hare, flying-fox, and musk-rat. Many articles are rendered entirely useless by the smell of musk, which this latter animal communicates in merely running over them. Mr. Percival asserts, and the fact 5 has been confirmed to us by the most respectable authority, that if it even pass over a bottle of wine, however well corked and sealed up, the wine becomes so strongly tainted with musk, that it cannot be used; and a whole cask may be rendered useless in the same 10 manner. Among the great variety of birds, we were struck with Mr. Percival's account of the honey-bird, into whose body the soul of a common informer appears to have migrated. It makes a loud and shrill noise, to attract the notice of anybody whom it may perceive; and 15 thus inducing him to follow the course it points out, leads him to the tree where the bees have concealed their treasure; after the apiary has been robbed, this

feathered scoundrel gleans his reward from the hive.
The list of Ceylonese snakes is hideous; and we become 20
reconciled to the crude and cloudy land in which we
live, from reflecting, that the indiscriminate activity of
the sun generates what is loathsome, as well as what is
lovely; that the asp reposes under the rose; and the
scorpion crawls under the fragrant flower and the 25
luscious fruit.

The usual stories are repeated here of the immense
size and voracious appetite of a certain species of ser-
pent. The best history of this kind we ever remember
to have read, was of a serpent killed near one of our 30
settlements, in the East Indies, in whose body they
found the chaplain of the garrison, all in black, the Rev.
Mr. —— somebody or other, whose name we have for-
gotten, and who, after having been missing for above a
week, was discovered in this very inconvenient situation. 35
The dominions of the King of Candy are partly defended
by leeches, which abound in the woods, and from which
our soldiers suffered in the most dreadful manner. The
Ceylonese, in compensation for their animated plagues,
are endowed with two vegetable blessings, the cocoanut 40
tree and the talipot tree. The latter affords a pro-
digious leaf, impenetrable to sun or rain, and large
enough to shelter ten men. It is a natural umbrella,
and is of as eminent service in that country as a great-
coat tree would be in this. A leaf of the talipot tree is 45
a tent to the soldier, a parasol to the traveller, and a
book to the scholar. The cocoanut tree affords bread,
milk, oil, wine, spirits, vinegar, yeast, sugar, cloth,
paper, huts, and ships.

Which sentences are serious, which humorous? Use care in judging
of the last in the selection.

THE LAST LEAF

I saw him once before
As he passed by the door,
   And again
The pavement stones resound,
As he totters o'er the ground   5
   With his cane.

They say that in his prime,
Ere the pruning-knife of Time
   Cut him down,
Not a better man was found   10
By the Crier on his round
   Through the town.

But now he walks the streets,
And he looks at all he meets
   Sad and wan,   15
And he shakes his feeble head,
That it seems as if he said,
   "They are gone."

The mossy marbles rest
On the lips that he has prest   20
   In their bloom,
And the names he loved to hear
Have been carved for many a year
   On the tomb.

My grandmamma has said —   25
Poor old lady, she is dead
   Long ago —

That he had a Roman nose,
And his cheek was like a rose
   In the snow.   30

But now his nose is thin,
And it rests upon his chin
   Like a staff,
And a crook is in his back
And a melancholy crack   35
   In his laugh.

I know it is a sin
For me to sit and grin
   At him here;
But the old three-cornered hat,   40
And the breeches, and all that,
   Are so queer!

And if I should live to be
The last leaf upon the tree
   In the spring,   45
Let them smile as I do now,
At the old forsaken bough
   Where I cling.

The skill shown in the metre and rhymes is very great. The exquisite fourth stanza is as natural as conversation. The poem is eminently worth learning.

___

Plan of Summary. — Reviewing the chapter, (1) enumerate the kinds of metre, designating them by the number of accents, and by the predominant foot. Then (2) say which poem is most noticeable for melody; (3) which for beauty of suggested sights; (4) which for pleasure of suggested sounds; (5) which for pleasure of suggested activity; (6) which for pleasure of suggested odors or tastes; (7) which is most easily understood; (8) which moves the reader most deeply; (9) which shows most skill in character drawing; (10) which has the best unity; (11) which, your critical judgment tells you, is the best piece of work; (12) which you like the best, — without regard to its deserved rank, or its fame.

2 C

CHAPTER X

THE FAR GOAL

At fifteen life seems very long. To be of that age is like being up very early in the morning. If man's life of seventy years be likened to the day of twenty-four hours, then when one is fifteen years old it is only five o'clock in the morning. At that time of day, what may one not expect to happen before night!

The golden plans of the youth have always been dear to the poet, for the latter recognizes in them much that is of high promise. Even if the things dreamed of are very vague, still they are not to be despised. The boy who never owns air castles will never own granite castles. Lowell, in his poem of Aladdin, regrets the passing of the day when he possessed many a golden-roofed palace of dream-stuff. George William Curtis, in a very beautiful essay, lingers over his Spanish châteaux with the same affectionate remembrance. He finds that he is not the only man who holds large possessions in the sunset clouds. All around him are these capitalists, some happy in their dreams, though these never come true, some soured and sad because they can never reach their cloud-land estates.

There are countless dreams that must come to naught, for we know very little of human nature, and less of the plans of Providence. We expect to find money-making, or learning, or truth-telling, easier than these things are. We are constantly surprised to observe how rapidly our own wishes change. We tie ourselves down to a certain

My Châteaux, p. 391.

386

place, expecting to pass our days there; next week we wonder why we ever set foot in that place. Nevertheless, dreams are a good thing. If we are sanguine about nothing, how shall we get anything done? If we do not believe there is much goodness in human nature, how shall we find any? Suppose life does cheat us and bully us; cheats and bullies can sometimes be bettered, and at heart they are never wholly bad.

The chief value of a dream, however, lies in the action that grows out of it when it is fading. This is the thought in Charles Kingsley's *One Grand Sweet Song*. When young people begin to awake from their day-dreams, they abandon the hope of reaching quite all their air-castles, but they have learned how to look ahead to a far goal. What can be said of this far goal as a sober possibility? Much, as we shall see. One Grand Sweet Song, p. 397.

One of the main differences between the beast and the savage is that the latter is the more provident, looks farther ahead. The same difference holds in turn between the savage and the civilized man. The higher up we look, the more dread do we find of living from hand to mouth. The poor white trash who never know where their next meal is to come from are immeasurably the inferiors of men like the old fur-trader Astor, who see ahead for months and years. Such prudence sacrifices, if necessary, the happiness of the present moment to the future gain. We avoid excess of sweets to-day that we may have our teeth ten years hence. Shakspere's old Adam, in *As You Like It*, declares that his old age is as a lusty winter because in youth he did not woo the means of weakness and debility. From this point of view virtue means foregoing a present pleasure in view of a greater one to come. Heaven itself is to be had for a small investment; and yet the famous Elizabethan poet Spenser had to argue himself into tak- Sweet is the Rose, p. 397.

ing no account of the little pain that buys an endless pleasure.

On the whole, education is one of the most nobly prudent institutions that the human race has managed to develop. Going to school may be said to have two prime objects; objects like the mere acquisition of knowledge are secondary. The first prime object is to find out what one is good for in life, — to discover one's goal. The second is to get the strength to pursue that goal.

It is extraordinarily easy not to find out what one is good for. Relatives tried to make a merchant out of Irving, but his firm failed and a great humorist was thus rescued for the world. Relatives tried to make a lawyer out of Lowell, but he insisted that he was "a bookman" by nature, and a bookman he became. The number of able men who have missed their calling or have lacked the circumstances which develop great possibilities is hinted at in three famous stanzas of Gray's Elegy Written in a Country Church Yard.

Some persons miss their calling by a hasty choice, for which years will not atone. Others miss it from neglecting opportunity, and these are probably the larger number. The well-advised youth will seize on just the right chance, as Longfellow's artist seized upon the burning brand of oak from which to shape his image, or as the prince in Sill's poem seized the weapon a coward threw down: —

Gaspar Becerra, p. 398.

Then came the king's son, wounded, sore bestead,
And weaponless, and saw the broken sword,
Hilt-buried in the dry and trodden sand,
And ran and snatched it, and with battle-shout
Lifted afresh he hewed his enemy down,
And saved a great cause that heroic day.

The second chief aim of going to school is to learn how, by training of will and intellect, to attain the far goal. Of these two forms of training, the first is the more important, because it brings about the second, too. Tennyson exclaims, "O well for him whose will is strong." Truly. Will, p. 399. But will is like anything else in human nature — it may be cultivated. Just as an inaccurate person may become accurate, so a weak-willed person may become strong-willed. The secret lies in a habit of doing somewhat hard things. It does not matter so much what the things are. The point is that when the resolve has been made to do something a little hard, it must be carried into effect at once. The power of habit is brilliantly explained in a Habit, p. 400. piece of prose by William James, a distinguished professor of psychology. The nobility of a habit of self-restraint is the subject of Emerson's poem called *Forbearance*. Forbearance, p. 401.

Progress toward any goal seems slow if the goal is distant. The goal of a chicken is soon reached, and therefore nature gives him the satisfaction of seeming to get on fast. He can run alone as soon as he is out of the shell. The man's goal is infinitely distant, and therefore, as Professor John Fiske has shown, nature must give man a long infancy, developing one power at a time. The baby may not be able to run alone when a day old, but the time will come when he will be worth a wilderness of chickens. The strongest nations have been those which have developed slowly. Precocity is as dangerous a sign in a people as in a boy. See the deliberation with which the Saxon race has spread, "winning by inches, holding by clinches" — as Robert Collyer puts it.

A person who grows is not much conscious of the fact except as others tell him, or he looks back upon what he was long since. This is the thought in Clough's *Say not,* Say not, the Struggle nought Availeth, p. 401 *the Struggle nought Availeth*. In the east the sun climbs slowly, but while you look at his imperceptible ascent the western land behind you has become bright. It is a curious fact that we think ourselves to-day the same persons we were ten years ago. Yet to our friends we were probably very different then, and, the chances are, much more disagreeable. By exercise of the will we do come after a while to the acquisition of power. The great theologian of the early Latin church put this truth into poetic form when he declared that every evil impulse conquered may be made a round in a ladder. Longfellow has set Augustine's thought in good verse.

The Ladder of Saint Augustine, p. 402.

It is desirable to find out what one is good for in life; it is delightful to find out that one is good for something more than one thought. The boy who aims to get a year of school-life (it must not be forgotten that school *is* life) does well if by Christmas he learns that he cannot get along without two years. The girl who wishes to be a nurse does well if she discloses real capacity for being a doctor. The youth who goes into business is fortunate if he early learns that he must have more training, more sympathy with education, and science, and civic life, and religion, and literature, and art, if he is to be a man among men, or capable of enjoying his money. He is a human being before he is a business man. If he does not learn this he will become a mere cog in the world's machinery.

Dr. Holmes's best poem has aspiration for its theme. He saw one day a section of the shell called the chambered nautilus. While wondering at the delicacy of its irised interior, he reflected on the way the spiral grew. The dim, dreaming life of the little tenant spent itself in building each year a new and larger cell. It

> Stole with soft step the shining archway through,
> Built up its idle door,
> Stretched in its last-found home, and knew the old no more.

The sight of this series of abandoned dwellings stirs within the poet a high aspiration, and he calls upon his soul to forget the low ideals of the past, and to build a statelier mansion with each returning season.

Whittier has a poem on this theme, or one very similar. He and his friends pursued through the woods the noise of a waterfall, and seemed to catch glimpses of its signals, the white scarfs of its foam; but, search as they would, the waterfall eluded them. Meantime however they had seen every other lovely thing the landscape afforded.

The final poem in this chapter has a very different conception from any of the others. The figure of struggle and battle used so often before is now changed for the peaceful flight of a bird. The goal of a life sometimes seems too far away to be reached. Moving toward it is like moving through trackless air. Bryant asks of the Water-Fowl, *To a Water-Fowl, p. 404.* whither lies its way through the depths of the evening sky. The bird could not answer if it heard. It cannot see the distant lake toward which it is moving steadily and swiftly. The bird is being guided by a Power. It is lone-wandering, but not lost.

MY CHÂTEAUX[1]

GEORGE WILLIAM CURTIS

In Xanadu did Kubla Khan
A stately pleasure-dome decree. — COLERIDGE.

I am the owner of great estates. Many of them lie in the West, but the greater part are in Spain. You may see my western possessions any evening at sunset, when their spires and battlements flash against the horizon.

It gives me a feeling of pardonable importance, as a 5 proprietor, that they are visible, to my eyes at least, from any part of the world in which I chance to be. In my

---

[1] Reprinted from "Prue and I," by permission of Harper and Brothers.

long voyage around the Cape of Good Hope to India (the
only voyage I ever made, when I was a boy and a super-
cargo), if I fell homesick, or sank into a revery of all the   10
pleasant homes I had left behind, I had but to wait until
sunset, and then looking toward the west, I beheld my
clustering pinnacles and towers brightly burnished as if
to salute and welcome me.

So, in the city, if I get vexed and wearied, and cannot   15
find my wonted solace in sallying forth at dinner-time to
contemplate the gay world of youth and beauty hurrying
to the congress of fashion — or if I observe that years are
deepening their tracks around the eyes of my wife, Prue,
I go quietly up to the housetop, toward evening, and re-   20
fresh myself with a distant prospect of my estates.   It is
as dear to me as that of Eton to the poet Gray ; and, if
I sometimes wonder at such moments whether I shall
find those realms as fair as they appear, I am suddenly
reminded that the night air may be noxious, and descend-   25
ing, I enter the little parlor where Prue sits stitching,
and surprise that precious woman by exclaiming with the
poet's pensive enthusiasm : —

> Thought would destroy their Paradise,
> No more; — where ignorance is bliss,   30
> 'Tis folly to be wise.

Columbus, also, had possessions in the West ; and as I
read aloud the romantic story of his life, my voice quivers
when I come to the point in which it is related that sweet
odors of the land mingled with the sea air, as the admiral's   35
fleet approached the shores ; that tropical birds flew out
and fluttered around the ships, glittering in the sun, the
gorgeous promises of the new country ; that boughs,
perhaps with blossoms not all decayed, floated out to
welcome the strange wood from which the craft were   40

hollowed. Then I cannot restrain myself. I think of the gorgeous visions I have seen before I have even undertaken the journey to the West, and I cry aloud to Prue, —

"What sun-bright birds, and gorgeous blossoms, and celestial odors will float out to us, my Prue, as we approach our western possessions!"

The placid Prue raises her eyes to mine with a reproof so delicate that it could not be trusted to words; and, after a moment, she resumes her knitting and I proceed.

These are my western estates, but my finest castles are in Spain. It is a country famously romantic, and my castles are all of perfect proportions, and appropriately set in the most picturesque situations. I have never been to Spain myself, but I have naturally conversed much with travellers to that country; although, I must allow, without deriving from them much substantial information about my property there. The wisest of them told me that there were more holders of real estate in Spain than in any other region he had ever heard of, and they are all great proprietors. Every one of them possesses a multitude of the stateliest castles. From conversation with them you easily gather that each one considers his own castles much the largest and in the loveliest positions. And, after I had heard this said, I verified it, by discovering that all my immediate neighbors in the city were great Spanish proprietors.

One day as I raised my head from entering some long and tedious accounts in my books, and began to reflect that the quarter was expiring, and that I must begin to prepare the balance-sheet, I observed my subordinate, in office but not in years (for poor old Titbottom will never see sixty again!), leaning on his hand, and much abstracted.

"Are you not well, Titbottom?" asked I.   75

"Perfectly, but I was just building a castle in Spain," said he.

I looked at his rusty coat, his faded hands, his sad eye, and white hair, for a moment, in great surprise, and then inquired, —   80

"Is it possible that you own property there too?"

He shook his head silently; and still leaning on his hand, and with an expression in his eye as if he were looking upon the most fertile estate of Andalusia, he went on making his plans,— laying out his gardens, I suppose, 85 building terraces for the vines, determining a library with a southern exposure, and resolving which should be the tapestried chamber.

"What a singular whim," thought I, as I watched Titbottom and filled up a check for four hundred dollars, my 90 quarterly salary, "that a man who owns castles in Spain should be deputy bookkeeper at nine hundred dollars a year!"

When I went home I ate my dinner silently, and afterward sat for a long time upon the roof of the house, look- 95 ing at my western property, and thinking of Titbottom.

It is remarkable that none of the proprietors have ever been to Spain to take possession and report to the rest of us the state of our property there. I, of course, cannot go, I am too much engaged. So is Titbottom. And I 100 find it is the case with all the proprietors. We have so much to detain us at home that we cannot get away. But it is always so with rich men. Prue sighed once as she sat at the window and saw Bourne, the millionnaire, the President of innumerable companies, and manager 105 and director of all the charitable societies in town, going by with wrinkled brow and hurried step. I asked her why she sighed.

" Because I was remembering that my mother used
to tell me not to desire great riches, for they occasioned 110
great cares," said she.

" They do indeed," answered I, with emphasis, remem-
bering Titbottom, and the impossibility of looking after
my Spanish estates.

Prue turned and looked at me with mild surprise ; but 115
I saw that her mind had gone down the street with Bourne.
I could never discover if he held much Spanish stock.
But I think he does. All the Spanish proprietors have a
certain expression.. Bourne has it to a remarkable degree.
It is a kind of look, as if, in fact, a man's mind were in 120
Spain. Bourne was an old lover of Prue's, and he is not
married, which is strange for a man in his position.

It is not easy for me to say how I know so much, as
I certainly do, about my castles in Spain. The sun
always shines upon them. They stand lofty and fair in 125
a luminous, golden atmosphere, a little hazy and dreamy,
perhaps, like the Indian summer, but in which no gales
blow and there are no tempests. All the sublime moun-
tains, and beautiful valleys, and soft landscape, that I
have not yet seen, are to be found in the grounds. They 130
command a noble view of the Alps ; so fine, indeed, that
I should be quite content with the prospect of them from
the highest tower of my castle, and not care to go to
Switzerland.

The neighboring ruins, too, are as picturesque as those 135
of Italy, and my desire of standing in the Coliseum, and
of seeing the shattered arches of the Aqueducts stretch-
ing along the Campagna and melting into the Alban
Mount, is entirely quenched. The rich gloom of my
orange groves is gilded by fruit as brilliant of complexion 140
and exquisite of flavor as any that ever dark-eyed Sor-
rento girls, looking over the high plastered walls of

southern Italy, hand to the youthful travellers, climbing
on donkeys up the narrow lane beneath.

The Nile flows through my grounds.   The Desert lies 145
upon their edge, and Damascus stands in my garden.   I
am given to understand, also, that the Parthenon has
been removed to my Spanish possessions.   The Golden-
Horn is my fish-preserve ; my flocks of golden fleece are
pastured on the plain of Marathon, and the honey of 150
Hymettus is distilled from the flowers that grow in the
vale of Enna — all in my Spanish domains. ·

From the windows of those castles look the beautiful
women whom I have never seen, whose portraits the
poets have painted.   They wait for me there, and chiefly 155
the fair-haired child, lost to my eyes so long ago, now
bloomed into an impossible beauty.   The lights that
never shone, glance at evening in the vaulted halls, upon
banquets that were never spread.   The bands I have
never collected, play all night long, and enchant the 160
brilliant company, that was never assembled, into silence.

In the long summer mornings the children that I never
had, play in the gardens that I never planted.   I hear
their sweet voices sounding low and far away, calling
"Father ! father !"   I see the lost fair-haired girl, grown 165
now into a woman, descending the stately stairs of my
castle in Spain, stepping out upon the lawn, and playing
with those children.   They bound away together down
the garden ; but those voices linger, this time airily call-
ing, "Mother ! mother !" . . .   170

As the years go by, I am not conscious that my interest
diminishes.   If I see that age is subtly sifting his snow in
the dark hair of my Prue, I smile, contented, for her hair,
dark and heavy as when I first saw it, is all carefully treas-
ured in my castles in Spain.   If I feel her arm more 175
heavily leaning upon mine, as we walk around the squares,

I press it closely to my side, for I know that the easy grace of her youth's motion will be restored by the elixir of that Spanish air. If her voice sometimes falls less clearly from her lips, it is no less sweet to me, for the 180 music of her voice's prime fills, freshly as ever, those Spanish halls. If the light I love fades a little from her eyes, I know that the glances she gave me, in our youth, are the eternal sunshine of my castles in Spain.

ONE GRAND SWEET SONG

CHARLES KINGSLEY

My fairest child, I have no song to give you,
No lark could sing 'neath skies so dull and gray,
But, if you will, a quiet hint I'll give you
For every day, for every day.

I'll teach you how to sing a clearer carol   5
Than lark that hails the dawn or breezy down;
To win yourself a purer poet's laurel
Than Shakspere's crown.

Be good, sweet maid, and let who will be clever.
Do noble things, not dream them all day long;   10
And so make life, death, and that vast forever
One grand, sweet song.

SWEET IS THE ROSE

EDMUND SPENSER

Sweet is the rose, but grows upon a brere;
Sweet is the juniper, but sharp his bough;
Sweet is the eglantine, but pricketh near;
Sweet is the firbloom, but his branches rough;

3. *near*, keenly.

Sweet is the cyprus, but his rind is tough;   5
Sweet is the nut, but bitter is his pill;
Sweet is the broom flower, but yet sour enough;
And sweet is moly, but his root is ill;
So, every sweet with sour is tempered still,
That maketh it be coveted the more: 10
For easy things that may be got at will
Most sorts of men do set but little store.
Why then should I account of little pain,
That endless pleasure shall unto me gain?

14. *That* = that which.

GASPAR BECERRA

Henry Wadsworth Longfellow

By his evening fire the artist
    Pondered o'er his secret shame;
Baffled, weary, and disheartened,
    Still he mused, and dreamed of fame.

'Twas an image of the Virgin   5
    That had tasked his utmost skill;
But alas! his fair ideal
    Vanished and escaped him still.

From a distant Eastern island
    Had the precious wood been brought;   10
Day and night the anxious master
    At his toil untiring wrought;

Till, discouraged and desponding,
    Sat he now in shadows deep,
And the day's humiliation   15
    Found oblivion in sleep.

Then a voice cried, "Rise, O master!
    From the burning brand of oak
Shape the thought that stirs within thee!"
    And the startled artist woke, —   20

Woke, and from the smoking embers
    Seized and quenched the glowing wood;
And therefrom he carved an image,
    And he saw that it was good.

O thou sculptor, painter, poet!   25
    Take this lesson to thy heart:
That is best which lieth nearest;
    Shape from that thy work of art.

WILL

ALFRED TENNYSON

I

O well for him whose will is strong!
He suffers, but he will not suffer long;
He suffers, but he cannot suffer wrong:
For him nor moves the loud world's random mock,
Nor all Calamity's hugest waves confound,   5
Who seems a promontory of rock,
That, compass'd round with turbulent sound,
In middle ocean meets the surging shock,
Tempest-buffeted, citadel-crown'd.

II

But ill for him who, bettering not with time,   10
Corrupts the strength of heaven-descended Will,
And ever weaker grows thro' acted crime,
Or seeming-genial venial fault,

13. *genial* here means harmless.

Recurring and suggesting still!
He seems as one whose footsteps halt,　　15
Toiling in immeasurable sand,
And o'er a weary sultry land,
Far beneath a blazing vault,
Sown in a wrinkle of the monstrous hill,
The city sparkles like a grain of salt.　　20

HABIT[1]

WILLIAM JAMES

Habit is thus the enormous fly-wheel of society, its most precious conservative agent. It alone is what keeps us all within the bounds of ordinance, and saves the children of fortune from the envious uprisings of the poor. It alone prevents the hardest and most repulsive 5 walks of life from being deserted by those brought up to tread therein. It keeps the fisherman and the deck-hand at sea through the winter; it holds the miner in his darkness, and nails the countryman to his log-cabin and his lonely farm through all the months of snow; it 10 protects us from invasion by the natives of the desert and the frozen zone. It dooms us all to fight out the battle of life upon the lines of our nurture or our early choice, and to make the best of a pursuit that disagrees, because there is no other for which we are fitted, and it 15 is too late to begin again. It keeps different social strata from mixing. Already at the age of twenty-five you see the professional mannerism settling down on the young commercial traveller, on the young doctor, on the young minister, on the young counsellor-at-law. You 20

[1] Reprinted from the "Principles of Psychology," by permission of Henry Holt & Co.

see the little lines of cleavage running through the char-
acter, the tricks of thought, the prejudices, the ways of
the "shop," in a word, from which the man can by and
by no more escape than his coat-sleeve can suddenly fall
into a new set of folds. On the whole, it is best he 25
should not escape. It is well for the world that in most
of us, by the age of thirty, the character has set like
plaster, and will never soften again.

FORBEARANCE

RALPH WALDO EMERSON

Hast thou named all the birds without a gun?
Loved the wood-rose, and left it on its stalk?
At rich men's tables eaten bread and pulse?
Unarmed, faced danger with a heart of trust?
And loved so well a high behavior,   5
In man or maid, that thou from speech refrained,
Nobility more nobly to repay?
Oh, be my friend, and teach me to be thine!

SAY NOT, THE STRUGGLE NOUGHT AVAILETH

ARTHUR HUGH CLOUGH

Say not, the struggle nought availeth,
  The labor and the wounds are vain,
The enemy faints not, nor faileth,
  And as things have been they remain.

If hopes were dupes, fears may be liars;   5
  It may be, in yon smoke concealed,
Your comrades chase e'en now the fliers,
  And, but for you, possess the field.

2 D

For while the tired waves, vainly breaking,
　Seem here no painful inch to gain,　　　　　10
Far back, through creeks and inlets making,
　Comes silent, flooding in, the main.

And not by eastern windows only,
　When daylight comes, comes in the light;
In front, the sun climbs slow, how slowly,　　　15
　But westward, look, the land is bright.

THE LADDER OF SAINT AUGUSTINE

HENRY WADSWORTH LONGFELLOW

Saint Augustine! well hast thou said,
　That of our vices we can frame
A ladder, if we will but tread
　Beneath our feet each deed of shame!

All common things, each day's events,　　　　5
　That with the hour begin and end,
Our pleasures and our discontents,
　Are rounds by which we may ascend.

The low desire, the base design,
　That makes another's virtues less;　　　　10
The revel of the treacherous wine,
　And all occasions of excess;

The longing for ignoble things;
　The strife for triumph more than truth;
The hardening of the heart that brings　　　　15
　Irreverence for the dreams of youth;

All thoughts of ill; all evil deeds,
　That have their root in thoughts of ill;
Whatever hinders or impedes
　The action of the nobler will:　　　　20

All these must first be trampled down
　Beneath our feet, if we would gain
In the bright fields of fair renown
　The right of eminent domain.

We have not wings, we cannot soar;　　25
　But we have feet to scale and climb
By slow degrees, by more and more,
　The cloudy summits of our time.

The mighty pyramids of stone
　That wedge-like cleave the desert airs,　30
When nearer seen and better known,
　Are but gigantic flights of stairs.

The distant mountains that uprear
　Their solid bastions to the skies,
Are crossed by pathways, that appear　　35
　As we to higher levels rise.

The heights by great men reached and kept
　Were not attained by sudden flight,
But they, while their companions slept,
　Were toiling upward in the night.　　40

Standing on what too long we bore
　With shoulders bent, and downcast eyes,
We may discern — unseen before —
　A path to higher destinies.

Nor deem the irrevocable Past   45
    As wholly wasted, wholly vain,
If, rising on its wrecks, at last
    To something nobler we attain.

TO A WATER-FOWL

WILLIAM CULLEN BRYANT

Whither, midst falling dew,
While glow the heavens with the last steps of day,
Far, through their rosy depths, dost thou pursue
    Thy solitary way?

Vainly the fowler's eye   5
Might mark thy distant flight to do thee wrong,
As, darkly painted on the crimson sky,
    Thy figure floats along.

Seek'st thou the plashy brink
Of weedy lake, or marge of river wide,   10
Or where the rocking billows rise and sink
    On the chafed ocean-side?

There is a Power whose care
Teaches thy way along that pathless coast —
The desert and illimitable air —   15
    Lone wandering, but not lost.

All day thy wings have fanned,
At that far height, the cold, thin atmosphere,
Yet stoop not, weary, to the welcome land,
    Though the dark night is near.   20

7-8. Bryant felt the difficulty of a "painting" that moves, but he decided
not to change an image for which so much could be said.

And soon that toil shall end;
Soon shalt thou find a summer home, and rest,
And scream among thy fellows; reeds shall bend,
 Soon, o'er thy sheltered nest.

Thou'rt gone, the abyss of heaven 25
Hath swallowed up thy form; yet, on my heart
Deeply has sunk the lesson thou hast given,
 And shall not soon depart.

He who, from zone to zone,
Guides through the boundless sky thy certain flight, 30
In the long way that I must tread alone,
 Will lead my steps aright.

CHRONOLOGICAL TABLE OF BRITISH AND AMERICAN AUTHORS

Sixteenth Century

Author.	Date and Name of First Work.	1[1]	2	Work in Present Volume, and Chapter
Edmund Spenser	1569 Theatre of Voluptuous Worldlings	17	77	Sweet is the Rose VII
William Shakspere	1588? Titus Andronicus	24	52	Hark, hark, the lark VII A Fop VIII

Seventeenth Century

George Herbert	1631 The Temple	38	40	Sweet day, so cool VII

Eighteenth Century

Benjamin Franklin	1725 Liberty and Necessity	19	84	Remarks concerning the Savages of North America VIII
Earl of Chatham	1736 (First speech in Parliament)	28	70	The American Revolution II
William Julius Mickle	1761 Knowledge, an Ode	26	53	There's nae luck VI
Richard Brinsley Sheridan	1775 The Rivals	24	65	Mrs. Malaprop on Education IX

[1] The first number gives the age at which the author published his first volume; the second gives his age at death. There is a great deal of difference, in value, among the first works. For example, those of Herbert, Sheridan, Wordsworth, Scott, Lamb, Byron, Emerson, Ruskin, Barnes, Clough, Whitman, and Symonds are representative of their authors, while those of Mrs. Hemans, Bryant, Longfellow, Holmes, Lowell, and Patmore are crude juvenile performances, now forgotten. Bryant's best poem, *Thanatopsis*, was however written early enough (at 18) to entitle him to a place in the first of the lists just given. It must not be forgotten that some authors wrote much before they published. Some, like Mr. Watts-Dunton, Professor James, Miss Dickinson, and Mr. Canton seem to have courted obscurity as long as possible. A distinguished art critic, Mr. William James Stillman, recently published at seventy a volume of essays which, he

NINETEENTH CENTURY, FIRST HALF

AUTHOR.	DATE AND NAME OF FIRST WORK.	1	2	WORK IN PRESENT VOLUME, AND CHAPTER.
Walter Savage Landor	1795 Poems	28	89	Rhodopè and Aesop VI
William Wordsworth	1798 Lyrical Ballads	28	80	March VII I wandered lonely VII My heart leaps up VII
Sir Walter Scott	1805 Lay of the Last Minstrel	34	61	Helvellyn I
Sydney Smith	1807 Peter Plimley's Letters	38	74	The Products of Ceylon IX
Charles Lamb	1807 Tales from Shakespeare	32	59	The Young Montagu VIII
Lord Byron	1807 Hours of Idleness	19	46	Swimming IV
Felicia Hemans	1808 Early Blossoms	14	41	Landing of the Pilgrim Fathers III
William Cullen Bryant	1808 The Embargo	14	84	The Twenty-Second of December III The Yellow Violet VII June VII The Death of the Flowers VII November VII To a Water-Fowl X
B. W. Procter (Barry Cornwall)	1820 A Sicilian Story	33	87	The Sea VII
Charles Wolfe	1825 Literary Remains		32	The Burial of Sir John Moore II
Charles Tennyson-Turner	1827 Poems by Two Brothers	19	71	The Lattice at Sunrise VII
Alfred, Lord Tennyson	1827 Poems by Two Brothers	20	83	The Charge of the Light Brigade II The *Revenge* II In the Children's Hospital III Sir Galahad VIII The Shell VII The Eagle VII

said, he should have been glad to defer another ten years if he had been reasonably sure of ten years. Contrast such solicitude for ripeness with the childish eagerness of Mrs. Hemans, Bryant, and Coventry Patmore! Of course, essays worth the reading imply greater maturity than lyric poetry, — in which the writer needs to express only his own feelings, not a wise judgment on many matters. It is a natural and excellent practice for boys and girls to express their feelings in verse. Yet even in lyric poetry children rarely produce what is worth printing. It is different in music; musical prodigies are common.

NINETEENTH CENTURY, FIRST HALF — *Continued.*

AUTHOR.	DATE AND NAME OF FIRST WORK.	1	2	WORK IN PRESENT VOLUME, AND CHAPTER.
				The Voyage of Maeldune V
				Will X
Henry Wadsworth Longfellow	1826 Miscellaneous Poems, with other authors	19	75	The Arsenal at Springfield III
				Sand of the Desert in an Hour-Glass V
				The Secret of the Sea V
				Sunrise on the Hills VII
				Gaspar Becerra X
				The Ladder of Saint Augustine X
Oliver Wendell Holmes	1827 Poetic illustrations of the Athenæum Gallery, with other authors	16	85	The Height of the Ridiculous IX
				The Last Leaf IX
Edgar Allan Poe	1827 Tamerlane	17	38	The Haunted Palace IV
Caroline Norton	1829 The Sorrows of Rosalie	21	67	The King of Denmark's Ride I
John Greenleaf Whittier	1831 Legends of New England	23	85	The Angels of Buena Vista II
				Barclay of Ury III
Robert Browning	1833 Pauline	21	77	How they brought the Good News I
				Tray I
				Incident of the French Camp II
				Hervé Riel II
				Oh! our manhood's prime vigor IV
John Stuart Blackie	1834 Translation of Goethe's Faust	25	84	My Bath IV
Sir Francis Hastings Doyle	1834 Miscellaneous Verses	23	77	The Private of the Buffs II
				The Loss of the *Birkenhead* II
John Henry, Cardinal Newman	1835 Parochial Sermons	34	89	The Gentleman VIII
Robert Nicoll	1835 Poems and Lyrics	21	23	The Hero III
Ralph Waldo Emerson	1836 Nature	33	79	Concord Hymn II
				The Rhodora VII
				'Twas one of the charmed days VII
				The Humble-Bee VII
				The Snow-Storm VII
				Tact VIII
				Forbearance X
William Makepeace Thackeray	1837 Yellowplush Papers	26	52	The End of the Play VIII
				When Moonlike IX

NINETEENTH CENTURY, FIRST HALF — *Continued*

Author.	Date and Name of First Work.	1	2	Work in Present Volume, and Chapter.
James Russell Lowell	1838 Class Poem	19	72	Incident of the Fire at Hamburgh III · To the Dandelion VII
John Ruskin	1843 Modern Painters, v. i	24		The Bird VII Of Vulgarity VIII
William Barnes	1844 Poems in the Dorsetshire dialect	43	85	Mary-Ann's Child VI
Charles Kingsley	1844 Village Sermons	25	56	The Three Fishers III The Old, Old Song VI The Merry Lark VI One Grand, Sweet Song X
Coventry Patmore	1844 Poems	11	73	The Toys VI
Matthew Arnold	1848 The Strayed Reveller	26	66	The Forsaken Merman VI Sohrab and Rustum VI
Arthur Hugh Clough	1848 The Bothie of Tober-Na-Vuolich	29	42	Say not, the struggle X
Sydney Dobell	1850 The Roman	26	50	How's my boy ? VI

NINETEENTH CENTURY, SECOND HALF

George William Curtis	1851 Nile Notes of a Howadji	27	68	My Châteaux X
Gerald Massey	1854 The Ballad of Babe Christabel	26		The Deserter from the Cause II
Richard Doddridge Blackmore	1854 Poems by Melanter	29		The Great Winter IV Driven beyond Endurance IV
Walt Whitman	1855 Leaves of Grass	36	72	Reconciliation III Patroling Barnegat III The Runner IV Warble for Lilac-Time VII
John Antrobus				The Cow-Boy V
Theodore Watts-Dunton				Midshipman Lanyon II The Octopus of the Golden Isles VIII
William Schwenk Gilbert ·				He is an Englishman IX
Richard Garnett	1858 Primula	23		The Didactic Poem IX
Thomas Wentworth Higginson	1858 Woman and her Wishes	30		Decoration II
Thomas Ashe	1859 Poems	23	63	Sympathy VII
Kate Putnam Osgood				Driving Home the Cows VI
Robert Buchanan	1866 London Poems	25		Two Sons VI

NINETEENTH CENTURY, SECOND HALF — *Continued*

AUTHOR.	DATE AND NAME OF FIRST WORK.	1	2	WORK IN PRESENT VOLUME, AND CHAPTER.
Sidney Lanier	1867 Tiger Lilies	25	39	Song of the Chattahoochee VII
Sarah Williams	1868 Twilight Hours	27	27	Omàr and the Persian VIII
Andrew Lang	1872 Ballads and Lyrics of Old France	28		Scythe Song VII
George Cary Eggleston	1872 How to Educate Yourself	33		A Plantation Heroine III Two Gentlemen at Petersburg VIII A Breach of Etiquette VIII
Henry Morton Stanley	1872 How I found Livingstone	32		A Meeting in the Heart of Africa V
Richard Jefferies	1873 Reporting, Editing, etc.	25	39	The Physique of a Woodcutter IV The Lyra Prayer IV
Alice Meynell	1875 Preludes			San Lorenzo Giustiniani's Mother III
John Addington Symonds	1875 The Renaissance in Italy	35	53	An Episode VI
Robert Louis Stevenson	1878 An Inland Voyage	28	44	Heather Ale II
William Watson	1880 The Prince's Quest	22		Changed Voices VII
Emily H. Hickey	1881 A Sculptor	36		A Sea Story III
James Kenneth Stephen	1885 International Law, etc.	26	33	Lapsus Calami IX
Charles Cracroft Lefroy	1885 Echoes of Theocritus	30	36	A Football Player IV Childhood and Youth IV
Arthur Christopher Benson	1886 Memories of Arthur Hamilton	24		Winter Harvests VII
Henry Woodfen Grady	1886 The New South	35	38	The Confederate Soldier after the War III
Rudyard Kipling	1886 Departmental Ditties	21		The Drums of the Fore and Aft II Soldier and Sailor Too II
William Canton	1887 A Lost Epic	42		The Crow VII
William Ernest Henley	1887 A Book of Verses	38		Enter Patient III Operation III
A. Conan Doyle	1888 A Study in Scarlet	29		'Ware Holes III
William James	1890 Principles of Psychology	48		Habit X
Emily Dickinson	1890 Poems (posthumous)		56	The Railway Train VII The Humming-Bird VII
Norman Gale	1892 A Country Muse	30		Dawn and Dark VII
Ednah Proctor Clarke	1897 An Opal			Hannah the Quakeress III
Charlotte Perkins Stetson				A Man Must Live III

.

A First Book in Writing English

BY

EDWIN HERBERT LEWIS, Ph.D.

*Associate Professor of English in Lewis Institute and in the
University of Chicago.*

12mo.   Buckram.   Price, 80 cents, *net*

" Among the recent educational books that have come
to us from America this appears to be *one of the very
best.* Every page shows that it is the *work of a practical
teacher* who is able to combine a wide knowledge of the
theory of composition and a cultivated taste with remark-
able ingenuity and practical resource."

— English Educational Times.

" The book is one of the best for high school use that
we have seen, *clear in its statements, logical in its
arrangements of material,* and provided with a great
number of practical exercises and apt, illustrative quo-
tations. — *Dial.*

THE MACMILLAN COMPANY

66 FIFTH AVENUE, NEW YORK

From Chaucer to Arnold

TYPES OF LITERARY ART IN PROSE AND VERSE

AN INTRODUCTION TO ENGLISH LITERATURE WITH PREFACE AND NOTES

BY

ANDREW J. GEORGE, A.M.

Department of English, High School, Newton, Mass.

Cloth. 8vo. Price, $1.00, *net*

Principles of English Grammar

FOR THE USE OF SCHOOLS

BY

GEORGE R. CARPENTER

Professor of Rhetoric and English Composition in Columbia University

---

12mo. Half-leather. Price, 75 cents, *net*

THE MACMILLAN COMPANY

66 FIFTH AVENUE, NEW YORK

www.ingramcontent.com/pod-product-compliance
Lightning Source LLC
Chambersburg PA
CBHW021323110726
47900CB00005B/1324